Stop Whining— and Start Winning

Recharging People,

Reigniting Passion,

and PUMPING UP Profits

FRANK PACETTA

WITH ROGER GITTINES

HarperBusiness
An Imprint of HarperCollinsPublishers

ALSO BY FRANK PACETTA AND ROGER GITTINES

Don't Fire Them, Fire Them Up

HarperCollins books may be purchased for educational, business, or sales promotional use. For information please write: Special Markets Department, HarperCollins Publishers Inc., 10 East 53rd Street, New York, NY 10022.

FIRST EDITION

Designed by Kris Tobiassen

Printed on acid-free paper.

Library of Congress Cataloging-in-Publication Data has been applied for.

ISBN 0-06-662005-8

00 01 02 03 04 ❖/RRD 10 9 8 7 6 5 4 3 2

To my wife, Julie, "simply the best"
Love, Frank

Contents

Acknowledgments

There are many people responsible for this project. I want to first and foremost tell Roger Gittines thanks for putting up with me, getting the best out of me, and writing a great book. Roger, you are a mentor and, more important, a good friend.

Thanks also to:

Margret McBride, my literary agent, who has always had faith in me and knows how to make things happen for me.

Laureen Rowland, our editor, who challenged us, supported us, and created a better book.

HarperCollins Publishers, who has been terrific to work with and open to the many ideas I keep coming up with.

But most important to the people who made the book, my terrific mentors: Neil Lamey, Peter Rogers, Paul McKinnon, Paula Innis, Bill Locander, Bill Matthews, Neil Sessoms, Mark Donnollo, Kristen Miller, and Ron Nelson.

And to the men and women whom I've worked with and for over the years—who have done extraordinary things to make us successful.

To my best friend and attorney, Brian Chorpenning, who always looked for my family's best interest and whom I can always count on.

To the great people at the University of Dayton—Ted Kissel, Oliver Purnell, Megan MacAlister, Jaci Clark—you proved you can go home again. This book is about the impact of family—I'm fortunate to have a great one.

Tune-ups, Turnarounds, Transformations, and Take offs

I've been accused in print of having the attention span of an infant. I'm not quite that bad, but I have absolutely no patience with introductions to books that are more than a few pages long, and even when they're relatively brief I tend to skip through them. I'm definitely in a hurry. I want the information that's on the page, and I want it now!

Assuming that you're in a hurry too, I'm going to keep this short. *Stop Whining—and Start Winning* is filled with leadership and management techniques accumulated in the course of twenty-five years—and still counting—in sales, fifteen of which were spent in general manager assignments running operations with roughly $100 million in annual gross revenues.

This book contains no theory. Zero. It's a road-test report on what works and what doesn't. I'd describe myself as a fanatic for leadership and process except that "fanaticism" isn't a strong enough word to describe my passion for the two subjects. And yes, leadership and process are entirely compatible. In fact, without a disciplined business process, leaders doom themselves to failure.

If you quickly thumb through the pages, you'll see boxes, bulleted lists, and other displays that highlight information to make it as accessible as possible. Be my guest, grab a handful of ideas to help run your business, make deals, close sales, or move your career up to the next level. I've also included some slices of real life that don't normally show up in business books because most books tend to avoid a theme I'm about to pound on—emotion.

You've heard of E-commerce? When I use the term the "E" stands for emotion, and the Internet can't even come close to the profit potential. **My mission is to *emotionalize* your business, your career, and your life.** There's too much complacency and mediocrity poisoning what could be exhilarating, rewarding, and satisfying professional experiences. And don't sit there and tell me that some jobs are boring and grubby—that's baloney. That's an excuse for lousy leadership. I'm sick of hearing it.

I'm looking for a fight, actually. I'm willing to go toe-to-toe with any-one who believes that people are just another disposable commodity instead of the number one business asset. The stories I share in his book aren't the usual corporate case histories, but rather close up profiles of peo-ple who "won't take it anymore"; people who are determined to make a dif-ference—and you know what?—they have.

One of my specialties is turnarounds. I help losing operations win again. I love my work. If you're ready for a tune-up, a turnaround, a trans-formation, or a takeoff you're reading the right book.

Enough introduction, already. Let's get busy.

Part I

CHAPTER ONE

To Hell with Ho-hum

What are you doing?

I know that's not the customary way to begin a book, but play along with me.

I'll start again.

What are you doing?

I'm reading a book.

No, you're not.

I'm not?

It only seems like a book.

What is it then?

A chain saw.

Chain saw? Could've fooled me.

In a moment, we're going to crank this sucker up and rip through the barriers that make going to work, doing your best, and *being your best* such a royal pain in the butt.

This chain saw is the perfect tool for all those who believe life is too precious to waste on a job that's boring, frustrating, or pure torture. It's for all those who are fed up with the same old excuses and dumb ideas, fed up with no shows, no guts, and no for an answer. And it's for all of those who are tired of hearing:

> *That's the way we do things.*
> *If you don't like it . . .*
> *Just shut up and follow the rules.*
> *Hunker down and nobody will bother you.*

Phrases like that make my skin crawl, and should make yours crawl too. That's because we don't have to take it anymore; don't have to listen to it or live it anymore. Are you wondering why? Why we don't have to take what for so long has been standard operating procedure in many companies and organizations, large and small?

Because together we can be a part of a business leadership revolution. Not the usual, "rearrange the deck chairs on the *Titanic*" kind of revolution. But *one that's driven by bringing out the best in ourselves and others powered with passion, performance, and process.*

The best? You've got it.

I love the smell of sawdust in the morning! There are whole forests of deadwood and deadheads waiting to fall. There's no reason to settle for second-best, second place, and second thoughts. It doesn't matter whether you take orders or give them, your job is to make your job second to none.

I'll show you how to do it.

And if you own or manage a business, supervise a staff of one or one thousand, or are a team leader or team member isn't it time for that enterprise—the one that claims so much of your time and energy—to live up to its promise and keep its promises?

I'll show you how to make that happen.

It's going to be fun too. Businesses of any size in any industry, and the jobs they create, can be lots of fun, hugely rewarding, and personally satisfying. Mine have been. First as a sales manager and then as a district manager for Xerox, I led three $100 million a year operations that racked up high profits and performance records year after year and were also warm, friendly, exciting work environments. We had double-digit sales growth and nearly triple-digit customer and employee satisfaction ratings. "I couldn't wait to get to the office in the morning. I was afraid I'd miss some of the action," was the way one former colleague described the atmosphere. "We were family," another said. Many of them are now CEOs, senior managers for top corporations, or owners of their own successful businesses. Along the way, the customers we worked with also prospered and grew from struggling start-ups to regional and national market leaders.

The same was true at Danka America, a $2 billion office products company, where I led a national staff of two thousand sales reps, and at SinglesourceIT, the red-hot, cutting-edge Internet-based information technology provider that I'm now involved with. The experience was—and continues to be—*richly* rewarding—and I'm not just talking about the money.

In each case, the whining stopped— and the winning started.

 Boom Boxes, Etc.

Throughout the book I will use boxes like this to highlight key points and provide you with reminders, tips, and summaries. There will also be bullet points, arrows, and charts to maximize information access.

In the pages ahead, I'm going to be exposing a dirty little secret that isn't dirty at all and should never, ever be a secret. You probably once knew this truth but were told by the cynics to *fahgitaboutit*:

A job doesn't have to be dull, empty, or in conflict with our principles and personal priorities. Businesses large and small can be rewarding and fun places to work from the bottom up to the top down. Do I sound naive? I'm not. There are boatloads of techniques, processes, procedures, and proven ideas that can help you achieve both profound personal *and* organizational transformations. We can do well, do good, make money, and have a great time! What it takes is high personal expectations and low tolerance for failure, mediocrity, and lame excuses. What it takes is a commitment "not to take it anymore."

Here's another secret. Tolstoy got it wrong. I'm referring to the author of *War and Peace* and *Anna Karennina*, who wrote in the latter novel, "Happy families are all alike; every unhappy family is unhappy in its own way." No, at least in business, unhappy families are all the same. They make the same mistakes over and over again.

They don't:

- care
- plan
- devise and drive a process
- execute
- measure
- build teams
- demand accountability
- communicate
- enforce discipline
- have fun
- motivate
- lead
- change
- reward, or
- inspire.

They may try to address a few of these failings when the problems become too severe to shrug off, but the effort is haphazard and the results are inconsistent. Dazed and battered, the unhappy business family's most important defense mechanism never kicks in because, worst of all, these organizations are emotionally dead. They are places where business as usual is conducted, and it's usually dull, dispiriting, and unrewarding. I call them "ho-hum places." *People don't matter. The process is a mess. And the profits are pathetic.*

None of us need TQM, reengineering, or learning organizations to recognize ho hum. We feel it the moment we walk into the dingy, lifeless lobby, roll our car up to the littered drive-thru to order a lukewarm burger and fries, or listen to the first two minutes of a droning two-hour slide presentation. Ho hum is a major business liability and can become a crippling personal affliction. It poisons the best people and products, even an enterprise proud enough to boast of a tradition that will deliver door to door for pennies, and do it despite rain, snow, and the dark of night. Yes, the U.S. Postal Service is working mightily to escape ho-hum hell. The hideous term, "going postal," captures the cancerousness of ho hum.

I'm out to eradicate ho hum. Employees don't deserve the hassle or the heartache. Customers don't deserve to be disappointed. Neither do stockholders. And managers should feel they deserve the right to lead, or get out of the way.

The bulleted list on page 6 marks the path that this book will follow. Care is first and is a dominant theme throughout this book. Those who don't care are literally careless. People who care less fail more than those who are care full. Wait. Don't let the word put you off. Care is not nearly as soft and fuzzy as it seems at first. In fact, it's one of the toughest words in the vocabulary. If you *really* care, there's no choice but to take action. As a manager, the moment I say that I care about my team's success, I've got tough decisions to make: Are the right people in the right assignments? Are they trained well enough? What more do they need? Is the job getting done? If I don't care, it's easy; I can just sit back and relax. It's the careless managers who are soft and fuzzy.

Caring—or not caring—is a measure of how much or how little our emotions are engaged in the day-to-day struggles of life. Throughout my business career, I've found that personal and organizational success depend on a seemingly simple question: Do the individuals involved in the enterprise really give a damn? Too often the answer is no, and that's a shame. Don't give a damn about how one spends forty, fifty, or sixty hours a week? Come on! Anyone who says that's the price of success should be drawn and quartered. But much of what we do in business today results in banishing normal human emotions from the workplace. The very first casualty is the one we can least afford to lose—caring. You've heard it:

Oh, well. The customer is unhappy—Who cares?
We lost the deal—I could care less.
We got the deal—So what?
Profits are down—Yawn.
Mary may quit—Let her.

What I am going to do in this book is, 1), make it okay to care in a business setting and, 2), show you how to create a high-energy, caring organization and atmosphere that will guarantee success and fulfillment for you, your people, and the business overall.

I used the word "guarantee" and I mean it. If you care about making a difference, try just a handful of the many practical techniques that are in this book and you'll see major changes start to happen. Among other benefits, organization-wide morale will soar and you'll clock up gains in profits, productivity, and customer satisfaction. It's bottom-line stuff, but I'm not writing exclusively for managers and leaders. They're only a part of my intended readership. The other, and it's far larger, is one I encounter roughly ever week or so when I speak to the business organizations around the country that invite to me to share my experience and views on what's needed to gain and keep a competitive advantage these days. I don't pull punches. I slam bad bosses and goose the clock-watchers whose Rolexes, real and fake, are set to Eastern Pension Time, a zone where everyone gets paid a handsome salary for life and no one is required to do a lick of productive work. We laugh a lot and pretty soon there's an air of a revival meeting. Afterward, I'm usually approached by people whom I've helped become aware of the shortcomings of their jobs and bosses (and maybe their own attitudes). They'll say, "He's a loser" or "She could care less about me." There's a lot of anger, frustration, and despair about the way we are typically managed and led.

I listen sympathetically but in the end my advice often boils down to do your best to make a difference; "I Give a Damn" should be your personal motto and you should work to spread that attitude to others. Take it from me, and I have the scars to prove it, a hard head can punch through many a stone wall. Be patient and make compromises as long as your principles are not being sacrificed. However, if the climate and the culture of the organization is so saturated in cynicism, insincerity, or mediocrity—if your integrity and pride are being undermined, and your family's welfare jeopardized—go get another job. Take your hard head and special talent elsewhere. Go where they care, plan, devise and a drive a process, execute, and all the other things I mentioned earlier and will address as we move along.

Go? That's right. Keep performing till the bitter end. Earn the right to be listened to. By being among the organization's top performers, you gain credible experience and stature that's hard to ignore. The best players don't have to whine. So put big numbers up on the board. But at the end of the day, don't ever roll over and stop caring. Don't settle into the rut and misery of an unhappy business family.

Get Dirty to Clean Up

During speeches, I bring audiences to their feet stomping and cheering when I remind them of a scene in the film *Dirty Harry* where Harry's boss reams him out for various and sundry lapses, but the detective just shrugs it off saying: "I never give much credence to anybody whose butt is the same shape as their desk chair."

How true!

Get off your butt. Get your hands dirty. Get the job done. Everybody. If it's a business, that means owners, managers, support staff, sales teams, the whole crew. The same goes for every organization and institution—politicians and civil servants, teachers and students, military officers, troops, clergy and congregations. Even families—particularly families. There's only one way to ignite people power. Sitting in a desk chair doesn't cut it. Waiting for someone else to take responsibility for your success and happiness is futile.

This is a book for anybody who wants to make a difference. Whatever the occupation, organization, or industry—if people are involved—there are techniques, rules, and tactics that get the job done right. Specifically, for the business manager or owner, *Stop Whining—and Start Winning* is all about finding the right people, instilling a fighting and winning spirit, and providing leadership and a business process that really works to delivery productivity and profits. And if you're just beginning your career, read on. Too often inexperienced people miss the signs of a complacent, cynical, and condescending business culture that will waste their time and talent. I'll show you what to look for and what the very best companies expect from you. *What are you complaining about, it's a job, isn't it?*—That's over! We're not going to take that anymore.

 Now-To

How-tos are fine, but now-tos are better. I've collected dozens of them from my own business experience and from conversations with other successful managers, leaders, and coaches. Surf for now-tos with an alarm clock logo like this one.

The book offers a unique form of how-to. I call it a "now-to." Pages of ideas that have been road tested under real-world conditions. Now-tos on recruiting, team building, training, rewards and incentives, customer retention, growth, and communication. Now-tos on issues that consistently trip up and stymie talented individuals and organizations that never seem to be able to break out of the pack and live up to their potential. By delivering "plug-and-play" solutions for typical problems, you'll encounter ideas that can be put into effect immediately. For those who use "to do" lists, these now-tos will help you develop an indispensable "do now" list.

I don't do things halfway. I'm out to help everyone who reads this book become a successful leader. Everyone. By demystifying and decoding the leadership process, I'll make it possible to—and here's the phrase again—make a difference.

People-ology: Loop-the-Loop

Business school professors and consultants have written hundreds of important how-to books. For all the solid concepts that are laid out, there's still one big problem: execution.

The loop is never closed. Some of the key pieces are in place, like a commitment to customer service or a state-of-the-art communications infrastructure, but an unbroken connection is not being made. How can we make that happen? By giving people a simple, consistent, and inspectable business process that is focused on building high-value relationships.

People without leaders are lost. But leaders without a process are doomed. I'll show you how to take a process—basic or complex—and wire it in to complete the circuit so that what needs to be done actually gets done without having to depend on luck, crisis management, or brutal downsizings.

My word choice here—"circuits" and "wiring"—suggests high technology, but hardware and software, gizmos and gadgets can *assist* with implementing a process; only "high people-ology" can actually *execute* a process effectively, consistently, and repeatedly. The people process comes first. It's the number one priority of leadership. Why? Every other process—no matter how slick or high tech—depends on talented, committed, hardworking people. I'll give you an example. An ATM—automatic teller machine—is the key hardware component of a process for delivering basic bank services to the customer without the need for a living, breathing, flesh-and-blood teller. But without an effective people process, the ATM cannot be maintained and serviced properly. Let the machine break down, eat cards, and foul-up accounts and it quickly becomes an irritating customer-killer. It may be that the only contact that hundreds (if not thousands) of people have with the bank is through the ATM. All it takes is one employee who doesn't give a damn—because there's no people process to ensure that he or she does give a damn—and the marvelous process to deliver service automatically is ruined.

I've got to be blunt, though. People-ology is all or nothing.

No faking.

No phoning it in.

It's full time, all the time.

If I can't convince you that, 1), people-ology is doable, and, 2), worth all the effort, forget you ever read this book. In the hands of a cynic or a faker, these techniques are ruinous. You'll frustrate, disappoint, and enrage the people around you. Plus, you'll cripple yourself. There may be short-term advantages, but in the end you'll crawl home in pain.

Harry and Frank

We know who *Dirty Harry* is, but what about Frank Pacetta? If you read my first book, *Don't Fire Them, Fire Them Up*, published in 1994, you may remember me as a maverick, whiz-kid Xerox executive who sort of specialized in climbing out on limbs in an effort to turn around failing business units and teams. If you haven't read the book, all I can say is— Amazon.com, BarnesandNoble.com, or your-neighborhood-bookstore.com. Pacetta is spelled with two *t*s.

I've moved on from Xerox (you'll see why in the final chapter of this book). But "fire 'em up" and creating people power, leadership, and motivation are still my game, a game I work at and play at full time, full out.

Between Xerox and the plunge into Internet entrepreneurship at SinglesourceIT, I was Vice President of Sales for Danka America. In roughly twenty years, my career went from being a scared knocking on doors in order to selling one copier at a time to leading a 2,000-person national salesforce.

Cold calls—been there, done that.

Team play—that too. And hiring, firing, strategic planning, leading, executing, training, recruiting, communicating, and all the other crucial elements of running a major league business operation. I've changed a lot and learned a lot—not the least is how to move from traditional brick-and-mortar corporate enterprises to the wired world of e-commerce. But I am still the same guy described in a front-page profile in the *Wall Street Journal* in 1991, who told a group of shell-shocked men and women at Xerox's district office in Cleveland that they could and would rise from the bottom to the top in one year's time.

We did it too. People—talented, motivated, well-trained, and well-led people—made it happen. That story is in the first book. This one is different. I took to heart Clint Eastwood's line and got my butt out of the chair to find what it is that makes the very best organizations keep getting better. I will be offering you not only Now-To's drawn from personal experience as an executive, motivational speaker, and Internet entrepreneur, but also insights, advice, and warnings from managers, leaders, and coaches who care deeply about helping people achieve financial success, personal fulfillment, and professional excellence.

 What got you there can't keep you there.

Pretty scary. If success isn't a safe haven, what is? There's no place to hide. Comments and expertise like this are highlighted throughout the book. Each one is a gem of wisdom that can have immediate positive impact on your business or career. Don't worry about theories or untested ideas. The stuff is pure, unadulterated street smarts. These men and women walk the walk every day.

Some of it's common sense. Some of it's genius. All of it worked or—get this—flopped big time. Yes, we're going to talk about failures because success doesn't happen without the willingness to risk falling on your face. What went wrong and why is as important as what went right. Most anything can be fixed, but we've got to know it's broken in the first place and why.

By escaping from my desk chair and going on this people-ology quest, I'm able to offer you the ultimate how-to and now-to:

What a great place to work!

- Do you say it?
- Do you hear it said around you?

Find out why not. It's the first major step to eradicating ho-hum.

How to turn ho-hum into "What a great place to work!"

The Power of People-ology

Overall, as an author, I've made an effort to draw out the most practical tactical information and keep it in the broadest possible context. My objective is to the make the book useful to a wide readership that cuts across industries and occupations. No matter what the business's specialty or unique requirements, the common denominator is people. From manufacturing on one end to service industries on the other, there isn't a single business that does not have people at its core. Yet, people skills, people policies, and people processes tend be treated like afterthoughts—"Something for human resources to worry about."

I'm convinced that competitive advantage *always* flows to those who are the most adept at practicing people-ology. They motivate, manage, train, and recruit better. Their customers are more satisfied, productivity is higher, and the bottom line is healthier. People make it happen. Why do we think that indifference, coercion, or cruelty make for a reasonable methodology for tapping this resource? Only a fool lets his or her hardware technology become outmoded, but allowing leadership development, training, or recruitment to languish is commonplace.

I've heard plenty of excuses, ranging from the solution to the problem is too expensive to there are other more important priorities. Most of the time these lame comments come from operations that are in trouble or heading for it. However, they never made the connection between cause and effect. My own experience at Xerox in the 1970s, '80s, and '90s confirmed that until the company realized there was a direct link between customer satisfaction and employee satisfaction efforts to improve overall quality and profitability would be erratic at best. Only when it made the people connection—and stayed connected—was Xerox the company it talked about being.

This book makes that connection. Not because it's the "nice" thing to do, either. Nice has nothing to do with it. To maximize profits these days, businesses need all the help they can get. A sullen, suspicious workforce, with poor motivation and lackluster skills cannot summon the energy levels and problem-solving abilities to get the job done in an increasingly complex and competitive world. Finding and keeping the best people is the key to gaining a competitive advantage. By treating people as a valuable, self-renewing resource instead of raw, disposable commodities, businesses can weather crises, seize unexpected opportunities, and turn on a dime.

Squaring Business Success with the Family Circle

When I head for work in the morning I'm actually going home, back to Far Rockaway in the New York City borough of Queens where I grew up.

I mean it. Sure, the office is really in the Midwest—it could be anywhere, really—but the values I rely on every day are still rooted in a small spit of land just east of Coney Island, squatting under the flight path to Kennedy International Airport.

I had a wonderful childhood. It was a warm, loving, tight-knit Italian-American family. My mother and father are my heroes and, to this day, they are mentors whom I still rely on for business and personal guidance.

Mom is the best manager I've ever known. Dad, a retired executive with Chase Manhattan Bank, is no slouch, either. Both of them held my sister and me and squeezed us. By that I mean we had plenty of security and reassurance, but at the same time we had just the right amount of pressure and incentive to make the most of our talents.

When I went off to the University of Dayton in Ohio—the first time I'd ever been outside New York—my father said he wanted me to do two things, "Have the best four years" of my life and "Don't let Mom and Dad down." Well, I ended up having the best *five* years of my life. After my freshman year I came home for the summer with a 1.6 grade-point average. Talk about letting them down! You have to work at it to be that lousy.

I'll never forget my father's welcome: "You cheated me," he said, sadly and quietly. Dad wasn't going to be cheated again, and he made me pay my tuition and other costs from then on. My screw-up had consequences and that got my attention.

I wish I could say that I matured on the spot. I didn't. The learning curve was a long one. Eventually, the lessons sank in. Years later, when I received my first management opportunity at Xerox, I unconsciously fell back on the leadership style I knew best—high expectations, trust, loyalty, commitment, and emotion. Lots of emotion. Mom and Dad didn't let me cheat and fail. They cared; they made a difference. The least I could do as a junior manager and aspiring leader was to care and to try to make a difference to the people who reported to me.

Ever since, I've run my business organizations like big, crazy, Italian-American families. They've been happy families, and no two of them have been alike. So Tolstoy got it wrong on both counts.

In my families nobody cheats, and nobody fails if I can help it. We dream, work, and win together. We have fun, make money, and build solid, satisfying lives. Why choose as a basic business model something that is joyless, wracked with tension, and soured by small-mindedness and boredom? When I hear, "It's only business . . . nothing personal," I want to gag.

I have another question or two for you:

Is it personal?
Do your bosses care?
Do your colleagues care?
Do you care?

That's the bottom line isn't it? Do you care? If the answer is yes, dream big dreams and I'll do all I can to help you make them come true. This book is packed full of ideas that have worked for me and other *dream-doers*. I'll introduce you to the incredible power of people-ology and even give you some Italian lessons along the way. Ready? Repeat after me:

To hell with ho-hum!

Say it again.

To hell with ho-hum!

Now you've begun speaking the language of success. Welcome to my productive, profitable, and happy family.

CHAPTER TWO

Accomplishing the Hard Part—

Going from Good to Great

*F*rankie was crying and I was on the verge. It was fall of 1997. We were trudging across the parking lot outside Jacobs Field. The Cleveland Indians had just defeated the New York Yankees and blown them out of their last chance to play in that year's World Series.

My (then) twelve-year-old son was born in Columbus, Ohio, and that's where our home is these days. Naturally, most of his buddies are nuts for the Indians, but he's a die-hard, scorched earth, take no prisoners New York Yankees fanatic. Who's to blame for making my kid an outcast?

I am. It's in his genes. I grew up about ten miles from Yankee Stadium. In reality, it might as well have been right next door. I don't care where I live today, that team belongs to me! Frankie does his share of rebelling, but on the subject of the greatest baseball organization in the cosmos, father and son are in sync.

Why am I telling you this? Fair warning. We're going to break some conventions in this book because I believe in practicing what I've always preached as a business manager and leader. Over the years the people who have reported to me have heard this mantra:

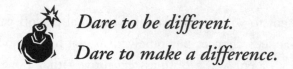

> ### Dare to be different.
> ### Dare to make a difference.

And I dare you, too. Treat this book differently. Don't just read it—*do it*. What I am doing now, on this page, by launching into a story about Frankie and the Yankees, is showing you who I am. My purpose is to get you to do the same. I want you to go to the office, the factory, the store—wherever you work and do business—and show them who you are. No more hiding from the customer, from your colleagues, or from your employees.

Not interested? Too risky? Not businesslike? Then you'll never be a genuinely successful leader or manager. And for those who aren't drawn to seeking an executive position or running your own business, your job is just going to be ho-hum, if not pure torture, without the courage to show the boss who you really are and demand that he or she reciprocate.

Example: I know a young executive named Dan. He's dedicated and hardworking. One night he got a call from his boss, who, without so much as a "hello" demanded to know what his quarterly numbers had been. Dan took a deep breath and said, "I'll give you the numbers *after* you ask me how I'm doing and about my family." The shocked manager immediately apologized.

Good for Dan. He wasn't going to allow his boss to dehumanize and depersonalize their relationship. It may have been an innocent mistake, but the message Dan heard from the boss was, "I care more about the numbers than I do about you"—and he wasn't about to stand for it.

You shouldn't either. By taking the easy way out and allowing business relationships to exist in a twilight zone devoid of kindness, courtesy, caring, and respect we make life miserable for ourselves and for others. Furthermore, there's not even a justifiable tradeoff. Minimal courtesy and caring does not yield maximum productivity and profits. The reverse is true. To dehumanize an organization is to demotivate its people.

So what's this got to with Jacobs Field? That final playoff game in 1997 wrecked the Yankee's chances but renewed my faith in a style of leadership—both as a parent and a business executive—that I've practiced for nearly twenty years. A style that made my reputation, got me on the front page of the *Wall Street Journal,* and provided the opportunity to write books like this one. Rather than telling you about it in theoretical terms, I'll finish my story about Frankie to *show* you what I mean.

Frankie bugged me to go to that playoff game, and I didn't want to. Why? I was busting my butt as the senior vice president for sales of Danka, a $2 billion office products corporation that I had joined after leaving Xerox. Leading a field operation of two thousand reps along with P & L responsibility for the entire office imaging division kept me pretty busy.

Going to the playoff meant a long drive from Columbus to Cleveland and back on the eve of a major business trip. A baseball game was not a good idea. To avoid disappointing my son, I said okay, immediately regretted it, and started looking for excuses. The day before the playoff final, I gently suggested that it would be a much better idea to watch the game on TV. We'd relax in the family room, have lots of pizza and soda. Our tickets weren't all that good, I pointed out. We'd see more of the action on TV.

Great pitch, eh? And I'm supposed to be a super-salesman.

Frankie wasn't going to buy that in a million years. I had promised, he reminded me—we were going and that was that.

It was a great game. The place rocked. The Cleveland fans were screaming their guts out. We were both thrilled to be there.

After the final out, our beloved Yankees crushed, the tumult was even worse. We could have surfed the sound waves back to the car. We were almost there when I noticed Frankie's tears, and I instantly choked up myself. As an Italian-American, who grew up in a Jewish neighborhood, if you scratch me I will bleed drops of guilt. There I was, standing beside a boy who had just had one of the great experiences of a lifetime—win or lose—and I had done my best to cheat him out of it. Watch it on TV!

Yes, Frankie was disappointed that his team had come so close and lost. But he'll forget those pangs—he has already—what he will always remember is the rush we felt together in the stadium. The idea that I had been willing to settle for ho-hum—for canned, for boring, for autopilot, for ruining a precious moment for my son—drove me nuts. I knew better than that.

I vowed then and there: No more ho-hum!

On the drive home, I thought about all the times my corporate superiors had told me, "You get great numbers, build top teams, and run first-class operations, but you're too emotional, Frank." Rather than respond with, "How else am I supposed to get great numbers, build top teams, and run first-class operations?"—I did my best to fix the problem. I dutifully turned down my emotional thermostat. But I eventually came to realize that that was cheating. Regardless of how good your numbers may look, if you wake up in the morning and don't feel good about what you're doing and know that it's the very best use of your talent and passion—you are cheating yourself and your family.

Thanks to Frankie, I came to my senses: I stopped cheating. I tore the damned emotional thermostat off the wall.

I'm going to show you how to do the same thing. As scary and "dangerous" as it may sound, I promise it will work wonders for your career, your business, and your life.

To truly succeed and to escape from make-work foolishness, the pointlessness of marking time, and all the other forms of mediocrity that numb and deaden our lives, this kind of energized, committed leadership is not optional. It actually starts with you, no matter who you are or what your job. Whether you're a CEO or a receptionist, some things—like career development or personal satisfaction—are too precious to delegate or leave to chance. Those are strictly do-it-yourself propositions, along with self-respect, family responsibilities, and—oh, I almost forgot—and happiness.

Yes, I'm suggesting that business success and personal happiness are not incompatible, and that both are products of effective leadership. But don't panic, you haven't inadvertently purchased one of the more than three thousand leadership books that are currently in print, which, for the most part, treat leadership as another form of management. My approach is different—quite different. It's likely, in fact, to irritate and outrage all those who believe a business book must be neat, orderly, and unfold in a methodical way. I've got news for them: Business is rarely neat, orderly, and methodical.

Have you noticed? I'll bet you have.

So don't expect to see a lot of carefully crafted structure serving as a platform for carefully crafted theories and strategic thinking. In fact, when I see the words *strategic thinking* I have all I can do to avoid falling into a coma. You're going to get an impressionistic, gun-and-go approach that puts as much usable stuff on the table as fast as possible. There's twenty years' worth of tips and techniques to draw from that I've used to get organizations out of trouble and ahead of the competition.

If you're like me, you don't have time to mess around. I want you to be able to read a page or two, pick up a workable idea, put the book down, and go to it. I know you'll come back because you'll want another idea that works as well as the first one did. Actually, it would be safer to try keep you glued to these pages right to the end by suggesting that until you learn the whole system it's premature to take action. But as much as I'd like to think that every reader will read and savor each word, I know there are going to be dropouts who think that when they read the chapter on communication, emotion, or what have you that they've received their money's worth.

Okay. If that's what you want, good luck. But be warned. This book comes in two parts. It almost like a pair of cookbooks. The first one, chapters 1 through 8, lays out the necessary ingredients. The second provides the recipes and the cooking lessons. If you leave the table before chapter 8, you're skipping the main course. I'll even look the other way if you violate another sacred literary convention—sequentiality. Read chapters 1 through 7 in any order that you want. Chapter 8 serves as a review and checklist. Then hit chapters 9 through 16 at random. Shuffle the deck. Or don't. Your choice.

In the end, if you've been using this stuff right along, you'll have a personal leadership and management system up and running that will deliver higher productivity and profits, not to mention a lot more fun and satisfaction that you ever thought an adult had a right to expect in an activity that doesn't involve food, sex, or speeding.

Now, let's take a shot at ripping that emotional thermostat off the wall.

Make It Personal

When businesses fail, it's rarely because of a lousy product or a poor economy. It's because people were allowed to fail. A culture was created policy by policy that did not recruit, train, reward, deploy, and energize people. Those in charge could not or would not lead. They thought they didn't need to bother, didn't know how, or figured they didn't have time.

What a shame. Leadership skills are the oldest and most effective "management" tool at our disposal. You don't have to be Gandhi or Attila the Hun to use them.

The first requirement is a genuine passion for people. As a leader, my overwhelming desire is to see the people around me succeed. Are they growing? Are they living up to their potential? Are they happy? In turn, that's how I measure my own success. This leadership characteristic is not unique to me. It too can be taught and learned. My first teachers were Mom and Dad. Yet it took Al Bird to call that to my attention.

I was a new district manager at Xerox running a $100 million operation. Al was the regional vice president. He summoned the members of his management team to Chicago for a get-acquainted session. Like me, there were several other managers new to the job. We were told to prepare a brief presentation that would serve as an introduction. Who are you? Where are you coming from? Bring some family snapshots, and that sort of thing. Hey, for a bunch of brash sales managers what could be easier?

The setting for the meeting was low-key: spacious hotel suite, early evening, a nice spread of snacks and drinks. The team members chatted and sized-up one another. When it was time for the main event, Al said he would go first.

I expected the same old thing. There'd be a few ice-breaking jokes, a story about the kids and college days, some rah-rah about vision and objectives. What we got from this suave, savvy, impeccably dressed African-American executive was electrifying. I remember most vividly Al's comments about the respect he had for his father, how strong and loving the man was, and how much he owed him. Al nearly broke down as he told us that his dad was dying of cancer.

Wow!

Emotions are said to alter a person's brain chemistry. I had never experienced it as vividly until this incident with Al Bird. After he shared this emotional story about his father, he became a totally different guy to me. He looked different, sounded different—my whole reaction to him changed.

It was completely unexpected, deeply revealing, and totally transformational. In just a few minutes, he had changed his relationship with us and altered the dynamics of the group. We knew who he was, the kind of leader he would be, and what we had to do to play on his team.

Al was a tough act to follow, but there were other managers who were also impressive. One woman showed a collage of pictures from her family album and high school yearbook. We got great glimpses behind the scenes. When it was my turn, I chucked my prepared presentation. I had planned to tell a bunch of jokes, keep things light and on the surface. Instead I told them about Joey.

He's my older brother. Joey was born retarded. Something happened during the delivery that deprived his brain of oxygen. His speech, coordination, and mental acuity were all badly impaired. For as long as I can remember, he's needed help with the most basic things, like tying his shoes and going to the toilet. But that was okay, Joey was Joey. Family life revolved around this chubby, laughing guy. Extra money earmarked for vacations, new cars, and clothes paid for medical care, tests, and the always fruitless search for a cure. But my sister, Carm, and I never had the slightest clue that our family was different or making a sacrifice. Our parents were always there for us. They never complained, never despaired. In word and deed, Mom and Dad let us know that we were blessed. And we were.

Family Money

Three years younger, I shared a bedroom with Joey. I was probably eleven or twelve years old when it began to sink in how long and hard my parents had worked to keep the family on an even keel, and how much I owed them. The realization meant that I had a really big job to do. I was going to repay my parents for the debt I owed them, and I would need to double it. One for me, one for Joey. He couldn't cover his share. I could. Years went by before I truly stepped up to that task. You've heard of the sixteen year old going on twenty-five? I was the twenty-five year old going on sixteen.

When at last I grew up, I found that I had inherited a fortune. There was discipline and love, loyalty and common sense, straight talk, hard work, and joy. Plus, accumulated compound interest of faith, courage, and perseverance that could have wiped out the national debt. I had been bankrolled by the ultimate venture capitalists—Mom and Dad.

I took the capital and we invested it—Joey and me—in people. The objective was to make the good ones great. Every time that happens, it's payback time for Mom and Dad.

The power of Al Bird's example prompted me to tell Joey's story for the first time. Now, I share it whenever I need to forge a leadership bond. And by the way, that team of Al's was a winner. The region's districts were among the highest performers nationally. From day one, the wall of suspicion and doubt had been torn down. He connected and so did we. There was a willingness to give other team members the benefit of the doubt and a helping hand because we knew them personally. Trust is the highest octane fuel of them all.

More recently, I was asked to stand before a group of beleaguered managers to give them the bad news that they were facing downsizing that included painful layoffs. They sensed what was about to happen. The room bristled with cynicism and hostility. I told them how I envied them. There was a snicker from the back of the room. I told them going from mediocre to good was easy; good to great was the hard part—the thrilling part. Then I told them about Joey.

Why? It doesn't sound relevant or "businesslike," does it? But that's wrong on both counts. Those men and women needed to make a quick evaluation of my credibility. I was there to show them how to survive the next ninety days of hell. I suppose I could have launched into a briefing on severance pay arrangements. If I had, I would have been sized-up as being cold, unfeeling, and businesslike. Much of what I planned to say over the course of the meeting would have been colored by that impression. If you've read Homer's *Odyssey*, you'll recall that in the ancient Greek world when strangers arrived in a strange land they were given food, shelter, and lavish hospitality. In return, they were expected to tell their story. How they had come to that place, who their ancestors were, the travails they suffered, and the triumphs they'd won. Everyone sat around eating, drinking, and listening to the free floor show. But more than entertainment was involved. It was the way the strangers were judged as friend or foe, worthy or unworthy. I doubt whether humankind will ever outgrow this instinct. I certainly hope not.

That's why Joe's story was and is relevant; here's why it was "businesslike."

What I wanted to do was to put the group in touch with emotions that were strong enough to counteract those they were already feeling—anger, fear, and confusion. I offered them perseverance and courage when I shared the story of my parents and Joey. The managers I was speaking to were all going to need perseverance and courage to carry on in the face of adversity.

Moreover, if you are going to lead people into and out of a business crisis, the least you can do is to take off your mask. If you don't, they won't. If they don't, you won't succeed. All the vision, all the goals, all the good intentions go right down the drain. Even the routine stuff becomes difficult. The leader has to earn trust, and to do that he or she must offer sincerity as the first token, sign, or amulet to demonstrate that the one who leads is, in fact, trustworthy.

What Al Bird taught me, and what I'm passing along to you, is the need to make a personal connection to override the natural suspicion, anxiety, uncertainty, and anger that may confront a new leader (old ones too). There is a craving to be led, but fear of being misled is the counterweight. You'll get just one shot, and, since emotion is the target, emotion must be the bullet. A heartfelt story that explains who you are and where you're coming from changes the relationship immediately.

"You thought you knew who I was before I told you about Joey, didn't you?" I said to the anxious managers. They all nodded.

"What do you think now?"

I made eye contact with a man in the front row and waited. After an awkward silence, he said, "I guess I trust you a little more."

Good. Let's go to work.

Eliminate the Question Marks

I'd like this book to be as interactive as we can make it. The traditional format—author pontificates while the reader nods—leaves a lot to be desired.

Take a sheet of paper and write down what you know about your boss. The personal stuff: hobbies, kids' names, likes and dislikes, birthplace, favorite color, and those sorts of things. Leave the job-related issues aside for now.

Number the items. You should be able to come up with fifty or a hundred of them without much effort. But I'll bet many of my readers can't get past ten. The boss is a mystery man or woman. Right off, it explains why there is a lack of leadership. A leader should be an exclamation point, not a question mark. A flag, not a veil.

Now turn the tables. List the personal things your boss knows about you. The tally may be even shorter. And if you are a manager with people reporting to you, take a moment to jot down where Bill or Ellen spent their last vacations, or if Daryl is responsible for the care of his elderly mother. What do you really know about their aspirations, problems, and preferences?

I see a swarm of question marks.

Truly, no personal news in a workplace is bad news. There's no connectivity. It's an inhuman and anti-human place. Fragile and unfriendly, such organizations crack and fall apart in a crisis, or lack the buoyancy to rise to meet challenges. Military combat veterans will tell you that most acts of battlefield courage are usually not prompted by thoughts of duty, honor, or country. Nor is it a question of following orders. Facing death, the Marine holds a position for the sake of his fellow Marines. In training, Marine and other military leaders struggle mightily to forge those kind of strong personal connections.

William Locander, who teaches and mentors students in business leadership at the University of South Florida told me about an exercise he does with consulting clients. He arranges to take a company's CEO onto the factory floor or wherever it is that the frontline troops are working. Bill structures it so that there is time for real give and take.

Invariably, the CEOs return to their offices surprised and impressed with the caliber of their workers. Not because they saw them bent over a drill press or driving a forklift on the loading dock, but as a result of the personal conversations that occurred. The executive will be stunned to learn that he employs expert horticulturists, prize-winning amateur astronomers, and museum-quality sculptors. If things really click, he may start wondering why it is that these bright people are leaving their talent at home instead of bringing it to the job.

Connection!

What can we do to tap that potential?

Connection!

What can we do to help our people develop and broaden their talent?

Connection!

But hold on. Don't even dream about sending around questionnaires demanding that people reveal personal information. That's no exclamation point—that's an upraised middle finger and you get (and deserve) one in return. The same goes for a sudden chumminess. *I've got a spare moment, tell me about the family.* That's phony and manipulative. In reality, it says, *I couldn't care less.* To care more, and care genuinely, it's necessary to practice people-ology the hard way: one on one. It can't be delegated or done by the numbers. Building empathy and rapport—which is what has to happen— is a lot like making friends. You share, you drop your guard, you open up. Shortcuts don't work.

Go to the loading dock or the retail outlet and make a connection. Tell them about your mom and dad, ask about theirs. The exchange will educate and energize both sides. Not only as a simple transfer of information but as an interchange of feelings. The isolated CEO or senior manager lacks sensitivity for people beyond his or her immediate circle. This an enormous barrier, and it is one that is a major contributing factor explaining why leaders and managers fail. Sensitivity is an acquired skill. You must be able to listen to others and be willing to reveal your own thoughts and emotions. Out of the process comes a set of responses from both sides. If you are an emotional blank, people will draw their own conclusions—she or he doesn't care about me—and shape their actions accordingly. Conversely, sincerity and trust engender sincerity and trust. It makes for a solid investment that will pay off in higher productivity, profits, and employee satisfaction.

People-ology Information List:
What You Need to Know About Your People

(What your boss needs to know about you
to be an effective leader)

- Career aspirations.
- Professional resume.
- Family situation.
- Spouse's background.
- Heroes.
- Recommendations for improving the company.
- Assessment of the boss's strengths and weakness.
- Expected support from the company.
- The five most emotional moments.
- Assessment of coworkers.
- Need for training.
- Outside interests.
- Biggest dream.
- Source of pride.
- Most significant accomplishment on the job.
- Most significant accomplishment off the job.
- Views on what characterizes an effective leader.

There are no "right" answers. This isn't a psychological test or an employee satisfaction survey. We're using the chain saw on a major barrier that's blocking one-on-one contact. Let 'er rip.

TAN—Take Action Now

The shelves of the Barnes & Noble near my home are stuffed full of business and personal development books that are avidly read from cover to cover. If you could measure ideas by the pound, megatons of good ones are dropped on readers with practically no effect.

I've read plenty of these books myself. Often, I'll see a neat new process or procedure, but I never get around to implementing it. One reason is that the author is presenting a system or methodology. By the time I digest the whole package, I've lost interest in the parts that initially caught my attention. As for the system, as brilliant as it may be, I simply don't have time for the kind of wholesale restructuring that would be required. Do you?

What I'm offering you is an array of off-the-shelf techniques that work right out of the box. None of them, however, are worth a damn if you don't use them. And the only way for you to verify my claim is to put the book down and try them.

There is something about business—any business—that fosters a "good idea, but won't work here" attitude. I've been in meeting after meeting where executives lament their problems. Every time a solution was offered the response was, "Good idea, but it won't work here . . . our situation is different." In the end nothing works here but the stuff that is already being used—and failing.

There isn't a single idea in this book that rises to the level of rocket science, brain surgery, or tightrope walking. That's why you can afford to put it down and go try them. Wall Street will not tremble because you decide to build trust by being trustworthy. When I told my new management team about nearly flunking out of my freshman year at the University of Dayton, Xerox's market share held steady.

Nonetheless there can be solid results. My team knew from that moment on that I was no academic superman. I was human. I needed their help. First, I had to earn their trust.

Put this book down. Go earn some trust.

Every strong, valuable relationship is trust based. It's the same for families, marriages, friendships, and jobs. Governments rise and fall based on trust or the lack of it. Customers walk away—no, they run away—from businesses they cease to trust.

A few years ago, I accompanied a team of senior executives on a barnstorming mission to rally and inspire a newly restructured corporation's far flung national workforce. At each stop, we rolled out the inspiration and the vision. We told them great things were going to happen, that there were terrific new products in the pipeline, and how rewarding it would be. After a while I started getting a queasy feeling: The reception wasn't what I expected. The walls weren't coming down.

Finally, at the end of a presentation, I moved to the rostrum and asked, "Do you guys even believe us?"

I looked around the audience and got my answer in the form of silence and classic body language.

No.

They had heard it before. Promises weren't enough.

And they aren't enough. I have a different take on the famous *Jerry Macguire* catch-phrase, "Show me the money!" It's "Show me the honesty." To build trust, we have to keep our promises.

It's that simple. Keeping promises. I'm going to show you how to do that by offering you an example of how not to do it. When I was a young sales rep and just coming into my own by racking up respectable numbers, I got a new boss who was a dream come true. We all loved the guy. He was fun to be around and he knew the business cold. Or so we thought, prior to the appointment.

Peter Rogers, another hot shot rep, and I were overjoyed. We were going to slaughter the competition and retire at thirty! It was probably the single greatest kickoff that I've seen a leader deliver. He booked the hallowed local arena where the university team played championship basketball and laid out a vision that had us all standing on the seats cheering. The PA announcer introduced each member of the team. "We are the champions" blared out of the loudspeakers. He even had ladders ready at the end so that we could cut down the nets to symbolize the champions that we were going to become.

Within a month, we knew the guy was an unmitigated disaster. Good guy, empty suit. He was incapable of delivering on his promises and didn't really even try. The team just collapsed. He was our guy, so Peter and I tried to defend him, but before long we just closed our eyes as the thing went from bad to worse.

He *said* all the right things; he *did* nothing. And his superiors did nothing to help him. It was a valuable lesson for me: I keep my promises, large and small. In fact, I'm crazed about it. My personal "do now" list is filled with follow-through items to fulfill promises that I've made.

I'm equally obsessive about seeing to it that promises that have been made to me get fulfilled. My people know that's the deal. I keep my promises; they keep theirs. Amnesia is a fatal disease in business and, for that matter, personal life as well.

I hate the old cynical line—what have you done for me lately? Far better is, *What have you done to keep your promises to me lately?*

This sacred promise reciprocity is a key to building trust. It flows both ways and must be established at the outset of the relationship that a leader seeks to build with those he or she is leading.

 Now-To: Post Your Promises

Put them on public display and track them day-to-day, week-to-week. When they are fulfilled, make sure the word gets out.

Before we move on to the next chapter, I'll give you a peek behind the scenes of book publishing. At an early meeting with my editor and publisher to discuss titles, one participant suggested *Failure Is Not an Option.* Sounds like the motto for a death squad, doesn't it? *Blow it up or blow yourself up!* Give me a break.

I was so adamantly opposed to it that I told Laureen Rowland, the editor, that "*Failure Is Not an Option* is not an option."

You know why? Failure *is* an option. People opt for it all the time. The whole idea behind this book is that we can opt for success every time.

You want to know what isn't an option?

Insincerity. Insincerity poisons trust.

Sincerity is the starting point. Out of all the business leadership material in this book, sincerity is the only thing that must be treated like a cornerstone concept. It gets dropped into place first, or the whole edifice will eventually crack and crumble. All the rest can be jumbled around, mixed and matched, and plugged and played to your heart's content. While other concepts are important, sincerity is essential. You've got to get the sincerity bit straight right here and now. If not, you'll blow yourself up as a leader. I've got big ears and I can hear the explosions all over corporate America, twenty-four hours a day, as leaders shade the truth, do a little spinning, selectively present the facts, or flat-out lie.

Puff. They're gone. Sure, they may still have a job and management responsibilities. But their credibility and effectiveness are shot.

Sincerity also extends to your motives. Better check them closely because the people who work for you are going to give them a thorough going over for signs that you're just looking out for yourself. If you are, then failure is not an option—it's a certainty.

Going from good to great—the comment I made to the group of apprehensive managers that faced the prospect of severe downsizing—is the hard part precisely because it takes qualities of greatness that have nothing to do with business models, market timing, or the competition. It comes down to emotional engagement, personal commitment, perseverance, trust, keeping promises, and sincerity. All the things we've been focusing on. These qualities can only be found at the source—within ourselves and our people.

Starting from scratch or moving from mediocre to good is easy because it can be achieved through sheer muscle, luck, or cunning. The breakthrough to greatness comes through making person-to-person connections. I call it turning on the people juice.

"Just Do It," Nike's famous slogan, is meaningless without the next part, which is left unspoken: "because we know each other, trust, each other, believe in each other."

Try a few other combinations:

Just do it . . . because you have to do.
Just do it . . . because I say so.
Just do it . . . because I need to please my boss.

If that's the message, then truly, going from good to great isn't an option, it's an impossibility.

CHAPTER THREE

Deploying the High Five—

Simplicity, Preparation, Perfection, Pride, and People

*A*nd "productivity" makes for the slick six. "Profit" gives us the magnificent seven. There are so many important *P*-words. Process? No, put that one back in the box, we'll get to it later—much later. Let's do the high five, plus productivity.

Productivity is sort of a downer after all the excitement in chapter 2, isn't it? Jacobs Field, Al Bird, Joey, and the need for building sincerity. I deliberately took you for a spin in the people-ology hot rod to give you a feel for what it's like and what you can do with it when you're behind the wheel. Now I'm going to shift gears.

So, here we are facing a blob called "productivity."

One of the dirty secrets of leadership is that its purpose is to maximize productivity. The idea isn't very poetic: "Let my people go . . . be more productive," or "Productive at last, productive at last, Thank God Almighty, productive at last." But think about it. A leader helps build a pathway to success. In the end, those who take the pathway are happier, wiser, more fulfilled, stronger, and richer in material and spiritual goods. They've become more productive by making full use of their talent.

It doesn't harm leadership to think of it this way as long as the primary purpose is recognized as *personal* productivity. Who can argue with the benefits of being smarter, more effective, efficient, and satisfied? But the abstract, quantifiable productivity of a business organization is always secondary—yes, always—because it comes as *a result of* personal productivity. The benefits flow from the individual to the organization and then back to the individual.

If you replace the words "personal productivity" with the words "personal enrichment," you can see what I'm suggesting. Leadership is a means of enrichment in a sense that has little, if anything, to do with money and everything to do with inner value. When personal productivity is shortchanged, business productivity is undermined as well. People can't or won't rise to the challenge. There is no way to have strong productive organizations built around demoralized, unproductive people.

We're going to have to cut down the complications that grow up in any organization as a result of the tendency to try to make business productivity the primary purpose. By neglecting individual development and enrichment, organizations then must attempt to substitute procedures and systems to fill the gaps. With the increasing neglect of personal development, the organization grows bloated and cumbersome. Bureaucracy is the scar tissue of corporate dehumanization. The more of it you see and feel, the more advanced the disease.

Each system, each complication creates a barrier that interferes with productivity—for both the individual and the business organization. Adjusting to barriers, learning to live with them, and accepting them is my idea of hell. It's one of the reasons why I was ready to leave Xerox when I did. I learned a lot there—good and bad. My belief in process is pure

Xerox. I'm zealous about process execution—as you will see as this book unfolds—because of the company's failure to live up to its own high standards. A good process should always be flexible and capable of mid-course correction; often Xerox's wasn't. A good process also turns up deficiencies that must then be corrected; again and again, Xerox's did the former but not the latter. It became frustrating and demoralizing as the layers of complication got thicker and thicker.

In some ways, Xerox is a unique case—and not unique at all. Spawned from the fiendish complexity of xerography, the copier giant seems bewitched by the need to balance technological complications against bureaucratic ones. The tangle led to the creation of cadres of highly skilled, often highly frustrated, barrier-busting leaders paired off against highly skilled, often highly complacent, barrier-building managers. It made for an ongoing civil war, much like the wars that are being fought in companies all over the world. I think it's time for a cease-fire.

Simple Smarts

Make par, not war. I love to golf, I could play every day. No, twice a day. What other sport lets you play a game and do business at the same time? One of the senior members of my home club is a distinguished business executive with a national reputation. One afternoon, he and I were discussing a company that I was researching for a possible acquisition. One of its minuses was a glaring lack of leadership. We both agreed that the weakness could be fixed.

My friend offered some wise suggestions, and as we parted, he turned to me and said, "Frank, it really is very simple." He bore down slightly on the "it" to signify that he wasn't just talking about one faltering company, but about them all.

He was right. *It* is.

Easy simple? No, not necessarily. Hard simple is more like it: long hours, important decisions, heavy responsibilities. But the notion that creating and running a viable business must be riddled with confusion, difficulty, and intricacy is off the wall. Or you have to be a lot smarter than me. And that may explain why I do what I do. At my college graduation, there were parents honoring *summa cum laudes*. Painfully aware of their son's horrendous academic record and their tuition-paying days were over, my mom and dad were there asking in amazement, *Lordy how come!*

As an executive, I can't complicate my life. I'm not smart enough. I've got to keep it simple. How simple? Here's how simple.

- Hire the best people
- Provide them with the best training and development
- Offer them limitless opportunities
- Create a high-energy, caring environment
- Recognize and reward success
- Make it fun and challenging
- Fashion and execute a business process that delivers these promises
- Build high-yielding, high-value relationships internally and externally
- Forge an enriching experience for everyone

And there's one more:

- Deliver now!

If you don't think that's simple, maybe you are not approaching the task like a good manager. I'm not being facetious. While I'm writing about leadership, the best leaders are good managers. They know to ask a basic question: How do we do that? Assuming "that" is what needs to be done to run a profitable business.

If we know what we have to do, how to do it—and then do it—we're 90 percent of the way to success. Still simple, right?

The next question then comes down to this: How can we do it better than we are doing it right now?

Can you walk me through what you have to do to survive and prosper, and how you actually accomplish these requirements? The basic stuff?

Now for Pete's sake, don't commission a study or hire a consultant to do research. If you can't answer off the top of your head, there is a problem. Or if the answer involves more than a sentence or two, you are getting tangled up in complications. Xerox, for example, is in the business of making and selling copiers—like it or not. It may aspire to be a "document" company or have another grand vision, but if they don't sell copiers today, tomorrow, and the next day it's *adios.* Anything that gets in the way of that purpose is a barrier.

Barriers are the enemy of productivity. It's amazing how extraneous activities—complications—are allowed to get in the way of primary business purposes. Gobs of rationalizations are laid down to protect them from people like me. I've heard anything from "I've got to attend a meeting" to "We can't do that until the proposals have been submitted."

Are face-to-face meetings important? Absolutely. But if they don't directly impact the customer, meetings become barriers to executing the bottom-line business activity. Purposeless meetings are productivity killers. Likewise, proposals, analysis, paperwork of all sorts are important parts of a business process. But the basics come first. Ben's Kansas City Steak House better take care that it serves up the best prime beef *before* it gets preoccupied selling lottery tickets or opening a sports bar. Ben can do those things, but only after he takes care of his bottom-line activity (and keeps taking care of it).

How can you hire the best people and give them the best training and development if complications are allowed to get in the way of the fundamental business purpose and the fundamental action to achieve that purpose? You'll probably end up hiring the wrong people and giving them the wrong training. It would be like poor Ben using lottery specialists to burn steaks back in the kitchen and wait on tables. It would be a disaster. The promise of limitless opportunity and an enriching experience for all are empty without a disciplined focus on what it is we do to stay in business.

If leadership is the art of cutting down barriers to create a pathway to success—and it is—the very first barrier is blocking answers to these questions:

- What do we have to do?
- How do we do it?
- Are we, in fact, doing it?

Once you know that you should be able to tell me:

- How often did you take that action today?
- How does that compare to yesterday?
- How often do you expect it to happen tomorrow?
- How many times did you take this action personally?
- How many times did your average worker perform this action?
- How do those figures compare to last quarter or last year?

If you don't know the answers, what do you know? I suspect you know about a lot of complicated stuff. Good for you, but it's bad for business. Bad because the emotion, the trust building, the vision, the communication, the recruiting, the training, the relentless leadership—all the things we focus on in this book—will be of no use. Once you've put your heart on your sleeve as a leader and offered sincerity, you'll have to roll up your sleeves and get busy clearing away the complications and using a chain saw to cut down barriers that interfere with personal productivity. It's part of the job. Make that it's the *best part of the job.*

We've got to get beyond the notion that equates high productivity with slave-driving and downsizing. The usual drill is for new managers to come on like the "productivity Gestapo" by announcing an enormous increase in output without going to the trouble of discovering what is actually interfering with current productivity levels. I don't care how sincere you are and what family stories you share, if you don't make an immediate effort to cut down barriers people will start humming the words to the famous "Who" tune—"Here comes the new boss, same as the old boss." They'll know that nothing is going to change except the stress level and the frustration factor: Both are headed higher.

It's the new boss's responsibility to swing the chain saw so that his or her people can deliver the productivity gains that will benefit everyone.

And after the cloud of exhaust fumes and sawdust settles, what's left? I realize that I'm reverting to my sales background, but I firmly believe that frequent high quality customer contact is the simple core of every business—and for that matter every relationship.

Okay, here's *the* question again: What do we have to do?

Answer: Delight our customers by fully meeting their needs and doing it better than the competition.

If in good conscience you can say, "My business doesn't work that way," take this book back to where you bought it and maybe, if they believe in delighting the customer, they'll return your money. But I don't think bookstores will have to worry about being overrun with returns. Everybody has customers. So can the pat answers and take a hard look at what you do to stay in business. If providing a product or a service to a customer is near the top of the list, the next "now-to" is a no-brainer.

 Now-To

Cut down three barriers that are obstructing your path to the customer. Don't spend a lot of time thinking, meeting, or talking about it. Do it today, tomorrow, and keep doing it every day.

The now-to is adamant about quick action because I want you to avoid falling into the trap of taking action eventually. Forget eventually. Don't wait for the study to be completed or the consultants to sign on. This will boost the customer contact rate, and even a modest increase is of great benefit. It will get your people busy and focused, and motivate you to keep your promises (like, "I will cut down three barriers a day"). When the rate is abysmal—which it can be in businesses that have been overwhelmed by complications—the effect is like a turbocharger kicking in.

After Danka acquired Kodak's color copier division, I discovered that Kodak had equipped each of its district sales offices with sumptuous demonstration rooms. They were gorgeous setups. The problem was that Kodak never used them. To jump-start sales and energy levels, I ordered a three-month demo blitz. It prompted a customer contact rate for the period that exceeded the entire previous year. The order rate rose dramatically, as well. But I didn't just say, "Let the demos begin," and snap my fingers. I made it my mission to clear the obstacles that had kept those demo rooms out of action.

In the same way, before joining Danka, in my last assignment for Xerox, I took over the Columbus district, which had been allowed to fall to close to the bottom of the national sales rankings. At the first meeting with my teams I said, "We're going to run the next four laps as fast as we can and then we're going to pick up speed." They thought I was crazy, but that's exactly what we did. After four quarters the district was near the top nationally and gaining steadily. That turnaround didn't happen because the productivity Gestapo had arrived, it came about because—first—I had to clear the obstacles off the track. Once that happened, talented men and women were able to run faster and faster and faster. As the speed increased, so did the exhilaration, the fun, and the rewards.

Get moving. Get productive—now. It's simple.

The Red Notebook

You want simple? Here's simple-plus preparation, the second of the "High Five." Go to an office supply store and buy out their stock of red spiral-bound, wide-ruled, single-theme notebooks; the kind you probably used in a college or high school; the pages are 8.5-by-11 inches and have pre-punched holes for use in a three-ring binder.

Keep one on your desk or in your briefcase to record leadership ideas, experiences, pieces of good advice, mistakes, and so forth. When it's full, stash it away and start another.

For example, "Frank, *it* really is very simple," went into my red note-book for future reference. I've accumulated hundreds of pages of material that way. Here's an item from several years ago after I attended a meeting run by a senior manager who announced plans for a "surprise attack" on the competition.

 From the Red Notebook

Nobody believed a word the guy said. Afterward, I heard somebody say, "Yeah, a surprise attack. I'll be surprised if we attack."

The guy had zero credibility going in and even less coming out. He was notorious for never following through, and the cynical comment from my colleague caught the moment precisely. Without the red notebook, the gem would probably have been lost. I also use the red notebook to record important decisions. I can go back and re-create one-on-one meetings with my sales reps that occurred ten or fifteen years ago. But I get even more value out of noting and then using good ideas that I pick up from other leaders. And I'm not afraid to flag the ideas—mine in particular—that don't work.

You might want to go back and pick up a few items from chapters 1 and 2: Al Bird's story is a good candidate as is Bill Locander's advice about heading for the loading dock to make some personal connections.

Every manager I talked to in compiling this list has mended his or her ways and is now a successful leader. Nobody's perfect. Mistakes happen all the time. But the worst mistake of all is the mistake we don't admit and therefore can never correct. Use the "terrible twenty" to determine where you stand today—or where your boss stands. It's a humbling experience. I probably was doing number thirteen—didn't have a process or stick to it— early in my leadership career. I tried to get by on energy and aggressiveness. What I was actually doing, as is the case for the rest of the "terrible twenty"

The Terrible Twenty

Now that your red notebook is up and running and the preparation is underway, I want to appropriate a page or two to establish a leadership baseline. For years, I've been asking managers to candidly share with me examples of what they did wrong early in their leadership careers. Here's the list of the terrible twenty:

1. Didn't do pre-work to learn the background or record of the people on the team.
2. Made snap decisions to demonstrate decisiveness and failed to gather the necessary information to make a solid, fair, tough decision.
3. Left a poor first impression that led to a failure to inspire, to enunciate expectations, and to establish open communications.
4. Went suddenly out of character, became aloof, and began acting like the boss.
5. Started talking instead of listening, telling rather than showing.
6. Became a lapdog by barking, "This is what management wants."
7. Hunkered down behind the desk, instead of getting dirty.
8. Didn't recognize or reward.
9. Turned inaccessible with no time for the team or the customer.
10. Didn't put his or her heart on the sleeve right away.
11. Put off addressing performance concerns.
12. Took too long to act once the data was collected.
13. Didn't have a process or stick to it.
14. Lacked energy.
15. Became overbearing and talked down.
16. Didn't insist on accountability.
17. Made too many compromises.
18. Turned into a workaholic and expected others to be the same way.
19. Changed everything for sake of change.
20. Delivered mixed messages.

was turning myself into a barrier that interfered with productivity. My people would have been even more productive if I had gotten out of their way by cutting down the no-process barrier instead of creating it. As we go though the book, look for ways to reverse the equation and make the list the "terrific twenty."

Special Ed

I'm going to do an entire chapter on training, but I want to touch on it here because it is the key to preparation.

My middle name should be Gallup or Roper. I am always polling. I have standard questions that I ask the business people I meet on my travels. One of them is about training. I'll wait until I hear how well the person's company is doing (or not doing) and then ask, "How's your training?" The answer is always a variation on, "Frank, it's lousy."

How's your new notebook computer?

Great.

How's the video conferencing system?

Terrific.

How's the roomful of high-speed color copiers?

Love 'em.

How's the Internet?

Wow!

How's your training?

Lousy.

Business literature is filled these days with sports analogies. Just imagine how that exchange would go if it involved the San Antonio Spurs or the New York Yankees. Something tells me that the *wows*, *terrifics*, and *greats* would involve training players to slam-dunk and hit home runs; the front office technology would come in second or third or not at all. Sports teams know what their primary business purpose is—win games—and to achieve it they must hone their *playing* skills. Preparation that does not relate to basic business purposes becomes a barrier.

Home Schooling

Most everyone knows the Boy Scout motto: Be Prepared. Okay, be prepared for what? That question mark has left room for the creation of a huge training industry that knows what its primary purpose is, even if you don't. Feeding your complications makes perfect sense to these entrepreneurs. There are thousands of nonessential skills to be taught and learned. It's a wide, wide world. And what's wrong with education for education's sake? Nothing, as long as it doesn't interfere with primary purposes or eliminate training time for those purposes.

I get particularly irritated when people are pulled off the job for training on high-tech software and hardware. It goes right back to the question—What are we preparing for? Companies that would, in the blink of an eye, downsize 3 or 4 percent of their workforce to fatten the bottom-line will divert manpower from activities that could quickly and directly earn the same amount of revenue. Put those people out on the street in front of customers, not on an unemployment line.

People can learn how to use a Palm Pilot or a notebook computer at home, in the evenings—with their kids helping them—instead of sitting in a classroom with an instructor who probably doesn't have the foggiest notion of what they will end up doing with the technological skills he or she is trying to impart.

As we attempted to integrate Kodak's high-end color copier operation into Danka, I was impressed by the state-of-the-art technology that had been provided to the sales reps and support staff at Kodak. What didn't impress me was that hardly anyone used the equipment or skills, which had been purchased at considerable expense. It was a rerun of the empty demo rooms. On one of my first visits to division headquarters in Rochester, New York, I asked an executive to access the computer system and show me the thirty- and sixty-day sales forecasts for key district offices. He looked at me as though I were crazy.

"Then show me that order rate broken out office to office."

"We don't have that."

"The rate per rep?"

"Can't do that either."

For the Red Notebook: Major Suspects

A major suspect list review trains everyone involved to pay attention to the fundamentals of the business. But don't do them if you're not going to follow-up. The blank spots need to be filled quickly and problems dealt with promptly.

It was embarrassing for both of us. "What can it do?" The answer was a lot of complicated stuff that had little or no bearing on the simple purpose of selling color copiers fast enough to pay the rent. Having a bunch of names in a computer database doesn't mean anything. It's what you do with the names. Preparation was being done, but not the right kind of preparation because Kodak lost the connection between what it had to do as a basic bottom-line business activity and what, in fact, it was actually doing. You don't have to be computer literate to employ the MSLR technique I introduced in my first book. MSLR, or major suspect list review, is the ultimate low-tech preparation process. Basically, it amounts to sitting down with the rep and asking him or her dozens of questions about key prospects: What's the status of each account and what is being done for each one? What's the competition up to? Who's the key decision maker? When will a decision be made? The point is to get five or six levels down inside the business. You can do that by candlelight—forget about digital technology. A MSLR should take place once or twice a year if you're running a sales operation, and a similar in-depth preparation process can be devised for *any business*. Find out:

- Are we doing what we need to be doing?
- Are we really doing it?
- Is it working?
- How can we do it better?

Is MSLR preparation or process? Both. The prospect of facing such an intense grilling forces people to prepare. At the same time, preparation is requiring everyone to think and act in a way that will yield the kind of in-depth knowledge that will result in high performance results. You can't wing an MSLR.

Almost Heaven: Perfection, Pride, and People

Am I naive enough to believe that preparation makes perfect? You bet I am. I'm so naive that zero-defect management has always been my objective. Nirvana. How can you be passionate about anything less?

If you tolerate one defect, why not two? Why not three or four? Without a leader's relentless drive for perfection—actions not words—quality inevitably slips and takes pride along with it. Here again, the issue loops back to simplicity. If we are going to generate passion and pride, there can't be a 2 percent or .5 percent defect policy. Defects are evidence that someone is screwing up. That someone includes the person at the top when he or she shrugs it off. I say don't be afraid of perfection. It may never be achieved, but it is well worth trying for.

 From the Red Notebook: Intolerance

I recently sat in on a management discussion of a competitor's policy of zero tolerance for workplace injuries. The participants were veterans of a heavy manufacturing industry that long ago made its peace with a high accident rate. "What's our policy on zero tolerance?" one person wanted to know. There was dead silence. Is it possible? Maybe not. But it certainly is worth shooting for. Just the effort alone will probably reduce the accident rate. It's also the *right* thing to do.

Baseball fans love no-hitters because they get to experience perfection. Pitchers and their teams who have come close to no-hitters are deeply disappointed when the other side gets on base or scores. Perfection denied. But none of them would ever stop trying to make it perfect. There's always a chance—unless you stop trying.

Telling the people in Xerox's Cleveland district office that they were going to be number one when they stood dead last in the rankings was pure Nirvana-seeking on my part. But it wasn't BS. I believed it could be done. Just the way I believe in trying to achieve zero defects. My chances of a turn-around would have been nil if I had gone into that demoralized, defeated operation and said, "Here's the plan: We'll finish in the top ten this year. Next year we'll be in the top five. The year after that we'll finish two or three."

No one would have bought that. As it was, they thought I was nuts or on drugs. Still, I gave them a vision of what they really wanted to be—number one. They wanted to be perfect. As Daniel Goleman put it in *Working with Emotional Intelligence*, this kind of passion appeals "to people's sense of meaning and value. Work becomes a kind of moral statement, a demonstration of commitment to a larger mission that affirms people's sense of sharing a valued 'identity.'"

The Xerox team in Cleveland had an identity the day I arrived in January 1988—loser. What I gave them back was their pride and the passion to fashion a new identity. There's a powerful link between passion and pride. It is hard to feel good about yourself if you are not doing your best. Hard? Impossible, actually. Leaders who tolerate mediocrity or, worse, contrive to institutionalize it, are cheating people of their pride.

 Now-To

Ask ten people, starting with yourself, "What makes you proud to work here?" If they hesitate or fumble, you know there's a problem. With those who answer right away, ask yourself, "What did we do today to merit that pride?"

If you regularly monitor the PQ—pride quotient—by asking a representative sample of your workers if they are proud to be working for your company, the exercise will serve as an accurate barometer of your operational effectiveness and prospects. Like the canaries that coal miners once took into the mines to detect dangerously high concentrations of methane gas, a fall off in PQ is a telltale sign that as explosion is imminent.

Quick PQ Test

(Answer on a scale of one to ten)

- Are you proud to work here?
- Are you proud of our product?
- Are you proud of the way we treat our employees?
- Are you proud of the way we treat customers?

Take PQ seriously. It's a guide the barriers that leaders need to cut down. Not long ago, I was invited to speak to key managers and supervisors of a major American steelmaker. Before lunch, my principal host held a get-acquainted session for a small group; the discussion ranged over the many problems the company faced. Locally, there had been progress, but it was an uphill battle in the face of indifference from top management. There was reference to a recent survey of corporate-wide employee attitudes that had been commissioned from a major consulting firm. The plant manager who had invited me said that the survey findings were shocking. "The workforce," he said, "hates everything we do. Everything." And bear in mind, this was one of the good guys speaking. He was trying to make a difference.

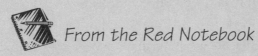 *From the Red Notebook*

Want to know why motivational business speakers are in such demand these days? Home-cooked motivation and pride are in woefully short supply. So companies resort to carryout. But motivational speakers cannot fill a vacuum. After we leave, the real culture sans motivation and pride resumes.

I agreed that it was grim news. "What's been done about it by corporate?" I asked.

He shook his head. "Nothing."

Nothing? That was even more shocking to me than the survey's findings. Nothing? Your employees tell you they hate everything you do, and nothing is done about it? I felt for the guy. He was trying, corporate wasn't. As a result, the steel company's PQ was flat-lining. There wasn't a wiggle. I confirmed it later during the speech by telling the audience how proud I was to speak to a company that was as historic as theirs. I spoke of its role in building America's bridges, skyscrapers, and industrial output. When I asked how it felt to be work for a firm that had helped the American dream come true, I got a shout of enthusiasm from one lonely person out of about two hundred.

It was sickening. I glanced at the plant manager and he looked like he was ready to dive under his chair. Poor guy. What a devastating PQ check!

Adding Up the High Fives

In the final analysis, what PQ tells us is whether an operation is winning or losing the war for talent. The August 1998 issue of *Fast Forward* magazine used the same military metaphor to assess how American businesses are preparing for the talent crunch that is shaping up. It concluded—and I'm using my own G.I. terminology—that 80 to 90 percent of us are destined for KIA, MIA, or POW status.

Fast Forward used a McKinsey and Company study of almost six thousand executives to show that there is a consensus that over the next twenty years, the most import corporate resource will be talented people. A nice round number—six thousand. They made it sound pretty cut and dried: increased competition, globalization, capital availability, strategic transparency, and the flexibility afforded by rapid technological innovation and the commensurate speed of obsolescence all mean that victory will go to those who have the best and brightest people. The one problem is that the best and brightest will increasingly be in short supply.[1]

What I found disconcerting about the study is that only 10 to 20 percent of the executives questioned felt that the improvement of the talent pool was one of their company's three top priorities. And 75 percent of them said their companies didn't have sufficient talent, or that talent was in chronically short supply.

Let's run through that again. Everybody seems to agree that talent will determine who wins and who loses, and practically no one is doing very much about it. Maybe I'm missing something, but it doesn't make much sense to me. I'll bet 80 to 90 percent of the people reading this book are nodding in agreement. And you are also likely to agree that finding and developing talent is not a priority.

Another nod.

Hold on. I'll bet you've been nodding a lot. As a native New Yorker, I'm an expert on the New York nod. There's the quick New York nod, a couple of shallow up and down bobs of the head to signify agreement to a "what else is new" proposition. Then there's the yeah, yeah, yeah New York nod, a series of jerky nods that says, "Enough, already. I understand." A half nod, half twitch usually means, "I haven't the faintest idea what your saying but I'm not about to admit it." (This may come with a "deer in the headlights" look in the eyes.) Finally, there's the slow, steady New York nod, accompanied by a slight shrug of the shoulders. It's sort of like a downbeat of punctuation. That one means, "I gotcha, but what the hell can I do about it?"

Don't nod your way through this book.

We probably face the most fluid and changeable business environment in a century. If there's low water in your talent pool, when the fat boy jumps off the diving board, it's going to be very painful. And if you personally get pushed into the water, will you survive? Early, I talked about zero tolerance. You need zero tolerance toward a company that neglects you. I spell talent—Y-O-U. What the respondents to the McKinsey survey were really saying was, "My company could care less about me. I'm not getting the backup I need to do my job, and, if my colleagues' talent and development are being neglected, I'm probably in the same boat."

Face it. The paradigm has been broken. We don't have to work an entire career for one company, and that frees us to say, "I'm not going to take it anymore. I'm out of here."

But what a waste! It doesn't have to happen if we practice people-ology. I love being a leader. What a thrill it is to play even a small part in helping another person develop his or her talent. What a privilege and heavy responsibility. That's why I am trying so hard to sell you on leadership. It's the next best thing to being a parent. My daughter Alle was given a school assignment to tell the class about her father and what made him special. I was dying of curiosity so when she came home from school, I asked her what she had told her classmates about me. Here's what she said: "My dad tells me every night how beautiful I am and how proud he is of me."

Alle, that's what dads are for. And it's a pretty good definition of what leaders are for too. Dads get to help their children grow; leaders get to help their friends grow. What a great life.

There I go again, using perfection, passion, and pride to circle back to family and emotion just as we seemed to be getting "businesslike" and dealing with things like productivity. That's right, and I'm going to keep doing it until I establish that emotion is the high-octane fuel that can propel any business organization higher and faster, and take its people along for the ride. And what a ride it can be! It baffles me when I encounter ho-hum business environments that seem to be plastered with invisible "no smiling, no laughter, no pleasure, no pride" signs. Why do people take it? Don't the owners, stockholders, or managers realize why the organization's performance—its productivity—is as lackluster as the mood?

Gimme five! It really is very simple.

CHAPTER FOUR

Do Get Excited—

Reaping the Rewards of Emotion

*E*motion is not a four-letter word, but it's treated like one in many businesses and other organizations. Don't ask me why—I'm an Italian-American, after all. If that seems like an offensive stereotype, I apologize. But I'm not sorry about being emotional or for being proud of my ethnic heritage. I think the two are linked. I laugh, I cry, I cheer, I groan. For better or worse, I express my feelings. It's made me an effective leader, business executive, parent, and husband.

There's magic in emotion. Do I really have to convince you of that? I'll start with Winston Churchill's emotionally charged speeches during World War II. By all rights, Great Britain should have crumbled before the Nazi blitz. But Churchill used words—fighting and winning words—as a weapon. Martin Luther King gave the civil rights movement an emotional battering ram with his "I Have a Dream" speech. How many sports teams have left the field or court at half-time losing badly and returned invincible fifteen minutes later? Is it something in the locker room drinking water? No, more than likely it was the emotion evoked by the coach in his pep talk. And now I will rest my case for the magic of emotion: Pedro Martinez of the Boston Red Sox is a superb pitcher, but when he struck out a record four batters in a row at the 1999 All-Star game—including Sammy Sosa and Mark McGwire—it was talent plus the emotion of watching a frail old man by the name of Ted Williams throw out the first ball. You don't stand on a pitcher's mound in front of the Green Monster in Fenway Park wearing a Red Sox uniform and shrug that one off. Every pitch was powered by emotion.

Emotion is not just a feeling. It is a powerful, powerful tool.

Showing emotion and evoking it in others is so natural to me that after all this time in business I have trouble accepting the idea that open displays of emotion and deliberately creating an emotional business environment aren't standard operating procedures everywhere. Emotion provides the winning edge. It's the switch the turns on people power.

I know not everyone is as comfortable showing emotion as Italian-Americans. Different cultures have different attitudes toward expressing one's feelings. There are gender differences too. Some men prefer to bottle it up inside. But come on! We're talking about a society that rants and raves on radio talk shows, screams itself hoarse for $90 million baseball players, and waters Stephen Spielberg's hedge fund with its tears. Maybe Spielberg has nothing to do with hedge funds, but it's a good line and I'm sticking with it.

The fact is, we are not a culture that is reticent about emotion. The business bias against emotion in the workplace has got to go. Study after study has demonstrated that feelings profoundly and positively influence behavior. It doesn't mean that intellect, rationality, and free will aren't involved. And the emotion that I'm referring to has nothing to do with sexual intimacy or sexual harassment in the workplace. I'm talking about caring. I'm talking about trusting. I'm talking about being fed up with losing to the competition.

Giving a damn is a strong emotion. But strong emotions don't mean that a person will stop doing his or her job professionally. Neither does it imply that if I "feel" a policy or decision is misguided I will fly off the handle. I feel lousy, for instance, whenever I'm forced to pay a traffic ticket—but I write the check. "Feeling" is irrelevant. Rationally, I don't want my car booted or towed. The same thing applies at work. There are responsibilities and requirements that I don't relish, yet they've got to be faced up to. Feeling emotion and doing the job are entirely compatible.

But many businesses have created an atmosphere that assumes that what we do to make a living is like paying traffic tickets, eight hours a day. Nothing we accomplish to stay gainfully employed, according to this model, is worthy of a smile, let alone a cheer. Emotion is therefore taboo, because it's assumed that the real operative feeling is irritation, anger, outrage, or whatever. I don't buy that at all. I like to work. I think most people do too—except when they find themselves spending their precious time incarcerated in a minimum-security facility that requires them to hide normal human feelings—*Let it show, and out you go.*

Folks, you can't hide them. It doesn't work. Feelings come out, for better or worse. It makes more sense to channel the positive feelings of pride and accomplishment that come from a job well done than to let those feelings ferment into resentment. Better to structure a business culture that can make productive use of emotion. We've turned a huge part of the workforce—perhaps the vast majority of it—into a legion of zombies. And it's not fair. As a business practice, it's also pretty damned stupid. And it is the reason I'm offering a full chapter on the subject of emotion and how to make it work for you.

Now-To: Conduct an Emotion Inventory

- Pinpoint the last time your organization shared a highly emotional moment. Was it planned? Was it bad news or good? What happened as a result?
- Identify a positive emotional moment that got away. Consider what should have been done to maximize its positive effects.
- Find out who your "emotion leaders" are. They're the people who can engage their emotions and use them effectively. Make them emotional role models for others.
- What do you *really* care about? Do others know? See that they do.

Competition Taps Emotion

Daniel Goleman, the author of the bestsellers *Emotional Intelligence* and *Working with Emotional Intelligence*, helped introduce the concept that success in life is determined by our capacity to effectively manage our emotions. I love his books, but I probably shouldn't use the word "manage" because it may be misinterpreted as meaning suppress or repress. What Goleman is saying is that we can put ourselves in charge of our emotions and make them work on behalf of our own best interests. If we don't, though, emotions take charge. Instead of getting angry and deciding to solve an annoying problem, we just explode and smash furniture.[1]

By pretending that emotions can be banned from the job, we invite uncontrolled and unchanneled emotional discharges. It may not come in the form of violence. Calling in sick, tuning out, or being argumentative are three other ways to unload anger. Know anybody who behaves that way in your office or company? I'll bet you do.

What I have done as a leader is to try to give the people who work for me more productive outlets. Don't kick the desk chair across the room; kick the competition out of the market. Don't tune out; tune into a high-energy, highly demanding, and fun environment. When I became district manager of Xerox in Cleveland, Kodak was our principal competition for the high-end market. I announced that we weren't going to rest until we had replaced every Kodak machine in the district. Kodak was the Evil Empire! It really got the juices flowing. Several years later when Danka bought out Kodak, my former adversaries told me that the declaration of war had cost them a tremendous amount of lost business.

As I've gotten older and more experienced, I'm less obsessed with creaming the competition as the primary motivating force in my life and in the lives of those I manage. But the old Frank Pacetta still exists alongside the new Frank Pacetta. Old Frank used to hang pictures of the other guy's sales reps on his apartment walls to remind him that the enemy was out there and never slept. New Frank reads Robert K. Greenleaf's writings that emphasize leadership as a teaching and servant role. Old/New Frank teaches his people the joys of serving the customer by taking a big order for a terrific product away from the competition and having a party to celebrate.[2]

The Value of Us Versus Them and Us Versus Us

I'm probably never going to be fully persuaded that conducting business without resorting to the traditional competitive strategies, tactics, and weaponry is either possible or desirable. Every customer who is being served by the competition is one less customer for me. I want that business, and don't like it when somebody else has it.

"Like" it? Right. Emotion is involved. The customer has been persuaded that the competition's product or service is superior to mine. I don't like that. If it's true, I better get busy improving what I sell and selling what I improve. If it's not true, that's even more galling because a superior product or service is being undercut by inferior sales, marketing, and other support efforts. Shame on me!

Competition triggers emotion. There's nothing like winning or losing to get people up or to knock them down. There must be other incentives as well, but the competitive instinct is too powerful to ignore. That's why sports are so popular. We win; they lose. An entire process and culture is built around ensuring that it happens. Being a servant—or to use the currently fashionable term, a customer service consultant—doesn't get adrenaline going in quite the same way. Winning—head to head, them against us—creates a buzz and it's a great feeling.

Start-up companies or those that are being challenged by adverse market conditions usually can't take the time and care necessary to build a high performance noncompetitive culture that can get them off the ground or turn the tide soon enough. Going after the "enemy" is fast and effective. People understand what's happening and what's expected.

I insist that my teams know who they are competing against.

- What's their strength?
- What's their weakness?
- What do the customers say about them?
- How do their products compare to ours?
- What's our major vulnerability?
- What can we do to fix it?

Intellectually, I can accept the proposition that it's better to work hard to build such massive market dominance that competition becomes irrelevant. It's the reasoning behind the so-called "category killers" like Home Depot. However, few businesses ever get to that point. You may be able to ignore the competition for a time, but eventually it starts to make itself felt. When that happens, it's time consuming to invent or reinvent a culture that thrives on competition. If you're the New York Knicks, the San Antonio Spurs may clean your clock, but at least you don't have to learn how to play basketball at the same time. It's a particular mistake to ignore the competition when your rival is on a roll. Wallow in bad news. Whenever the other team scores, your players should know about it and it should be an occasion for soul-searching. Show me somebody who doesn't mind losing, and I'll show you a loser.

- What did we do wrong?
- What did they do right?
- How do we get back in the game?
- Is this the start of a trend?

I want people to sense danger—to feel it. What's the old line? If you hear footsteps, don't look back, somebody may be gaining on you. I always look back. How else do you know if it's time to get your butt moving? And when I don't hear footsteps—that's when I really get nervous. At times like that I reach for my security blanket: I notch up customer contact and the overall activity levels, and I throw some logs on the emotional fires.

One more point about lost business: Always ask the customer why he or she chose the rival product. It's important information that all of your people need to hear. Get them to *care* enough so that it won't happen again.

Although it seems like a quick way to stir up emotion, bad mouthing the competition is not something I recommend. For external consumption, it's better to treat the competition with respect. The customer won't be impressed by a hatchet job. Acknowledge what they do well and emphasize what you do better. Internally, I prefer to cast the competition as a formidable opponent not to be taken lightly. But of course, if they aren't a serious threat, don't invent a straw man. People will see right through that and your credibility will be damaged.

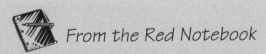 *From the Red Notebook*

"Life'd not be worth livin' if we didn't have our inimies."

—Finley Peter Dunn

Talk about the competition frequently. Bring their products or promotional literature into meetings. There are few better ways for getting attention than holding up a rival's product and saying, "This is better than ours." Or ask a volunteer to sell the group that product based on what he or she knows about its strong points.

At least once or twice a year, launch a direct assault on the competition. The emotional blast is good for morale and it is excellent training to periodically go head-to-head with the competition. Seek to take measurable market share or to persuade customers to replace a rival's product with your own. Be careful not to get carried away in the rush of adrenaline, though. This can be an expensive and time-consuming venture. Getting to the new business opportunities before the competition is even aware of them is a long-term approach. But taking business away from the enemy is fun and worth crowing about.

It's worth rewarding, too. Special recognition, extra compensation, or other incentives amount to tangible evidence that beating the competition is important. If a company isn't willing to pay for it, how crucial can it be? And the honest answer is—not very. Without rewards—and it doesn't have to be money—the only emotion you'll evoke is resentment. People value their time, and if you tell them that their time has no value, their response will be to tell you to shove it.

I'd prefer another more productive set of emotional responses, wouldn't you? I think if an IBM employee in the 1980s or a Xerox employee of the 1970s had been asked who their competition was, the answer would probably have been, "We don't have any." And that's why both corporations had near-death experiences. Competition keeps you sharp and focused. Without it, organizations turn flabby. When the competition does surface, they're almost defenseless. I'm willing to be a servant or even a customer service consultant, but I'd sure hate to completely lose the thrill—and the practical business value—of winning.

As for "us versus us," friendly competition between an organization's teams or individuals also generates emotion. Many managers worry that internal rivalry will be counterproductive or lead to bad blood. I haven't found that to be the case. An attentive leader will know pretty quickly if things are getting out of hand. One sign is lack of cross-talk among teams and a falloff in collaboration. Or lone wolves will break away from their teammates to pursue their own objectives.

The best remedy is a set of clearly stated organization-wide goals that can only be reached if everyone pulls their own weight. If I find that one team is lagging behind and another is far out in front, I'll assign the hotshots to work with the underachievers to get them up to speed. This kind of inter-team collaboration and contact is a must anyway. You've got to allow your best people to model their behavior for the others. Excellence rubs off—*If he can do it, so can I.*

By using a variety of internal rankings for teams and individuals, there's an objective standard to evaluate performance. Go ahead, make a big deal about who's leading and how they're racking up such a stellar performance. Ask the stars to share their best practices and also do some mentoring. This alone is a tremendous tonic for many individuals who have been ground down by corporate cultures that are stingy with praise. Sometimes I think the "gratitude misers" actually fear that saying thank you will lead a worker to demand a seat on the board of directors or his or her own parking space.

 *Now-To*

Set a measurable performance standard that applies to all teams and rank each of them against the benchmark. Post it. Publicly recognize and reward the number one team.

Ignition by Recognition

I've touched on recognition a couple of times already. The subject deserves its own book. Here, it pertains directly to emotion. As we were writing this chapter, my sister-in-law stopped by the house one evening. She was glowing with happiness and enthusiasm. A new job? No, same old job with a vending machine company that, to put it kindly, is a trifle boring. A raise? No, the money's okay. Jane was on her way back from an annual company meeting in Orlando, Florida. It was a great meeting, then? No, the same old thing—with one exception. Jane unexpectedly got an award for being one of the top five account executives in the country.

It made her year. Hey, Jane! Go girl!

And bravo to her company. People love to be loved, honored, respected. They just like hearing the words—"Thank you. Nice job."

Researchers into human behavior believe that the need to achieve and the need to affiliate are two primary motivational factors. Basically, affiliators are people persons. They identify with others, the group, or family. Achievers may or may not also be affiliators, but they measure themselves against high standards and strive to meet goals. It seems to me that recognition, therefore, is the ideal way to reach both types. The affiliator is honored for contributing to the family; the achiever wins acclaim for accomplishing difficult tasks.

So, end of subject, right? What more needs to be said? A lot. Because most companies, large and small, simply do not dispense enough recognition.

- When was the last time you recognized your team or organization's top team and individual?
- Do you recognize annually, quarterly, monthly, weekly, daily?
- Do you even have an objective evaluation standard to allow for meaningful recognition?
- Have you made a special point to thank somebody today?

I'll take the last point first. When I ran the Danka sales operation, managers were told to supply my administrative assistant, Sandy, with the names of reps and support people who needed to be thanked personally by me for making a special effort. Sandy was my director of queme. I spent the end of every work day, sometimes until ten or eleven o'clock, leaving voice-mail, e-mail, or talking to them in person. Basic stuff like, "Thanks for making that extra call. It really paid off and it means a lot to us."

When was the last time you got a compliment? I bet it made you feel pretty good—both about yourself and about the person who offered it. Psychologist Richard Carlson advises people to spend a moment every day thinking of someone to thank. He points out that gratitude is worth practicing in that it creates a sense of inner peace by countering resentment and frustration. Those are benefits that accrue to the one who says thank you. I believe it also extends to those who hear it. Don't just think of someone to thank—go do it.[3]

 From the Red Notebook

Criticize group shortcomings in public, but never knock an individual in front of others. The only example you give by "dragging the body through the street" is an example of your own brutality.

Since I'm a die-hard advocate of "management by walking around," I never miss an opportunity for thanking people for good work within earshot of their colleagues. I'll just stop at the individual's desk or cubicle and let it rip. But be careful not to get a reputation for empty flattery or playing favorites. If things are going badly in one of my operations, days will pass by without a word of praise or a thank-you being uttered. It's a signal that everybody reads loud and clear: I'm dissatisfied and disappointed. At those times, the "walking around" mode turns into a question and answer session: "What do you hear about . . . ?" "How long before . . . ?" "What's the story with . . . ?"

As far as I'm concerned, insincere recognition is worse than no recognition. It turns people into cynics. Another Jane, this one married to my coauthor Roger Gittines, has a wall of plaques from her former career as a news correspondent for the Voice of America. She regards them as a joke because the VOA handed them out indiscriminately. Jane and Roger laughed uproariously when their car was broken into and a box full of her awards was stolen. The only thing of value was the cardboard carton.

The VOA is an international news service, and it's nuts to send that kind of a message to its hard-working employees.

The Other Pay Day

Leaders forget how much every word and deed are scrutinized, analyzed, parsed, and gossiped about. People are paying attention to what you do—and don't do. Failure to recognize extra effort and success is a message that hard work is not all that important. As a result, I rarely open a meeting without some form of recognition. I'll ask people to come up front or stand at their seats. When I don't, like my walking around periods when there's no praise, everybody battens down the hatches.

I expect team leaders to do the same thing. Studies have found that one of the major reasons that people leave a job is that they feel their work is not being appreciated. And you know what? You can ask people if they feel appreciated by their boss. It's really simple: Do you feel your work and your extra effort is appreciated around here? Yes or no. Why wait to find out that it is no, and too late to save a valuable employee?

If the answer is no, and he or she is a top performer, you better get off your butt and give them a hug. Only the top performers? Come on! They get the biggest hugs, but the others aren't forgotten. We want to make everyone feel important to the success of the operation. Kristen Miller of Xerox is among the top three best sales reps I have ever worked with. She started in Cleveland at twenty-two, fresh out of college and, of course, needed every bit of encouragement she could find. The year she started, we were on a drive to become number one in the region and I set an "impossible" number for one crucial month—$7 million in sales. That was roughly two and a half times higher than our total for the previous year. I asked everyone to go all out. We made it, just barely. When I researched this book, Kristen told me she remembered that some of her colleagues came through with six-figure deals, and that the best she could do was sell two measly $5,000 copiers. At the meeting, when I announced the results, I asked Kristen to stand up. I told the group that her two machines had put us over the top. And they had.

Kristen says today, "From then on I was ready to run through walls." And she did.

She single-handedly changed my definition of what to expect from a sales trainee. Before she came along, I figured two or three orders a month from a novice was acceptable performance. She'd write eight or nine. The more I told her how important her work was to the organization, the more she sold. I finally took a chance and put her in an important territory with a heavy budget; within a few months she owned every inch of it.

She loved what she did and couldn't wait to get to work in the morning.

In the spring of 1999, Kristen was on medical leave from Xerox due to a difficult pregnancy. I'm sounding like Woodward and Bernstein, but sources told me sometime after I left the company that Kristen's bosses were hands off, in terms of their management styles. They left her alone. This is a woman who doesn't like that. She needs to be in the thick of things and to be pushed for results.

Kristen was feeling restless and adrift during her leave and wanted to continue her business career, but wondered whether it was worth it. Xerox, I believe, had managed to do the impossible—dampen her spirits. That's unforgivable.

 Now-To

Have you done any of this stuff yet? Pick one.
Now is a good time. *Now* is always a good time.

Partying for Profit

Recognizing achievement is a good excuse to party. I try to arrange one big bash each year, usually in January to kick off the new year's activities. The affair can be built around a business theme or a message. But don't overdo it. Let people take the night off and have fun.

Yeah, fun. Isn't that a subversive idea! One of the most successful formats I've used over the years has been a variation on Hollywood's Academy Awards. Try it. Rent a classy venue, hire a video crew to tape the event, book a band and a good master-of-ceremonies, and go for it: red carpet, black tie, and mink coats. The awards angle lets you pay tribute to your stars. Come up with fifteen or twenty "best" categories to honor individual and team performance. Welcome your newest employees, salute the veterans, and say farewell to those who are about to retire or move on. Don't forget to honor families too. There will be high school and college grads to congratulate and "net adds" (a copier industry term that I use to tease new parents). Dish up pure, unadulterated emotion. No one will accuse you of being corny.

These celebrations are just as important for spouses as they are for the employees. They should get to hear the applause for their husband or wife and to take part in the business family experience. I believe in integrating our two families—the one at home and the other at the office—as much as possible. I don't want my people to leave work and forget about it for the next twelve hours. Nor do I want them to leave home and blank out family issues while their on the job. The two should support and compliment each other.

I learned the value and emotional power derived from celebrations at Italian-American weddings, birthdays, and anniversaries—even funerals. In the afternoon you cry your eyes out and that night you're screaming with laughter remembering the great times you had with the deceased. Celebrations make for traditions, and traditions create a strong family.

And besides, I'm a genuine party animal. I do a mean air guitar. Ask Paul MacKinnon, who has served as my deputy in many assignments over the years. In terms of our personalities, Paul is my exact opposite.

He's steady as a rock. I call him Padre. In 1990, we were having a huge party to celebrate a major victory at a ski resort to the east of Cleveland. The room was packed and the troops were egging me on to accompany the band, which was playing the Ramones' "What I Like About You." There I was on top of a table doing my riffs, the crowd clamoring for the band to crank up the volume louder and louder. The tune ended and somebody shouted, "One more time." I was ready and I let loose with, "Yeah, one more time!" Padre calmly seized the microphone, reached up and took me by the arm, and said with a smile, "No more times." And the party was over.

Thanks, Paul.

The Sound of Business: Turn up the Volume

Time for more interactivity. Take the red notebook and list your top ten favorite songs. I'll start you off with my numero uno: "Stairway to Heaven" by Led Zeppelin.

When you get the list completed, think back to a moment connected with a particular piece of music. Chances are you'll rediscover some emo-

---

Pacetta's Top Ten

"Stairway to Heaven," Led Zeppelin
"Rosalita," Bruce Springsteen
"Times They Are A Changin'," Bob Dylan
"Piece of My Heart," Janis Joplin
"Layla," Eric Clapton
"The Weight," The Band
"Taxi," Harry Chapin
"Volunteers," Jefferson Airplane
"Maggie Mae," Rod Stewart
"American Pie," Don McLean

tional blasts from the past. Music is pure emotion. It has the capacity to form an almost chemical bond with whatever other stray molecules of emotion that are whirring around to form unforgettable and powerful combinations that heighten energy and excitement.

I rarely make a presentation that does not include music. The ears, not the eyes, are the quickest route to our emotional core. I do, however, draw the line at the theme from *Rocky*. I'm pretty hokey, but not that hokey. In 1990, when one of my operations was coming off a particularly bad year, I needed an anthem that would rally and inspire. I chose Tom Petty's "I Won't Back Down." That line says it a lot better than any words I could utter. They didn't need another talk from me. They needed to rock! And that's how the meeting ended—people on their feet, shaking, rattling, and rolling it. The next day they were rolling the competition again.

I love music. In college, I played "Four-Way Street" so often that one night my roommate Don snapped and threw it out the window. No problem, I went out and bought another copy. In the early eighties, when I was a Xerox product specialist, I traveled with Keith Davis, a terrific sales rep who always planned out great days. We almost always got an order. The two of us had a marvelous time cruising his territory with the stereo blasting out Bob Seger tunes.

What fun!

There is no reason a job can't be fun. And every reason that a job must be fun; if it isn't, people will tune out and switch off. Is that because we are frivolous and foolish at heart? No. Work is hard. Fun lightens the load and makes its inevitable routine and repetitious aspects easier to endure. My children's sports coaches have caught on to this. Basketball practice for the eighth-grade girls' team is always accompanied by hard driving, upbeat music. There's a huge boombox sitting in the bench blaring disco tunes. Those who aren't at the line taking shots or doing lay-ups are on the sidelines skipping rope or dancing. It's great! With the boys' team, in contrast, all you hear is the sound of balls hitting the floor. Boring! The girls' team won their championship in 1998 and, along the way, got a chance to polish their dance steps. The coach of the freshman boys' baseball team must have been paying attention. At batting practice that spring, his music was even louder. Playing a sport is a blast, but those drills—while absolutely essential—are sheer drudgery. The music keeps the kids focused and pumped up while they are mastering the fundamentals.

We can do the same thing in business. When I ran district sales operations in Cleveland and Columbus, I used music for special events to set an exciting and inspirational mood, but I didn't use it in the office on a regular basis. I now realize that I should have. There are periods during the day when people can use a lift or a change in the atmosphere. Select a piece of music that becomes the signature for success and play it whenever a key goal is met or a major sale is booked. "Dress down days" have become popular in many offices; how about "music days"? If things generally get off to a slow start on Mondays, launch the week with some hard rock. Or if Wednesdays bog down, hit them with one of my favorites, Harry Chapin's "Taxi."

TV shows have theme songs. Why? The music conveys a message: Stay tuned, here comes fun, drama, excitement, inspiration—whatever. When viewers hear the music, they think of the product. The same goes for advertising jingles, college football fight songs, and love songs that couples adopt as "our song." We play "Pomp and Circumstance" at graduations, "Ave Maria" at weddings, and the "Star-Spangled Banner" at sporting events in order to raise those moments to a higher plane of significance, to make them memorable, special, and—here's that word again—fun.

Work is the last bastion of puritanism. We treat work with the reverence that used to be reserved for church. If you're having fun something's wrong! Even church is more fun these days than most jobs. The priest, rabbi, or minister has an inspirational message to share, the music is great, some congregations applaud the soloists in appreciation or to celebrate a christening, and there's genuine fellowship and community. I walked by a United Methodist Church one Sunday recently and Motown was rocking the place instead of Rock of Ages. It sounded like they were having a ball.

How ironic! Religion, which in many traditions was steeped in sacrifice and suffering, has become the domain of joy, while business is a place of

darkness and agony. And the double irony is that many companies sell a spir-
ited and spiritual message to their external customers through touchy-feely
ads, while smothering their internal customer, the employee, in bleakness.

Come off it!

Doing serious and important work doesn't mean that we have to suffer.
To me, there's an element of mistrust and distrust at the core of this aver-
sion to fun in the workplace. People who are enjoying themselves, the reasoning goes, aren't being efficient and productive.

Huh?

Author Daniel Goleman points out that the key to building peak performance during periods of prosperity and the resilience to get through
slumps is creating work groups that can joke together and enjoy good
times. Without this bond, groups are more likely to lose their effectiveness
and fall apart at the seams when the going gets tough.

You know from experience: Good times do not last forever. Business success is a mixed blessing. The good news is that you're successful; the bad news
is that you're successful. Complacency and caution set in. The competition
increases the pressure. The higher the climb, the harder the fall. Companies
that have weathered their share of adversity know this and hang on to practices
and procedures that helped them survive the last downturn. Once a crisis
strikes, it may be too late to build strong work groups, welded together by the
enjoyment that they jointly experience. Pay cuts, downsizing, and twelve-
hours days aren't much fun, particularly if the culture is grim and joyless to
start. It is a lot easier to go the extra mile in the company of people you've
laughed with and celebrated with than to be thrown into a life or death struggle depending on people with whom you lack emotional ties and a reservoir of
good feelings.

The power of music in this respect comes from its shared nature. From
tom-toms to trombones, music is a feature of communal life: lullabies,
marching bands, hymns, funeral dirges, rap, and opera. It seems absurd to
me that the community that we are immersed in for a minimum of forty
hours a week would be one that is devoid of music. Sure, some places have
Muzak or other elevator music services. But the purpose is to soothe and

tranquilize. Is that because the atmosphere is tense and riddled with conflict?

While I'm not knocking Muzak, my personal choice is for musical selections that generate high energy, excitement, and electricity. That's what I'm listening for when I walk into a new place of business. The ears are just as perceptive as the eyes. I don't have to look for trouble, I can hear it.

If I'm not hearing music, what am I hearing?

Silence?

Hushed voices?

Complaints?

Bickering?

Scolding?

Each environment comes with its own soundtrack. What's yours? What message does it convey?

One of the songs on my top ten list is "American Pie." Don McClean's line grabbed me when I first heard it and it still does—"I knew if I had my chance, I could make those people dance."

That's what great leaders do—they make 'em dance.

The Uses and Abuses of Fear

We've been talking about normal human emotions, so it's time to consider fear. Is fear a legitimate leadership technique?

No.

Is fear an element in the relationship between leaders and those they lead?

Absolutely.

The biggest fear—and the one that's justified—is that a leader will fail. All of us have a direct interest in our leader's success. Naturally, we worry about it, and that's why leaders are put under the microscope. We want to be the first to know when there's trouble shaping up. In addition, the assumption most of the time is that the leader will crater. Blessed is the pessimist for he is never disappointed. I suppose this attitude comes from watching unprepared leaders self-destruct and having to deal with the fall-

Make a Soundtrack

- Ask your people for their personal top-ten lists.
- Assemble a CD collection based on these lists and play them at company events.
- Compile your own top-ten list.
- Designate music zones in lounges, reception areas, hallways, and snack bars.
- Feature music at *all* meetings.
- Encourage your teams to develop their own distinctive soundtracks.
- Pipe in "pump-up" music before and after business hours to the work areas. (Take a vote to determine the selections, but the leader is the chief disk jockey.)
- Hold occasional disco nights and invite staff families to attend.
- Celebrate a good quarterly performance by taking everyone to a concert or musical. (Incorporate the evening's program into subsequent events to remind everyone of the good time.)
- Find out how many members of the workforce are musicians, including their families, and hold in-house concerts that are recorded and distributed as commemorative CDs.
- Match contributions to support a local musical scholarship program.

out. All of us have pretty good radar for detecting the signs that the hot-shot new manager is "CC": Clearly Clueless.

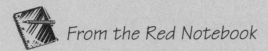

From the Red Notebook

"This guy"—roll your eyes—"is CC": Just about says it all, doesn't it? Clearly Clueless. At Xerox, if a meeting was going badly, you could almost hear the murmured CCs around the room.

This kind of fear breeds the cynicism, low expectations, and disengage-ment (emotional and physical) that contribute to the hapless leader's predicament and ultimate collapse. *This guy's going to go and take me with him? Not a chance.* I believe the only antidote is to give new leaders time to prove themselves. How much time? Oh, a day or two.

I have made best friends and lifelong enemies in less time than that—and you have too. Clearing a day or two "fear-free zone" for a new leader is plenty. You'll be able to tell quickly whether he or she is bound for glory or the gulag. That means, if you're the incoming leader, there's not much lee-way for mistakes (I talk about how to get off to a fast and effective start in the next chapter).

Take a swallow of Doctor P's truth serum and answer this question truthfully: Are you afraid of the boss?

No. That's what I thought. Hardly anyone is willing to admit it. *I hate the boss, disrespect the boss, think the boss is a dork, but I'm not afraid of him.*

Another dose of truth serum coming up. The first dose obviously wasn't strong enough: Are you afraid of the boss?

If the answer is yes, it's time to take stock. The boss may be a sadistic idiot, but you don't have anything to fear. Hand in your resignation and walk out the door. No one deserves to live or work in fear of anyone or anything. Don't tell me that jobs are hard to find or that the money is good. Pack it in. What sinks a bad leader faster than being hit by a nuclear-tipped torpedo is when his best people say, "I'm outta here." Saying bye-bye is the best revenge.

The other kind of fear—fear as a leadership technique—should have lost its legitimacy at about the time drawing and quartering went out of fashion. I was going to say thumb screws, but they're still in use in some places. Deliberately creating fear is a crummy technique.

You've got thirty days to turn this place around or you're history. It sounds good if you're scripting a made-for-TV movie. What happens, though, is thirty days of CYA—Cover Your Ass. Everybody runs off and hides. Seems kind of counterproductive to me. When the troops are dug in and camouflaged, then it's all up to you. A total do-it-yourself job. But aside from hot-dog stands and a few other enterprises, in today's business world success means doing-it-with-others. For the truly gifted, enforcing a reign of terror and making a profit can be done, I suppose, but is it worthwhile? The rewards just aren't commensurate with the effort to burn, loot, and pillage.

Seriously, it is one thing to make hard decisions that people disagree with, to rule for one side against another, to deal firmly with conflict, to tell another person that the time has come to seek opportunities else-where—it's another thing to play fear games. And that brings us to the crossover point between fear and the conscious awareness of consequences. If there is such a thing as good fear and bad fear, the conscious awareness of consequences is the former.

Effective leaders must make us aware of the consequences of our actions and enforce those consequences. Personally, I don't regard that as fear. It's discipline, responsibility, and accountability. Without those three essential elements, leaders and all those who depend on them are doomed to fail. Consequences are not a function of random chance; they're pure cause and effect. The leader's job is to remind us of that and to oversee a process that results in positive outcomes. If he or she doesn't do that, everyone—fearful and fearless—is in jeopardy.

Not long ago, my son Frankie went on a Saturday sleepover with his buddies at another family's home. When I went by to pick him up the next morning, the host's dad came out to the car and offered me congratulations. "Congratulations for what?" I asked. He said, "For Frankie not getting arrested last night."

That's an attention grabber.

He told me the boys had decided to go hang out at the nearby park to see if some girls happened to be around. If that sounds like a stupid teenage boy trick, you're right. Who happened to be around were the police enforcing the evening curfew for teens under the age of sixteen. Frankie was the only one who wasn't bagged. When I got him in the car, he explained that he had stayed behind to watch TV.

"Didn't you want to go with the guys and check out the girls?" I asked.

"Yeah I did, Dad."

"Why didn't you go, then?"

"I knew if I got caught you'd kill me."

Yessss! Is Frankie afraid of me? No, I doubt it. But he definitely has a conscious awareness of the consequences of his actions and, as a result, the outcome was positive—because I'm doing my job as a leader and a father. It isn't easy for either of us, but I'm too afraid of the consequences not to.

I do my job—and I *do* get excited. Both of us reap the rewards of emotion: The son stays out of trouble, and the father knows that his lectures and nagging haven't been for naught.

CHAPTER FIVE

Running the Trust Department

I went to Brooklyn Prep, a Jesuit high school in Brooklyn. The experience gives me the confidence to say that trust is the secular equivalent of faith. Both are precious. Both can be lost. Only one is easily found again, barring a miracle.

Faith can be restored with a flash of lightning or at the break of day. Bird song or the birth of a child will do it. Faith may take you—or retake you—by surprise, since it is a Divine franchise. But when trust goes, the door slams shut. Getting it open again is infernally difficult, especially in business.

This exit-only, one-way aspect of trust protects it and us from abuse. By design, trust is such a precious and powerful substance that it implodes the moment there is solid contact with duplicity.

So let's do trust. A few techniques, a little schmoozing, and we're in business. Right? Wrong.

I wish I could say that it were that easy. Actually, I don't wish that at all. I'm glad it's damned hard to "do" trust. Want to know why it's hard? You already do know, unless you've been skipping around in this book. Hopscotch right back to the end of chapter 2 and read my comments on sincerity.

Sincerity is not optional. That's why it's hard. Leaders build trust with one sincere action at a time. Oh, yeah—action. Isn't that an interesting and troublesome word? Some people actually think that leaders talk, everybody else acts.

No. Too bad there isn't a button right in the middle of this page that you could push to hear the alarm on the "insincerity meter"—otherwise known as a bullshit detector—go off in reaction to words that are intended to trick, jive, and pacify; words whose only contribution to the material substance of the world is to add another layer of ear wax and make us all a little more deaf each time we hear them uttered.

As a sales guy, manager, speaker, and business consultant with a reputation for full disclosure and the ability to look a person in the eye and tell the unpleasant truth, I am often asked to deliver bad news. But the last time I did it may turn out to be the last time I do it. I was invited to speak to a group of managers facing a round of painful layoffs that they would have to oversee, only they didn't know it yet. I asked the client if she was going to tell them before I spoke. She demurred. "I'll tell them then," I said. It was okay with her.

I'm a teacher at heart. I wanted her to learn that full disclosure is the only way to go. I also couldn't stand the idea of spending a couple of hours pumping up a group of people that would have a blowout the next day or the next week when the whole truth and nothing but the truth was delivered. What happened was what always happens: shock, disappointment, and anger. Then, as the objectives were made clear and the humane procedures to be used laid out, the group's leadership instincts and mechanisms kicked in.

I was involved in an ugly, gut-wrenching downsizing at Xerox, which I will go into later as an example of how good companies do bad things. But the reason I was willing to deliver the news to this group was that I wanted to share an insight that I had during the worst of the Xerox episode. I told them they had the consolation of knowing that if what they were doing didn't work, their names and the names of their bosses belonged at the top of the list for next layoff. Every head in the room nodded—and they weren't New York nods.

Together we had tapped into the hard core of sincerity and emotional commitment. Maybe the boss couldn't deliver the bad news to them, but they were going to be able to do it for their teams and keep trust intact to rally the survivors and rebuild the organization.

The epilogue to this story, which explains why it could be the last time I deliver somebody else's bad news, came a few weeks later when I told the story to Bill Locander of the University of South Florida's Leadership Center. We were speaking consultant to consultant, and I was pleased with my ability to step up to the plate for the client. Without a moment's hesitation, Bill told me I had made a mistake. His reasoning was impeccable: You cannot establish trust as a leader if you are not willing to communicate both good and bad news yourself. I got the senior executive off the hook, but I didn't do her any favors. I should have coached her through the process instead of doing the dirty work for her. She had to deliver the message to keep her bond of trust from busting wide open.

Bill Locander was right. Along with the button to activate the bullshit detector, I would like to figure out a way to deliver a dose of Doctor P's truth serum to you. Maybe one of those peel off things like they put in fashion magazines for perfume samples. Peel it off, lick the page, and tell it like it is. Not like the character in the Jim Carrey movie *Liar, Liar,* who couldn't stop saying whatever dumb and inappropriate thought popped into his head, but building trust by telling people exactly what's going on around them and what they need to do to succeed.

A Breeding Ground for Sincerity

Full disclosure isn't complicated. It is the utmost simplicity. Spin, evasion, and half-truths destroy trust.

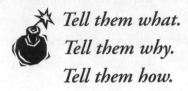

Tell them what.
Tell them why.
Tell them how.

This formula shouldn't be read as turning back the clock and the calendar to the era when the maximum leader dictated the script to his troops and they saluted. What, why, and how are parameters, not hard and fast edicts.

What—the goals
Why—the thinking that led to selecting the goals
How—the process we will use to achieve them

Selling the policy is not the point here. Information is the point. Trust is the point. Even though people may not agree with what they are hearing and seeing, full disclosure is a demonstration of *your* sincerity and *your* trust in *their* sincere commitment to fulfilling *their* responsibilities professionally. A lot of pronouns went into that sentence. Every one of them is essential.

A leader pays for trust with sincerity. The trust he or she receives back is underwritten by sincerity from both sides. Sincerity breeds sincerity. If you don't believe that, we just hit the wall. Leave this book on the train, plane, or bus. Maybe someone else can make good use of it.

Trust me on this—it works.

Whole Foods Market, Inc., the country's largest chain of natural food supermarkets, knows enough to trust its employees. The firm makes its financial performance information available throughout the organization. It even provides salary data by name. You want to know what one of your team members makes, look it up. The boss? Look it up. Whole Foods knows that if you treat someone with trust and respect, you get trust and respect in return. Denying access to information implies that someone can't be trusted. The policy seems to be working. In 1998, Whole Foods Market had a 24 percent increase in sales over the previous year to $1.39 billion with net profits surging 55 percent to $46.5 million. Also in 1998, *Fortune* magazine named the company to its top 100 Best Places to Work list.*[1]

Don't buy it? Try it. Do full disclosure for six months and carefully measure the results. Zero in on team productivity and performance. Look at employee satisfaction stats. Oh, you don't measure those. I think you will after we go over the need to collect those numbers in chapter 12. In the meantime, you won't even have to wait six months.

 Now-To

First, do an anonymous survey asking if your people buy into stated goals—goals without whys and hows.

Adopt a full-disclosure policy with a thorough presentation of what, why, and how. Follow up by asking your people if they support the policies.

Compare the two sets of results.

I predict you'll see a 10 to 20 percent upsurge in support. If that extra margin doesn't seem impressive, think in terms of what another 10 or 20 percent would do to your bottom line. Wall Street goes ape when companies increase their productivity by 10 to 20 percent. And it's hard to beat the cost. Write out a check for what, why, and how.

A Help that Hurts

Do I really have to say what I'm about to say? Yeah, I'm afraid so.

Don't lie.

Little white ones don't count, or so we tell ourselves. But they do count as credibility killers and the same goes for fibs and half-truths. I've heard that it's a gospel among managers at Coca-Cola that two quick ways to get fired are, 1), not to achieve your numbers and, 2), to lie. But the fastest and most direct route to the door is to lie about your numbers. Good for Coke. That's exactly as it should be. Lying is so destructive that it cannot be tolerated.

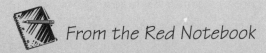

From the Red Notebook

It's okay to feel bad about delivering bad news, but not okay to withhold it.

Ironically, most of the time, when a leader lies, he or she is trying to be kind. It's rare to find someone brazen enough to say, "I'm going to fake these suckers out!" But it is common to sugarcoat bad news or to soft-peddle messages that will lead to conflict and bad feelings. Another motive for lying is to buy time to work out a solution to a problem. It was Adlai Stevenson who said, "A lie is an abomination unto the Lord, and a very present help in trouble."[2]

I know all about that kind of help. When I was a kid I used to hide report cards and papers that had lousy grades on them. I didn't lie to my parents, but I was trying to avoid conflict and maybe solve the problem by getting a better test score or a few As instead of Cs. My younger sister Carm didn't have the same problem. She was a star student and loved it when I did my "Report card, what report card?" number. She'd go on a search-and-destroy mission all over the house until she found my book bag with the hidden evidence and hand it over in triumph to Mom or Dad.

You know what happened then. I had a bigger problem on my hands than if I had just 'fessed up to the bad grades in the beginning. Something happened in the intervening years—maybe I grew up—but now I'm obsessive about solving a problem the moment I become aware of its existence.

It's an obsession I hope to convince you to share because, like a dead tree that falls into a rushing stream, an unresolved problem acts as a barrier that snags other problems, which soon clog the flow of business.

Lying gets in the way of a fast solution because it hides the evidence— just like my attempts to keep Carm's hands off the book bag. Lying makes a problem worse because you can't get at the problem; it festers and spreads the longer it goes without attention.

I should have had Carm help me with my schoolwork instead of sneaking around. Today I dread postponements. Do it now and get it over with so that work can begin on a solution.

For me, lying isn't at all tempting because delivering bad news or dealing with conflict is the first step to a solution. If you don't take that first, possibly difficult, step, there can be no solution. Also, telling the truth gets easier the more you do it. People will still be shocked, yet they won't assume that you're being mean, callous, or vindictive. *Oh, that's just Frank. He believes in full disclosure and full solutions.*

Finally, there is no way to be a sincere liar. Without sincerity there is no trust. As President Clinton demonstrated, lying taints all your good and honest work and irreparably undermines credibility.

Move Fast to Build Trust

"Do it now" is also the best policy for building trust. People withhold their trust—it is our most precious asset, after all—until there's action that validates what they've seen and heard. But trust, in this not-quite-jelled stage between skepticism and belief, is extremely perishable. It's got a "sell-by" date on it that's measured in hours.

If you're a new leader, you can't wait. Or if you're reporting to a new leader, beware of the passage of time. It's not a good sign when the fresh face comes in and says, "I'm not going to make a changes for a while . . . just take my time to get the lay of the land." Inertia sets in quickly and hardens like cement. Before too long, the new leader finds he or she has inadvertently invested in the status quo. Ron Nelson, an executive with

Danka America, recalls having a new boss once who let 120 days go by before communicating with his teams. That's scary.

Why would people give their trust if they suspect that it's going to be business as usual? Waiting 120 days to hear from the boss has B.A.U. stamped on it. Generating or regenerating trust is doubly difficult for a leader who is already in place, if you personify business as usual. It's that perception that must be changed quickly and decisively to get back in the leadership game.

Wait-and-see leaders usually end up deserving to be *see-you-later leaders*.

New leaders are often cautioned about making snap decisions to prove they're bold and decisive. You know—change for the sake of change (second on the "terrible twenty" list of leadership mistakes). That's good advice. Shoot from the hip and you're likely to hit an innocent bystander. What I'm talking about is different. First impressions are crucial.

Even when the first impression is a second or third impression. In my first management job, I had been promoted from the inside. People who had been my peers suddenly found themselves reporting to me. Some of them felt it should have been the other way around.

Fortunately, there was time to prepare for the takeover. Not a lot—three days to be exact. I worked around the clock to get ready. Luckily, my predecessor had also won a promotion and was available to help with my research. He and I spent hours going over the files of each of my ten new team members. Of course I was interested in their territories and accounts, but I really focused hard on the individuals. I wanted to find out what made them tick as people. Mind reading? No. I started with what I had: the names of the spouse and children, where they had grown up and gone to school, and those other sketchy bits and pieces of the personal profile that find their way into the files. Bill, the outgoing leader, gave me briefings on strengths and weaknesses and overall performance.

I really crammed. The impression I wanted to make on them at our first meeting was how much I knew about them and cared about them as a team—and even more importantly—as individuals. And that's what happened. The reserve, the skepticism, the hostility in the air eased considerably.

I held the meeting at the best hotel in the city, ordered up the most expensive breakfast on the menu, followed by something money can't buy—sincerity. You better believe I talked about sales goals and revenue potential, but first I said I was going all out to build pride and that our team would do everything first class.

Pride? First class? That's it?

That's it. It doesn't get any more basic. People want to feel pride in themselves and in the work that they do. All of us hunger for it. Who says we have to check our self-respect and the respect we deserve from others at the workplace door?

I let the team see how honored I was to be given the assignment. I confessed it was a long-cherished goal. I promised them I would do my best and not let *them* down. Them, not the company. I said we'd formulate our goals together and pursue them as a team. On top of that I emphasized that I would help develop individual winning game plans for each of them. I laid out my immediate and long-term expectations, and then left the room to give my colleagues a chance to candidly discuss their reactions to me.

Looking back on it, I did four things that morning:

1. I let them see who I was.
2. I told them how we would operate.
3. I asked for their help.
4. And I demonstrated a keen interest in their welfare and success.

On the page, it doesn't seem very impressive. Yet, ask yourself how often it has happened in your business career or in your personal life. Rarely, I'll bet. And when it did happen, the effect was influential, if not profound.

Yes, life is complicated. But don't complicate a first impression. The leadership bond is created out of simple compounds—I like him or I don't; I trust her or I don't. My top priority was to impress them with how much I cared about their success. I banged away at that theme because I knew it would help accomplish my objectives, yes, but I also did it because it mattered to me.

When the team came out of the room, its members didn't love me. I wasn't looking for love. But they were willing to trust me—a little. As one of them said, "We're going to have to work awfully hard to keep up with you—but it sounds like it will be fun."

And it was fun.

A People-ology Tip

A few years into my leadership career at Xerox, I learned a great people-ology technique from Al Fagan, a senior vice president. Al had six hundred sales reps in his area. He collected information and a picture on each one. When Al was about to make a visit, he'd get the file out and go over it so that he could walk up to people and call them by name without having to be introduced. Cynics will say, "Oh, how manipulative!" But not those to whom it happened. It was impressive and appreciated. By the way, those same cynics will be bowled over when they arrive at the Four Seasons Hotel in New York City for their second visit and the doorman opens the cab door and welcomes them by name. Impressive. How do they do it? Ask Al Fagan.

"Frank, I'm not that lucky." I can hear a new leader complaining. I'm about to hit the ground as a total stranger."

Actually, you may be the lucky one. It's nice not to have to live down past mistakes or to suddenly have people you grew up with at the company reporting to you. Even so, first impressions are still key. Aware of this, and apprehensive of getting off on the wrong foot, many new leaders try to ease into the water by introducing themselves in bits and pieces.

Not the best idea. You're giving up control of the message. There are too many blank spots between the components that are filled in by conjecture and assumptions. If I'm new to an organization, I'll do my preparation work from off-site by having the files sent to me at home and working the phone. I don't want my colleagues trying to size me up with fragmentary contacts and glimpses. The first day I arrive at the office is show time. The new regime starts.

And don't be afraid of the show business metaphor. Our most respected corporations spend billions on show business aimed at the external customer. How about a few dollars on the internal customer? They'd like to have some—what's the word?—fun too. By dramatizing my arrival on the first day, I guarantee that attention will be focused on what I have to say.

On that day, first thing, I call a meeting of the entire staff or team, put my heart on my sleeve, and show them who I am and where we're headed. I ask for support and, by name, I thank those who have given their best effort to the organization in the past.

You can do that too. Make it straight talk: What you expect and what you'll inspect; what stops and what starts; what are the rewards of success and what are the consequences of failure. If you haven't been through one of these bell-ringer kickoffs, you are missing a great thrill.

Make them a part of your leadership repertoire. If you're not in a leadership position, *expect* a great first impression. If it doesn't happen, let it be known that you are disappointed.

Look for:

- emotion
- vision
- goals
- what to expect from the leader
- what he or she expects of you
- straight talk about rewards
- straight talk about problems and solutions
- and recognition for those who have performed

That's the bare minimum. And—and!—barriers have to start being cut down. It's time for the chain saw. When I took over as Xerox district manager in Columbus in 1993, I knew I had to set an example. The district had been lazy. There were good people, but they had been allowed to mail it in.

In the preparation process for the first meeting, I talked to several experienced sales reps who brought me legitimate complaints about the ways things were being done. Some, I wasn't senior enough to fix. So I surprised them by announcing that the Xerox president for field operations would be arriving in one week to hear what they had to say. That got their attention. Of course it did. Sincerity, direct communication, and immediate action are hard to ignore.

Then I went down a list of other barriers I had collected:

1. Orders take too long to process locally.
2. We spend too much time typing our proposals.
3. We fill out redundant paperwork.
4. We need a color copier on the floor for customer presentations.
5. We have only a few PCs to pull up necessary data.
6. The working mothers want later morning meeting times so they can take care of family business.

"Okay, I said, "here's what's happening. Admin has agreed that an order with the proper information will be processed in one day—guaranteed.

"We have hired two administrative assistants to be in the sales area to help process proposals and presentations—it's up to you to keep them busy."

I held up two sheets of common paperwork. "Fill these out completely and throw the other stuff away.

"When you return to the office tomorrow a color copier will be on the floor—I should see a lot more presentations going out the door.

"We will have six additional PCs up and running tomorrow too, and morning meetings will start a half-hour later."

None of the six items was a major issue. But each one was an irritation that got in the way of performance and interfered with employee lifestyle, work-style, and productivity. By tackling them right away, I was demonstrating two things: 1), that quick and decisive action was to be the norm, and, 2), I would listen closely to their concerns and treat them seriously. And by the way, I wasn't making idle promises on the spur of the moment. I had made arrangements for the new PCs, the color copier, and the administrative support *before* the announcement. I knew the changes would be in place the next day. I wasn't going to take any chances.

Far from earthshaking, right? But if we can't count on the leader to take care of the small stuff, why should we believe he or she will be effective when it comes to major problems? Most people are schizophrenic about new leaders: They harbor high hopes and low expectations. Teetering between optimism and pessimism, small things can push them either way. If tomorrow looks like yesterday, it's hard to believe that anything will change for the better, no matter how sweeping the promise and the vision.

Also, when excuses accumulate, action becomes increasingly difficult. A defeatist or complacent attitude is created that rests on self-serving rationalizations: *I can't do the presentation because I need a color copier. I wish I could make the extra sales call, but I have to type these proposals. I'll wing it on these numbers because I don't have a PC to call up the data.*

Clear the decks for action. My priority in this first rush of decision-making is to increase productivity. What is the operation doing? What can be put in place to make sure things get done faster and more effectively? Trivial matters create an amazing amount of friction and drag. Get them out of the way and start moving. The analogy of test driving a new car fits perfectly. Most of us are on our best behavior until we're out of sight of the dealer's lot and then we gun it. Let's see what this baby can do!

It's the same with new leadership responsibilities. Gun it. See what happens, listen for strange sounds, and look for black smoke.

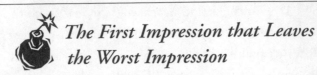

The First Impression that Leaves the Worst Impression

Please, none of this, "One year from now, a third of you will no longer be here," garbage. That's a great trust-builder. "Trust me, I'm out of here," is what many of your best people are going to say. Those are the ones you have to convince to stay. Star players in sports and business are never intimidated or motivated by terror tactics. They thrive on challenge. Pile it on.

I've probably made it sound too easy. It isn't easy. Who wants easy? Easy is boring. Effective leadership is like an iceberg, two-thirds of it is beneath the surface. Hours and hours of time have to go into preparation to make a high-impact first impression. Burn up the phone lines talking to your predecessors, superiors, mentors, and other colleagues with insight. Call on key customers. I'd even check with the competition to hear them crow about recent victories. You've got to immediately sponge up enough information to tell you what has happened.

The big problems will take time to fully solve, but you've got to make a start. If nothing else, every organization can use an extra blast of energy, enthusiasm, and efficiency. Take what they've been doing and do it faster, better, and with more fun and rewards. It's not necessary to lay out a carefully crafted agenda for the next five years. The next five hours, or the next five days, will do nicely, thank you.

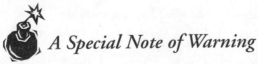

A Special Note of Warning

If your new team members go back to their cubicles after the meeting and pick up where they left off—you are a goner!

Bumping up a key activity rate is often the way to go initially. Take care of the fundamentals first—basic blocking and tackling. As I said in chapter 3, customer contact is a fundamental that is almost universal. If the rate per staffer is two a day, double it—for everybody. Even those who don't normally deal with customers get brought in. And you too. That can shake things loose. You'll be told there's not enough time and that other priorities will slip. Stick to your guns, and you will see who performs and who doesn't.

On that score alone—identifying the performers—you're now in the possession of priceless information.

The Leader/Manager As Impressionist

Use your red notebook to write down first impressions for a variety of situations.

 From the Red Notebook

- The first impression of a new colleague.
- The first impression of a new product.
- The first impression of a new restaurant.
- The first impression of a new service business, like a dry cleaner or florist.
- The first impression of a new teacher.
- The first impression of a new doctor.

Jot down a few reasons for your negative or positive reactions, including that you might not be able to identify a reason. In three months, revisit the sources of these first impressions and see how you feel. Whether you've changed your mind or not, I want you to realize how strong and vivid those initial responses were. Psychologists believe there's a primitive emotional mechanism that puts us on guard against possible enemies or signals us that it's okay to relax.

What if a new leader makes a poor first impression? The odds of his or her success have lengthened. Double check the first impression by asking for candid assessments (this too establishes openness as standard operating procedure). Also, keep a sharp eye on what the team does in response. If you suspect you've flopped, take a cold hard look at the message you delivered.

Effective communication is deceptive. It seems so easy and natural. Just crank out a vision and mission statement, send a memo, fire off an e-mail, or speak your mind. But the message—the real message—isn't like that. Unless it comes enclosed in an envelope of trust, it's bound to get lost in the mail, lost in the suspicion, cynicism, and paralysis that this fundamental shortcoming inevitably inflicts on people and organizations.

CHAPTER SIX

Make Big Dreams Happen—

What a Great Place to Work!

*P*icture a hundred men and women sitting at a hundred desks in a massive room without windows. The only sound comes from the ticking of a clock on one wall; its pendulum swings back and forth in a slow, hypnotic arc. On each desk there is only a single yellow legal pad. The men and women stare at the blank pages. Staring. Staring. Staring.

Occasionally, an individual stands up and paces in a circle around a desk, sits back down, and resumes staring, staring, staring.

The group has been assigned the task of creating a corporate vision and a mission statement to go with it. They're trapped in *Vision/Mission Statement Hell.*

By now everyone knows that we need a vision and a mission statement to define who we are, what we do, why we do it, and how we do it. All that's necessary is to drill deep within the corporate and individual soul, and out will pour a gusher of rich, pure vision. This elixir will bring profits and contentment to all.

Don't get me wrong, I'm not knocking vision and mission statements. It's necessary to have them, and it can be powerful and profitable when you do. But I have found that lifelessness leads to visionlessness. Most vision formulation and mission statements—the process that the imaginary group above is undergoing—do not grow out of a real, living, breathing context and therefore are dead on arrival. There's no way they can be brought into play.

The unfortunates who are assigned and consigned to Vision/Mission Statement Hell will eventually come up with something. They're disciplined, smart, and creative folks. But the end product will likely wind up in a filing cabinet or bottom drawer. That is, if they are lucky. Irrelevant and hollow vision and mission statements are acutely dangerous. Those who buy into them and then find out the hard way that the vision and mission statements are meaningless to senior management and investors, are destined to be confused, angry, and disillusioned. Those who see through it immediately withhold their trust and adopt cynical, self-protective attitudes.

Better no vision than a phony vision.

There are gurus galore available to help you create vision and mission statements. But beware. While it can be done—and is ultimately worth doing—it is a time-consuming and agonizing process. It's necessary to simultaneously run a bottom-up/top-down analysis of what makes an operation tick and square it with what makes its people tock. When I talk to executives who have gone through the exercise, they suggest it degenerates into a production that is made by and for top management purposes alone.

The greatest of all vision and mission statements, the U.S. Declaration of Independence, proclaims that "all men are created equal." The resonance of the statement comes from the word "all." Unless you are prepared for the effort to bring "all" into the process, your vision and mission statements are going to be seriously flawed—and probably more trouble and far more subversive than they're worth.

Connecting Vision to Action

If you've got your red notebook handy—and I hope you do—start a new page by writing I-O-N centered on the top line. Draw two lines radiating downward diagonally from the middle to the left and right bottom corners. Under the left line write A-C-T and under the right put the letters V-I-S. Connect them both with an arrow running left to right across the bottom of the page.

$$\text{ACT} \ (\bullet \ \text{ION}) \ \longrightarrow \ \text{VIS} \ (\bullet \ \text{ION})$$

This will serve as a reminder that action is the source of vision. *Act* derives from Latin: *actus*, to drive. *Vis* in ancient Greek means strength. There is no strength in a vision or mission statement that is not driven by action. The words could be attached with a hyphen: action-vision.

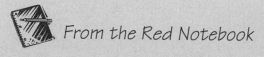

From the Red Notebook

Live the vision.

Living the action-vision is the true test of a vision and the accompanying mission statement. Measure every action against the vision, and you will see immediately how relevant the statement really is. Every hole needs to be filled to reinforce the integrity of the vision, otherwise it is being undermined or corrupted.

The action-vision connection offers the quickest, most direct role to creating and living a vision. Instead of addressing cosmic and semi-spiritual issues, focus on the nitty-gritty of your business. The way I've always done it is to set out to make my team the best.

It really is simple. Being the best is one of those universal human desires. Personally, we may not be overly aggressive or competitive, but there is still a instinct that drives us to claim a form of uniqueness that sets us apart and affirms our value. Knowing that we are the best or striving for it is powerfully reassuring. Conversely, being the worst—or believing that we are—is crushing.

My mom and dad had one hard and fast rule—do your best. I'll bet yours did too. Paula Innis, who started out at Xerox's typing pool in Columbus and now owns her own successful printing business, was kind enough to share her experiences and insights for this book. She recalls her own mother's insistence that as African-Americans, her children would have to do their best—even better than best—and refuse to allow the racial prejudice and unfairness they experienced become an excuse for giving up and not doing their very best at all times.

Paula told me that her mom's attitude was they were black—and so be it. If racial prejudice made it more difficult to succeed, she wasn't about to let it become an excuse for failure. Paula was promoted out of the typing pool and she became a terrific sales rep under conditions that I know I couldn't have surmounted. She was a single parent. Paula would pick up her kids after work, go home, cook dinner, and spend time with them. They'd all go to bed about nine o'clock. A few hours later, Paula would get up and start doing her preparation work for the next day. Three hours of sleep a night and she was still a great sales person.

 From the Red Notebook

"I will do everything I can to be the best sales rep. I have to be the best Mom."

—Paula Innis

Unbelievable. Nothing was going to stand in that woman's way of being the best—the best parent, the best businesswoman. She works hard at it. Today her printing business is one of the best in the Midwest.

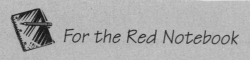

For the Red Notebook

Dream big dreams.

Paula's role model is Oprah Winfrey. She intends to be as successful and influential as her hero. And she lives the vision every day.

Why can't we all live big dreams?

Creating a Hard-Core Vision

A simple, powerful vision based on being the best is one that does not present difficulties in communicating its message and what's required to achieve it. What does being the best in your business entail? I'll give you a list of possibilities, starting with profits:

- Best overall profit margin.
- Best year-to-year profit growth.
- Best year-to-year revenue growth.
- Highest order volume.
- Highest year-to-year growth in orders.
- Best customer satisfaction.
- Best product quality.
- Lowest product return.
- Highest employee satisfaction.
- Highest employee retention.
- Best training.
- Best compensation plan.

You get the idea. Anything you can measure is a candidate for being cranked into the vision. What about the underlying philosophy? Remember the red notebook page: Action yields strength. The philosophy—a spiritual core—will follow and support the action. A genuine drive to be the best on so many fronts will require the best intentions, ethics, and professionalism.

Time and again, I've told my organizations that their performance—by objective standards—fell short of the best, that they were in effect cheating themselves and cheating me. I've never forgotten the words that my father leveled at me after my first academically disastrous year at the University of Dayton: "You cheated me." I wince when I read them on this page. By wrapping vision around hard-core performance, rather than softer sentiments, you're guaranteeing that you can live the vision and live up to it.

But let me emphasize that a vision of being the best is meaningless and destructive if it is not rigorously and systematically acted upon. An ambitious vision makes us feel good. It provides meaning and identity. However, proclaiming that you intend to be the best and then not achieving the vision or, worse, not trying hard enough, is just plain nuts.

Conducting a Reality Check

Another vision-making technique is to compile a list of the organization's ho-hums—the stuff that's boring and second rate. Ask your people at all levels to make ho-hum lists:

- The phones aren't answered promptly or professionally.
- The offices are dirty or shabbily furnished.
- Supplies are inadequate.
- Customer complaints are not handled expeditiously.
- There's too much redundant paperwork.
- Too many meetings.
- The product line needs to be updated.
- Sales reps only show up at the customer's workplace to write new orders.

- Team leaders don't listen to team members.
- There's no training.

Instead of a hundred people sitting at a hundred desks and staring at a hundred yellow legal pads in Vision/Mission Statement Hell, give them one of these ho-hum lists as a vision platform. The *visioneers* could then write a statement that prescribes action to rectify the shortcomings. Does this seem too prosaic? It's not. If you don't do the basic stuff to the best of your ability, all the highfalutin' words with their New Age connotations are meaningless.

Do a reality check on your vision and mission statements. Write them out from memory in your red notebook. Now. Don't look them up. Write them down cold. Take your time. If you can't do it, the vision and mission are as dead as doornails. If you were able to get some or all of it on paper, the next thing to do is identify the action elements: What do we do every day—or even occasionally—to realize the vision and mission. If that's difficult to tally up, the vision and mission need improving—Now!

A Leadership Lesson: The Red Towel and the Black Hat

A good rule of thumb to judge a vision is whether or not you can see it. We should see the vision all around us. If you read my first book, *Don't Fire Them, Fire Them Up*, you may recall the story of how I used a black knit ski cap to symbolize the reward I was offering for the achievement of a key sales goal in Xerox's Cleveland district office. If the teams achieved the goal they were going to celebrate by going to Peak 'n' Peak, a popular resort to the east of Cleveland, for an all-expenses-paid trip. Whenever I ran a meeting, I had the black Peak 'n' Peak cap in my hand as a symbol of the goal.

What I didn't include in that book was how I learned to use a symbol like that to accomplish leadership objectives.

I owe it to Coach Duffy. At Brooklyn Prep High School, we were fortunate to have a unique gym teacher and football coach named Bill Duffy. Coach Duffy looked like a shorter, balder version of the comic actor Drew

Carey. He was a character. Tough as nails, quick to criticize, with a lightning fast Irish sense of humor. It was a badge of honor among football players to get your head ripped off by Coach Duffy. We'd all sit around comparing notes afterward and laughing about it. He was one of those people you never forget.

Our traditional football rival was Saint John's Prep, another Catholic high school in Brooklyn. We played them every Thanksgiving and the competition was ferocious. The importance of "The Game" was drilled into you from the first day you arrived at Brooklyn Prep. We weren't a local football power by any means, but this matchup was for all the marbles.

I was a running back and quarterback—and not all that good, but that's another story. In my junior year, on the first day of practice, Coach Duffy met with the team and laid out the goals for the year. Naturally, he was determined to achieve a winning season and to cap it off with a victory over Saint John's. The goal was particularly important that year because it would be the last time the two schools would face each other. Sadly, Saint John's was being closed for financial reasons. More than sixty years of tradition would be lost. Coach Duffy wanted that final victory, and he wanted it bad.

As his locker room talk drew to a close, he pulled out a red towel. Red was Saint John's school color. The coach said that starting immediately one of the players would always be carrying the red towel. It would go with him to class and be on the field for practice. He said the towel would remind us what the season was all about.

Now you know where the black knit ski cap came from. But there's more to the Coach Duffy story.

He taught a me a lot that season about being a leader. We beat all the other Jesuit schools. As Thanksgiving approached only one remained—Saint John's, which, to be fair, had a much better team. But does Harvard admit that about Yale or Army give the edge to the Navy? No way! Even so, they were heavily favored. The game was to be carried on local New York TV—8 million people watching (okay, a couple of dozen relatives watching).

On the last day of practice before the game, rough, tough, aloof Coach Duffy did something unexpected. Traditionally, the student body was allowed to watch the final practice, but when the team got onto the field the stands were empty. The coaches were waiting in the usual spots for the team to begin warm-up calisthenics, so we got into the standard lines of six or seven deep and waited.

Coach Duffy told us to kneel on one knee and to look down. I remember thinking that this was a little odd. The coach was wearing the red towel in his belt. He spent the next hour going from player to player, standing over each of us, and in a quiet voice—though loud enough for the rest of the team to hear—thanking each boy for his contribution to the team. He summarized the highs and lows of our football careers, noted the special contributions we'd made, and how much each individual meant to him. As he went up and down the lines, you could hear the kids sniffling to fight back the tears. The Coach said he wanted to say thanks and wanted to us to know we were part of his family.

When he finished with the last player, the coach said a short prayer and walked back to the locker room. There was no practice that day. We didn't need one.

On Thanksgiving we creamed Saint John's. There was no way they could have beaten us. We were an emotional juggernaut. The Red Army would have been crushed by Brooklyn Prep if it had faced us on the field.

That night and the next day, there were wild parties everywhere. When I went back to the school to drop off my equipment for the last time, there was Coach sitting alone in his office listening to a replay of the TV audio that a parent had taped. Tears were streaming down his face.

Twenty-five years later, not only did I use the black knit ski cap as a symbol, I laid out a vision for Cleveland of how we would end the year as number one and how we would go about doing it. When the district went into the final three months of the year, I still had the hat when I convened a final review of the prospects for the remaining year and what we still needed to do. I went around the room and thanked each person for his or her unique contribution to our success to that point. My teams left the room, and at the end of the year we were number one.

Thanks, Coach Duffy.

Dealing with The Kinks in Kinko's Vision

The red towel taught me that if you can't see the vision you probably won't live the vision. When I walk into a business for the first time, I'm looking for the vision all around me. I can see it in the demeanor and attitude of the employees, the layout of the facility, and the decorations on the wall.

I was in a specialty printing operation not long ago that offered a classic example. Bear in mind that the firm probably brings in about $18 million a year in revenue. Not mammoth, but far more than a mom-and-pop store. The reception area was empty when I arrived and it stayed empty throughout my visit. When I say empty, there wasn't even a receptionist on duty. The welcome desk was abandoned and the phone console sat there blinking forlornly.

The walls were dingy and in need of a paint job. There wasn't a picture of a human face, nor a display of products, awards, or marketing material. I hardly noticed the company's logo. When I penetrated farther into the complex, the atmosphere became even more bland and unexciting. I wondered if a neutron bomb had gone off and wiped out the people. They certainly weren't to be seen in the common areas or the hallways.

I was there as the ultimate customer. I was exploring the possibility of buying the business. There was no mystery about why it was for sale. The place was lifeless. After thirty seconds or a minute, an untrained eye could describe the firm's vision—ho-hum. I didn't have to embark on due diligence to know that the company was in need of a serious fix up.

Any customer walking through the front door would recognize the operation for what it was. Low performance, low quality, low value, and low people-ology have an unmistakable aura. Another printing business, one you're probably familiar with, comes to mind and offers another example of how we live our vision, whether we know it or not, in large and small ways: Kinko's. While I was working on this book, I needed some quick copies. I went into Kinko's close to my home in Columbus, walked to the counter, said hello to the woman on duty, asked how she was, and, getting no response, requested a card to activate a machine. Without looking up, she flipped it at me. I went to a copier and it didn't work (ask me about copiers that don't work—I dare you). I waited, I waved for help, I smiled, I fidgeted, and finally I walked back to the woman and said politely, "You're going to be in my book." She looked up.

"Really?" she said with genuine interest.

I nodded. "This is the first time you've bothered to acknowledge that I'm alive, or even look at me. I'm never coming back to Kinko's—and you will be in the book," and I walked out. I now go to Staples instead. My coauthor, Roger Gittines, still uses Kinko's because he's mad at Staples for the same reasons. We're not going to take it anymore. I fired Kinko's; he fired Staples. We fired them because our experience as customers told us all we needed to know about vision. What we saw—or didn't see—was:

- leadership
- process
- consistency
- care
- execution

Vision is nothing more—and nothing less—than a promise. We promise to live and do business based on a set of higher values. Maybe your Kinko's or Staples does better keeping its promises. I hope so. But go out and fire somebody who doesn't deliver on their vision. Don't take it anymore.

Good Words, Bad Deeds

People make or break a vision. The woman at my Kinko's surely did. So does the manager in another store who sits chatting on the phone in a glass walled office overlooking the gridlocked checkout area and does nothing about opening another cash register; he's also a vision-breaker.

While I'm picking fights with national chains, I'll tell you about my experience at Circuit City during one Christmas shopping season. My wife,

Julie, and I decided it was time for a new stereo system after years of putting up with one that was long past its prime. However, neither of us knows much about stereos. We went to Circuit City, making a beeline for the room in the back of the store that is set up to demonstrate the tweeters and woofers and receivers and what have you. We walked in and music was blasting out of the speakers. Hey, that's what we came for! I looked around and there were two employees sitting side by side on a coach jiving away. They loved it. I caught their attention and said, "Great sound!" They nodded and stayed in the groove of the music, shaking their shoulders and wiggling their heads to the beat. We waited. They jived. We waited. They jived. Then we left.

Is that vision? Yeah, Circuit City was living its vision at that moment. It's was a vision that encompassed training, recruiting, leadership, motivation, and discipline. Like all visions it was the sum total of the existing—living—culture.

And that's why Julie and I walked out.

Now I fully expect to hear from Circuit City, Kinko's, and Staples (though Staples should take up their beef with Roger). And I'll probably get irate calls from America West Airline and Compaq, who will be held up to critical analysis later in the book. What I'll probably hear is that I'm being unfair to them based on isolated incidents involving a few employees who don't represent the high levels of professionalism shown by the vast majority.

Okay. Sounds reasonable. What happens next though, is the true test of vision, and you and I will see the results—or the lack of results—in the future. Customer complaints that are acted upon with a New York nod and its West Coast equivalent, the L.A. shrug, reveal how a company lives its vision. I have never examined Kinko's vision or mission statements, or those of the other companies I just mentioned. Maybe they don't have them, for all I know. But what they do have, and it's the same thing, is a companywide culture that reflects certain values and actions that support them.

We know you by your deeds, not your words.

Rollout a Vision Renewal

What I'd recommend to Kinko's or any company with a vision that may be showing signs of being lived down rather than lived up, is to call a time out. Take five days to check the vital signs of your vision to see if it's living or dying.

 Now-To

Day 1

- Call your people together and give them the hard-core vision.

> ### Our Employees Will Say:
> *What a Great Place to Work!*
>
> ### Our Customers Will Say:
> *What a Great Place to Do Business!*

- Make it a moment they'll remember, full of energy and emotion. Tell them you're not going to settle for anything less because you know they won't settle for anything less. Publicly thank your top performers for all they've done, name names and tell their stories for all to hear. Go shake their hands and look them in the eye. This is not a test. It's the real thing.
- Announce a full-disclosure communications policy (and mean it).
- Announce an open-door policy (and mean that too).

Day 1, Part 2

- The CEO follows up (or continues) by calling the top performers or holding one-on-one meetings to thank them personally and request their help and support. Then, each manager sits down with his or her teams to begin developing their thirty-day plan (to be followed by sixty- and ninety-day versions) to implement the vision. Rough cost estimates should be included.
- Senior management fans out to call and visit five accounts each. They should be told about the vision and asked for their advice on how best to achieve it. These five accounts should be asked to serve on a customer vision advisory council.
- Sales rep should begin scheduling meetings and making phone contact with all accounts in their territories.

Day 2

- All teams gather in one place to review and discuss the plans they've developed.
- Senior management gives the green light to team plans accompanied by announcement of performance expectations. There will be increased productivity and revenue mandated to pay the cost of the additional costs estimated by each team and forecast by top management to accomplish the vision.
- Teams are told to prepare to roll out elements of their plan on day 3.

Day 3

- Senior management personally inspects and takes part in the training and recruitment processes. Training curriculum is inspected with an eye for its ability to support the vision. The same standard applies for recruiting. All potential recruitment candidates are to be introduced to the vision within forty-eight hours.
- Teams begin vision rollout.
- Senior management spot checks rollout by personally contacting customers for reaction.
- Management at all levels seeks to identify speed bumps/barriers and remove them.
- Management's team leaders meet and decide how to tie compensation to vision achievement. A results-tracking mechanism is put in place.

Day 4

- Team vision-action rollouts continue.
- Management reports specific *actions* to eliminate speed bumps and other barriers to the vision.
- New vision-related compensation plan announced.

Day 5

- Teams gather to report on their rollouts.
- Teams that have contacted 100 percent of their accounts to brief them on the vision renewal are recognized and presented with appropriate awards to be displayed in the office reception area and headquarters.
- End the day early for a reception, including families and the members of the customer advisory board and other key customers.

By putting the vision blueprint on a five-day track, I've created a sense of urgency and given it an action orientation. As a leader, I am always concerned about complacency and drift. When you do it often enough, every job, including a high-wire act without a net, becomes routine. This blast of energy created by a vision renewal campaign gets people out of their ruts. Normal business can still continue, but it will have a different dynamic and more zest.

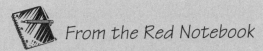

From the Red Notebook

"Vision and mission statements must be living documents."
—PAUL MACKINNON

Sure, people may grumble about the extra work and pressure. But if you look for ways to keep the emotion levels high, they'll breeze right through it. Think of the occasions when you said, "Boy, the time flew right by. I hardly realized hours had past." That means you were in a state of flow; in the groove. What we're looking for here is an atmosphere that will induce flow and the exhilaration that accompanies it. Deadline pressure alone, however, doesn't necessarily guarantee a state of flow. People have to be emotionally committed to and confident in their work and the outcome. A living vision can give them that confidence.

Even if your vision looks, feels, smells, and tastes healthy and fresh, it pays to periodically launch a vision and mission renewal program modeled after the one I've just laid out. Vision can go greenish-gray and moldy overnight. There's a tendency to take it for granted, which guarantees that it will lose effectiveness. Some people will groan and say, "No, not vision again!"

Yes, vision again. All actions, all policies must constantly be related back to vision and the mission statement, and it has to happen at all levels from the board room to the loading dock. If this isn't happening constantly, a vision renewal will help get you back on track. The cynics may not like it, but if the vision is genuine they will be in the minority. Cynicism is a product of disillusionment. A living vision is the antidote. The energy, electricity, and emotion it generates will jump-start the whole enterprise. But you have to go "do" the vision, and keep doing it after the renewal exercise. It won't happen by itself.

Yellow Submarines and Purple Hearts

Not long ago I was on hand for Nortel Network's yearly mission and vision relaunch and was impressed by the simplicity and directness of their message. Essentially, it was this—*Why you, the employee, should choose Nortel so you can help our customers choose us.*

There were a thousand people in the room. Exciting images flashed from huge video display screens. An MTV-style collage of customer testimonials helped build the excitement level. There was a preview of the new TV ad campaign. Yet there were only five speakers; each one hammered away at the basic people-oriented message.

You can do the same thing. Make the meeting as exciting as your resources will allow. Can't afford custom-made videos? How about a $15 music CD? Don't forget our earlier discussion—music is pure emotion. Nortel, it turns out, knows this too. In 1999, the telecommunications giant launched a marketing campaign to emphasize its goal of capturing a leadership position at the heart of the Internet revolution. Its theme was "Come Together," after the song from the Beatles' famous *Abbey Road* album, and the tune rock 'n' rolled nationwide under Nortel's ads on shows like *Chicago Hope* and *60 Minutes.*

Come together. Wow!

The corporation's CEO and vice chairman, John Roth, also proved he believes in emotional *Pacetta-fication* by sending out a letter to the corporation's 75,000 employees announcing that, in conjunction with the campaign, "we are involved in an all-out war on the competitive front."[1]

My kind of guy—the Beatles and the bomb.

But Mr. Roth needs to remember that those are fighting words. And that, forever more, he and Nortel will be judged by how they actually fought the war and whether it was won, lost, or ended in a draw. Vision is a powerful weapon as long you don't shoot yourself in the foot with it.

CHAPTER SEVEN

Four Deadly Words—

"It's News to Me!"—And What to Do About Them

I'm an old-fashioned communicator. I'm no communications minimalist. I don't believe less is more—more is more. There is no such thing as too much communication. It's like when your car stalls and won't restart: Check the gas tank first. The business is stalling? Check the communications. I could just as easily have titled this chapter "It's the Communications, Stupid!" And I believe in the primacy of the written word. Put it in writing.

Please.

 *Now-To*

For forty-eight hours, prohibit the use of voice-mail and e-mail. Remind everybody what it's like to communicate with words on paper, face-to-face, and one-on-one.

I'm serious. Try it for a limited period as a way to break the habit of using technology as a substitute for direct communication. Nothing infuriates me more than receiving a voice-mail from someone who could have reached me live and in person at my desk, but chose instead to wait until after business hours or the weekend to leave a message.

What's he hiding from? Me obviously. I might ask a question, say no, or otherwise complicate his life. But I'm still going to ask a question, say no, or complicate his life. He's just postponed the inevitable and forced me to take the initiative. And if it is bad news being left on my voice-mail or e-mail, that's a double bogie. It has the word "coward" written all over it. Bad news is always delivered face-to-face or, if there's absolutely no other alternative, it gets transmitted human voice to human ear on the phone.

If communications hide-and-seek is happening colleague-to-colleague within an organization, it's a bad sign. Never mind the internal chaos—which is bad enough—the customers are probably being treated the same way. Want to find out? Call them and ask. And please don't leave voice-mail. Ask:

- Are you satisfied with the contact you have with our organization?
- When was the last time you heard from us?
- Are you receiving enough information?
- How fast do we respond to your calls and messages?
- Are your calls always returned?

- Do we rely too much on voice-mail and other communication technologies?
- Would you prefer more one-on-one contact?
- How can we improve our communications with you?

Rarely will you be told that your company communicates too much with a customer—unless you're in telemarketing. But if that's the case, see if you can find out what purpose was served by the excess communication. Was it necessary? Pestering existing customers only alienates them and leads to doors being slammed in your face when there is a legitimate need to communicate. Try to set up a communication schedule when the relationship is in its early stages. There's also nothing wrong with checking in with a brief—live—phone call once every thirty days to see if there's anything a customer needs. Keep it brief and don't forget to ask about the customer's family, his or her health, and other personal matters.

Oh, that's so phony, Frank. The hell it is! What's phony is a business relationship that lacks a sincere interest in the human elements of life.

Personal relationships drive business relationships. We are all very busy these days, but if things get so hectic that we cannot establish a modicum of personal contact through our communications channels, we're going to be digitized into oblivion. Some people are delighted to do business on the Internet or push buttons on a Touch-Tone phone for ten minutes for what should be a thirty-second transaction. Others hate it. One size does not fit all.

If your motto is *That's the way we do business*, you deserve to be out of business.

A forty-eight-hour moratorium on dehumanizing communications technology is not nearly long enough. I'd prefer thirty days, but I know there'd be a backlash. You need enough time to rekindle personal contact and to demonstrate that it is not necessarily more productive in every case to rely exclusively on technology. For instance, there are ancient and honorable techniques for wrapping up a call or a discussion that's served its purpose and run on too long. "You probably need to get back to work . . ." is still effective. "I've already used too much of your time . . ." works too. It is so easy to forget these simple skills when e-mail or voice-mail becomes the principal means of communication.

Sure, some people talk too much. They waste your time and theirs. Figure out a way to deal with it without going into hiding.

One reason to be jumpy about an overreliance on communications technology is that it has yet to find a substitute for the inner ear or the gut-feeling that we use during one-on-one encounters to evaluate the importance of the information. What you should fear is that you won't pick up on the warning signs from voice-mail, e-mail, or the Internet and suddenly the bottom will fall out of your perfectly healthy business. "I've been meaning to tell you" are among the six scariest words in English, along with these four: "I thought you knew."

Technology is perfect for avoiding conflict. I hate conflict. But I hate the consequences of avoiding it even more. Most adults can sense when there is trouble brewing. We may choose to ignore it, but we know. You've probably been in too many meetings where you sensed that there was a hidden agenda or some camouflage draped over the proceedings. But instead of a meeting, if there's an exchange of position papers or a moderated discussion on the company Intranet, will you be as sensitive? I doubt it.

I'm a worrywart about a lot of things, so I'll introduce you to my standing list of communication worries. You might want to add these to your red notebook.

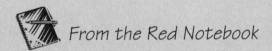 From the Red Notebook

Worry when the rate of communication falls off.
Worry when the rate of communication suddenly spurts.
Worry when communication turns impersonal.
Worry when nobody is griping or complaining.
Worry when everybody agrees with the consensus.
Worry about lack of specifics.
Worry when things are going great and no problems are reported.

Include conference calls in your moratorium, and, if you're really high-tech, suspend video conferencing as well. Conference calls (and video-conferencing) create the illusion of full group interaction. It's interaction, but it's not full. Take your truth serum. During your last conference call did the conversation have your undivided attention, or were you reading memos, checking your e-mail, or paying your bills?

Conference calls are not all that high-tech, but if you let them replace face-to-face gatherings, you'll regret it. I have been known to beg top management not to supplant face-to-face meetings with conference calls. One of my principal arguments is to remind them that their mission and vision statements call for a team-based enterprise. What if the New York Jets or the Denver Broncos practiced individually and only got together once a week by conference call before the big game? Great idea, eh?

Come on!

When we pay all this lip service to creating and empowering teams, we shouldn't then pull the plug on the personal interaction that teamwork requires. Teams are part of the communication circuitry. But there's a tendency for teams to lose their cohesion depending on how senior the members happen to be. It's illogical to expect the people on the loading dock to be operating face-to-face as a team, but not middle or top management. If it's important for the leaders of teams on the warehouse or factory floor to communicate goals and requirements to get buy-in and compliance, why isn't it just as important for the leader of a team of regional VPs to be held to the same standard? Decisions on the regional level tend to have a lot of impact, as far as I know. If the excuse is that top management is too busy, my question is, too busy for what? Too busy to communicate effectively? Maybe they're so busy because they're running around crazy cleaning up the mess that's created by communications breakdowns.

The last thing you want to have happen is to design different communication standards for different levels within the organization. One that's direct—for those who wear blue collars or are in the field with the customers. Another that's indirect—for those who are entitled to stock options and bonuses. That amounts to accountability for one, cover for the other.

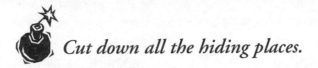

Cut down all the hiding places.

Poor communication is a favorite hiding place for all levels within the organization. *Whoops, communications breakdown.* Nobody's at fault. It's the adult equivalent of the dog ate my homework.

Other classic cop-outs:

- First I've heard about it.
- That's not my understanding.
- I was afraid of that.
- I was out of the loop.
- I wasn't briefed fully.
- It's news to me!

Establish a Presence with E-mail and Other Tools

After the moratorium is over, you'll probably realize that you honestly can't operate without e-mail. It can't be beat for establishing quick access to all parts of a far-flung operation. At Danka I used a judicious mix of e-mail and voice-mail to stay in contact with my two-thousand-member sales force. I tried not to spam them with broadsides on every topic, though. The idea is to establish your "presence." Nobody wants a manager and leader who is the recipient of the Caspar Award.

Caspar?

I guess I haven't told you about my not-so-coveted Ho-Hummer Awards for Mediocre Managers.

Here goes. Imagine yourself seated in the Dorothy Chandler Pavilion in Los Angeles. Billy Crystal is on stage finishing a joke about Jack Palance. They've heard it before but the audience howls with laughter anyway. He introduces the sexy actress Charlize Theron, who appears in a glittering designer gown with décolletage that extends so far south it gives new meaning to the term *beyond the Beltway.* "There are three nominees for this year's Caspar," she says. "Bidwell Morris of the Cooper Scooper Corporation for his acclaimed open-door policy. Bidwell's door opens on an empty desk, empty chair, empty office."

Applause.

Charlize smiles. "Kent Lockstep of the Gremlin Group. Kent worked at home as the company teetered on the edge of chapter eleven and only communicated by e-mail after midnight."

Applause.

"And Zoe Smirfler of Gotchas, the investment banking firm that specializes in underwriting hostile takeovers. Zoe hasn't been seen since July of 1989."

Applause.

The actress rips open the envelope and pauses dramatically. "The winner of the Caspar the Friendly Ghost Award for the Best Invisible Manager goes to . . ."

I think it has the makings of an annual event, don't you?

Which award do you qualify for? Which one does your boss deserve?

It's a fun way to address serious management shortcomings, and if you go through the list closely, you'll see that many of the major problems they address are communications related. Here's a statistic that should alarm you and alert you to the size of the problem. Fourteen percent of each forty-hour work week is wasted because of poor communication. Do the numbers. It comes to seven full work weeks of lost productivity each year.[1]

What that tells me is that I can add up to 14 percent to my bottom line if I can ramp up my communications effectiveness.

How? One of the best ways is to follow the three Rs of communications:

The Ho-Hummer Awards for Mediocre Managers

- The **Casper the Friendly Ghost Award** goes to the best invisible manager. He or she is never around when needed.
- There's the **Polly, or Polly Parrot, Award** for the manager who just repeats what the his or her boss says.
- The **Robo, or Robot Manager, Award.** It goes to the manager who does his or her job by the numbers and by the book.
- The **Eddie, or Eddie Haskell, Award.** The boss who always heaps praise on anyone who might help him or her, and doesn't mean a word of it.
- The **Dip, or Diplomat, Award** goes to the manager who feels strongly both ways about the issue.
- The **Sarge, or Sergeant Schultz, Award.** In honor of those managers who see nothing, say nothing, and hear nothing.
- The **Howie,** in memory of Howard Cosell. You qualify by telling it like it is, but offering no solution to fix it.
- The **White Glove, or Michael Jackson, Award.** It goes to managers who refuse to get their hands dirty.
- The **Phil,** name after Puxatawny Phil, the groundhog. This award is for the manager or company who makes every day seems as long as an endless winter of the same old things rerun over and over again.
- And there's the **Nicky,** in honor of the pugnacious former Soviet Communist Party boss Nikita Kruschev, for the manager who screams and slams shoes on the table.

repetition

repetition

repetition

As I'm writing this, it is spring and there is a bright red male cardinal outside the window sounding his mating call over and over again. If it's important—and it certainty is to that bird—it is worth repeating. Advertising agencies knows this. They fashion a slogan and hammer it home again and again until people can repeat it in their sleep.

At Danka I used "10–5–2"—it was in my memos, e-mails, speeches, and phone calls. It meant that my sales force was expected to have ten sales calls a week, five sales a month for the standard product line, and two special orders for our newly introduced color copiers. I had them stand up at meetings and chant "10–5–2."

Try it. Say it out loud: 10–5–2. Go ahead, don't be bashful.

What I just did right here on the page was to repeat 10–5–2 a total of three times (four if you count this sentence, and the fifth is coming right up). The slogan 10–5–2 would have been forgotten in a heartbeat if it hadn't been repeated over and over again.

When I was at Xerox, the corporation was into TQM, the Total Quality Movement. Hardly an hour went by when we didn't hear, see, or say the word "quality." Xerox wanted to win the Malcolm Baldridge Award as a way to demonstrate that it had bounced back from its slump in the 1970s and 1980s. TQM was the vehicle and the word "quality" was the gas pedal. Today, I'm told that quality is mentioned from time to time, but not nearly as often. It's too bad. Quality makes for a powerful mantra.

Listen Up and Down

One reason that repetition is so helpful is that our listening skills are dreadful. I suspect this is a fairly recent phenomenon. It seems only natural that our listening capability—hearing—would be as acute as our eyesight since primitive men and women spent about half their time in the dark.

Furthermore, listening was a way to be entertained and to gather folk wisdom. Reading is only a recently adopted skill. But something has gotten in the way of listening. To counteract the problem, I make a point of summarizing the key points of a meeting before it concludes. Or I'll go around the room and ask participants to recapitulate. This is also a great way to spot gaps, uncertainty, and confusion.

Your red notebook amounts to a hearing aide. Write things down, both as you hear them and later to summarize the stuff you don't want to forget. By taking notes, you are training yourself to listen and remember. What's the alternative title of this chapter? The one I offered as a possibility in the opening paragraph. Don't look back. If you had taken a note, you'd probably remember: "It's the communications, stupid."

And that, by the way, is a paraphrase of political consultant James Carville's technique for keeping the Clinton presidential campaign on message during the 1992 election. It's abruptness and borderline rudeness (redeemed by a sense of humor), calls attention to the message and highlights its importance. Business communication needs less jargon and blandness and more Carville-style bluntness in order to overcome the prevailing listening-ability deficit.

Don't take my word for it, though. Test me. Actually, test your people to see how well they listen. Present a policy change or announce a set of priorities in the usual ho-hum way. Include one variation on the Carville formula. It is easy to do: "It's the numbers, stupid, it's the execution, stupid; it's the _____ stupid." At the end of the meeting ask them to write a half-page summary. See what they remember.

Serving Pure Protein

I'm a feedback freak. I want to know what you think. Does it make sense? Do you see a problem? Can you add to it? How can you use it? Am I off base? Feedback is the report card of people-ology. If I'm not cutting it, I want to know.

Having a sales background helps. "No" is the ultimate feedback. It gets so that anything else—"You're an idiot," "This makes no sense whatsoever," or "Huh?"—is not a problem. All leaders must develop leather skin. It's never pleasant or easy to hear, but full-frontal feedback ensures that the communications gap is closed.

Many managers discourage feedback or dabble in it to create the illusion that they want to hear what the troops think. Usually, they've made up their minds and, as far as they're concerned, the feedback is irrelevant. But it's nice to know who's on board and who isn't, what their reservations are, and if better alternative possibilities exist that haven't been considered.

I've gone from hating feedback to making a living off it. I used to seethe when my team started poking holes in one of my brilliant schemes. Probably the most infamous episode was in Cleveland when I rolled out a special bonus plan for my managers and was thunderstruck when they started nit-picking. I had gone out on a limb with corporate to get the plan approved as a way to reward their extra effort and the district's success. Part of it was tied to customer satisfaction rates, and that's what drew the complaints. I was expecting gratitude, not carping. Tom Bill, the district's business manager, was about to make a presentation at the front of the room to lay out the exact details. I got up, walked to the overhead projector, and knocked his stack of transparencies to the floor. "We're not going to talk about this anymore, we're doing it," I said. "The meeting's over." There was dead silence. Finally, Tom, who towers over me said, "I guess you don't want me to bother making the presentation."

Today, I'd handle it differently. The decision to go with the plan wouldn't have been changed. And, no, that doesn't mean I'm advocating going through the motions on feedback. For one thing, the dispute involved additional compensation that Xerox had to be talked into paying in the first place. The customer satisfaction tie-in was a side issue. Corporate was not about to sweeten the deal. I should have explained that better and just allowed them to vent.

I got away with my temper tantrum because we had always practiced full-frontal feedback and the outburst was considered to be an aberration. But there was an element of calculation involved in it from my standpoint. As leader, I thought my managers were being petty and self-centered. They were all extremely well paid. On top of that, linking customer satisfaction to management compensation is nonnegotiable. I wanted to sober them up. After that the subject was closed. It never arose again.

To Advise and Dissent

Today, it's nerve-wracking to see a roomful of nodding heads. Are they tuned out? Am I getting the New York nod? The odds are that 20 percent of any one gathering of business people will disagree with anything you put on the table: *Let's give everybody the day off on December 25.* I know there's going to be somebody in the room saying, "What kind of a flaky idea is that?" I'd much rather confront that head-on than have to deal with it later in the form of covert opposition or half-hearted support. I'll keep probing and pushing until someone raises his or her head to offer a reservation. Usually that's enough to encourage others to speak out. Another way to go is to shoot holes in your own proposal, if no one else is willing to do the job. Play devil's advocate.

We owe the people we lead information and explanation. Pete Egoscue, the renowned exercise therapist and author, shared a communications story with Roger that I want to pass along. Pete is a former Marine combat officer who served in Vietnam. As his unit was preparing for its first patrol, the CO told his platoon leaders that the only way they could be certain of bringing their people back alive and uninjured was to make sure that each knew exactly what the mission was. "If I say we're going out there looking for three blue beebees, you better make sure they know that, know why, and know what we're going to do about it," was the way he put it. As they patrolled, the commanding officer would break away with his radio operator and drop in by surprise on various platoons. He'd head straight for the nearest Marine and ask him what they were doing out there in the bushes. Pete recalls, "If that kid didn't know, your ass was in a lot of trouble."

The Marine officer was using a formula that we discussed earlier—what, why, and how—and it's the backbone of effective communication. By discouraging feedback you never know if the what, why, and how has been effective. Don't assume that they get it.

Bear in mind, though, the purpose is not consensus building as much as information sharing. Consensus will come in time. Blunt feedback rankles so many managers and leaders because it is regarded as evidence of disloyalty, a bad attitude, or poor teamwork. The most disloyal act of all is to withhold the truth. If you believe I'm wrong—tell me, and at the same time tell me why and tell me what you propose that we should do.

In my first book I offered a hard and fast rule—no whining! And this book's title implies that the rule still holds. But—there is an exception. I'd rather hear whining than have silence. Constructive whining is okay. It's pointless to play the victim, however. Whining must be accompanied by an effort to improve the situation overall, offer alternatives, or to comply with the disputed policy to the best of one's ability. Winning requires listening and taking action. Encouraging feedback allows you to look for weakness in your own argument. I believe in making quick decisions, but I'm even quicker to seek as many different perspectives as possible.

I can remember any number of decisions that my bosses made that I did not agree with at the time they were announced. But the more I learned about the background and the reasoning behind their moves, the easier they were to accept. "I can understand that," is a far better reaction than, "Who knows what the hell they're up to!" Middle management frequently gets caught in a communications trap devised by senior management's tendency to dictate policy moves without providing adequate explanation. This leaves middle managers with the task of motivating their teams with the most demotivating words of all—*You don't need to know. Just go do it.*

Your best people hate that. They want to be included in the planning process and be part of the information loop. Top performers are always seeking to gain control—control of the ball, control of the agenda, control of the process. That's why they are good at what they do. Information is power. If you deprive them of power and control, they'll go elsewhere to find it. There are a raft of psychological studies that show that powerlessness and a sense of helplessness contribute to depression, resentment, and violent behavior. Information is good medicine.

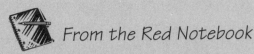

From the Red Notebook

Kristen Miller told me one of her secrets of success is that her customers think she's the boss. Not their boss, Xerox's boss.

You don't need to know. Just do it also hurts the manager's credibility, because he or she seems to be a candidate for the Robo Award—doing it by the book, doing what the boss demands no matter what the consequences. If middle management has the information it can at least put it on the table and let people make up their own minds. *You don't need to know. Just go do it* is read as an indication that an illogical, poorly thought out policy is coming down from the top, and it's time to hide.

Before I close this section of the chapter, I want to follow up on Pete Egoscue's Marine Corps communications experience with material sent to me by John A. Olsen, another former Marine officer. After hearing one of my speeches, Mr. Olson went home and dug out his own red notebook—and it was red—from officer candidate school. In it, he found these eleven points about effective leadership:

1. Be technically and tactically proficient.
2. Know yourself and seek improvement.
3. Know your men and look out for their welfare.
4. Keep your men informed.
5. Set the example.
6. Ensure that the task is understood, supervised, and accomplished.
7. Train your men as a team.
8. Make sound and timely decisions.
9. Develop a sense of responsibility in your subordinates.
10. Deploy your command in accordance with its capabilities.
11. Seek responsibility and take responsibility for your actions.

Curing Meeting Madness

Time for another Pacetta Poll. Ask your people:

- As an organization, grade our communications skills from A to F.
- Grade your team leader's communications skills on the same basis.
- Grade your team members' communications skills on the same basis.
- Is information shared from team to team, routinely, occasionally, rarely, never?
- Do you believe what you're told is the truth all of the time, most of the time, some of the time, or none of the time?
- Do you have more than enough information to do your job well, just enough, or not enough?
- Are you listened to by your manager and colleagues?
- Is feedback encouraged or discouraged?
- Are you made to feel comfortable or uncomfortable about expressing disagreement or contrary views?
- Have you been penalized for expressing your opinion, yes or no?
- How often is there a communications failure—never, occasionally, frequently?
- What is our strongest communications mode overall—written, verbal, one-on-one, group?
- Is our communications policy consistent?
- Are there too many meetings, a sufficient number of meetings, or not enough meetings?
- Are meetings very productive, productive, occasionally productive, unproductive?
- How often are you in direct face-to-face communication with your manager?
- Would you prefer those contacts to be more frequent, less frequent, or at about the current level?

- How often are policy changes imposed without explanation—never, occasionally, frequently, always?
- Is our communications with the customer poor, fair, good, excellent?
- Grade how well we listen to the customer—A through F.
- Would you describe your knowledge of company long- and short-term goals as good, fair, or poor?
- When was the last time we communicated our vision and mission statement to you—today, this week, this month, within the last six months, or can't remember?

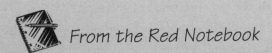

From the Red Notebook

"Lack of communication frustrates people."

—BRUCE SYPOD, BUSINESS CONSULTANT

This Pacetta poll is more detailed than most because communication is too important to be given ho-hum treatment. Communication is ground zero for Murphy's Law: What can go wrong will go wrong. We have to keep watching and working at it constantly. When you think it's finally perfect, there will be a breakdown a few minutes later.

Some communication sectors are more accident prone than others. The reason meetings are dreaded by many people is that we allow the communications value to leak out of the meeting and leave everyone wondering why they bothered attending.

We hate meetings because:

they are too long
have no agenda
are not pertinent
don't invite input
take place in an awful room
. . . with a terrible sound system
we've heard it before
there are too many people
nothing happens afterward

Meetings must be prepared as carefully as you arrange for an important dinner party at your home. The casualness and indifference involved in calling meetings is astounding. No wonder we consider them a waste of time. Most of them are a waste of time.

There are two questions to ask—one at the beginning of the meeting and one at the end:

- What's the meeting intended to accomplish?
- What are we going to do as a result of this meeting?

I never close a meeting without asking this question: What are we going to do now?

If we go to the trouble of having a meeting, shouldn't some action take place based on what was discussed?

Of course. But too many meetings are held with loose or impossibly ambitious agendas. Focus is lost, and at the end it's impossible to sort out what needs to be done. I rate my managers on their ability to conduct meetings. I'll tell them if they need to improve their skills and coach them along by inspecting the agenda for future meetings and exposing them to team leaders who have mastered the art of "giving good meeting." And while it is an art, the techniques can be learned. It's a mistake to lose this communications tool by using it badly or deciding that meetings are a waste of time.

From the Red Notebook

If you're in a meeting and it doesn't impact your customers, get up and end the meeting. This kind of strong stand will keep everyone focused on why we are in business in the first place.

I'm also a firm believer in unstructured meetings, otherwise known as bull sessions. Break your people into small groups and allow them to talk. Throw out a few topics and let the discussion flow where it may. Is this productive? Very. Among other things it builds a sense of openness. Talk is not just something that goes on through official channels and according to a strict set of rules. Some people will be more inclined to open up in a less formal setting. And the opposite is true too. Without official sanction and imprimatur, there are those who are reluctant to express an opinion or take a stand. They have to be encouraged to participate. Mix your teams together and do some cross pollinating with different departments and functions. I hate it when ghettos form. At Xerox, I made it a point to get "the wrenches" as the service people are known—how's that for white-collar snobbery?—to mingle with the sales, support, and admin people.

Whether they are structured or unstructured meetings, they can be utilized as accurate barometers of your operation's health. If they turn flat, rancorous, or ho-hum, you'll know in a minute that there's a problem. I went to one several years ago that featured a senior executive who spoke without a break for three hours and showed up to three hundred slides. You could have done open-heart surgery without anesthesia on most of the audience, that's how numb we were. There wasn't even a bathroom break. I concentrated on the wall behind him, hoping that if stared hard enough I could burn a twenty-foot "CC" into the wall. And he was "clearly clueless," but it took senior management about a year and a half to get up the nerve to move him out of his job, and in the meantime he did extraordinary damage to Xerox's field operation. And that meeting was a dead give away that he was trouble.

Perfecting the Write Stuff

Written communication is also accident prone. For many of us, writing is such an unnatural act that we'd rather send smoke signals. Our reading skills aren't great either. The combination makes for a disaster. It wouldn't hurt from a training standpoint to require remedial work in writing, reading, public speaking, and listening.

Take some truth serum. How's your writing? It could probably use a brush up, no matter how accomplished you are. Style is not the issue, clarity is. For all of its many drawbacks, e-mail has actually promoted clarity in written communications. I've received any number of one word e-mail replies:

Yes.
No.
Maybe.

 Now-To

Go to the bookstore and buy a copy of *The Elements of Style* by William Strunk and E. B. White. It's the best little book ever published on how to write effectively. Read it and "write with nouns and verbs" forevermore.

Pretty damned clear. But e-mail's brevity is also its weakness. Ink needs to go on paper to ensure complete comprehension. When it doesn't, there's bound to be trouble. I believe in writing nearly everything. Yeah, it's a pain, but the record is sure nice to have when you need it.

I wouldn't dream of operating a business without written contracts. We have them with our customers and our suppliers to make sure both sides know what's required and when. Management covers itself with paper to make sure there are generous pension, bonus, and stock-option provisions. But when it comes to employee and employer performance we tend to leave everything to chance.

Stop leaving it to chance. Chance has delivered many a cruel surprise.

And it is surprise that is the enemy of effective communications. Hand each new employee a copy of the company's vision and mission statements, short- and long-term goals, his or her team's plan to implement those two documents, and a description of the job being filled. Ask them to write a one- or two-page contract describing how they will personally carry out those requirements. This sounds more daunting than it really is.

Let's say I own a dairy farm, but I want to spend the winter in Florida. When I hire a substitute farmer, what do I expect him to do?

1. Feed the cows.
2. Care for the herd's health.
3. Milk the cows.
4. Deliver the milk to the processor.
5. Clean the barn.
6. Show a profit.

Here's what happens next. Two people, Mary and Murray, answer the ad I put in the paper. I show the requirements to Murray, who says okay, and I hire him. A month later I get a call from him to inform me that the cows are dying. What happened? Murray explains that he examined the farm's cash flow and concluded that we would not make a profit unless he cut overhead costs. His solution was to feed the cows only once a week.

I think we had a communication breakdown, don't you?

What I should have done is use a contract like the one Mary offered me in response to my job description.

1. I will feed the cows twice a day, morning and evening. They'll receive a balanced diet that I will develop in consultation with the local vet.

2. The same vet will be on call for emergencies and I will ask him to inspect the herd once a month. I will also get his recommendations on vitamin supplements and begin a program of regular inoculations.

3. The milking routine will be conducted twice a day. All equipment will be sterilized and checked for contamination prior to every session.

4. There will be one delivery a day to the processor. I am establishing an e-mail link with this company and will request biweekly price quotes which I will compare with other processors should we decide to take our business elsewhere.

5. The stalls will be cleaned twice a day and doused with non-toxic disinfectant. Waste products will be stored to be sold on the weekend to area gardeners and local nurseries. The return from selling the manure will add 2 percent to our annual profits.

Murray was an idiot. Mary is a saint. But I was a fool not to insist on a contract with Murray. And I'd have been an even bigger fool not to realize that the major contributing factor to Mary's sainthood is the contract. Sure, she's conscientious, but the contract tells me what to expect from her, gives me a standard against which I can measure her performance, and lets her know what she can expect from me. I can't come back to her and say, "Mary, you didn't give me the profit margin I wanted." It's there on paper, 2 percent. I can't say, "You shouldn't be consulting with the vet so much, it costs us money." The contract stipulates that she will have the vet visit the herd once a month.

From the Red Notebook

Personal performance contracts eliminate question marks by establishing responsibility and accountability.

To fully close the loop, I should also have offered my own contract to Mary:

1. I will check in with you by phone once a week.
2. You are authorized to spend up to $1,000 for medical emergencies involving the herd. Inform me within twenty-four hours should an emergency arise.
3. Please use Doctor Janice Brown for vet services.
4. Keep the farm's financial accounts balanced and up to date.
5. Attend the monthly grange meetings.
6. I will pick up 15 percent of the tuition costs at the agricultural college if you pursue part-time course work while on my payroll.

See what's happening? Mary and I are communicating our expectations.

Personal performance contracts should cascade from the top to the bottom of the organization. They provide a tight system of discipline and accountability. Contracts are not straitjackets or exercises in micromanagement. Get some parameters in place instead of flying blind or making things up along the way. By establishing understanding and agreement on both sides, there is a process in place for achieving long- and short-term goals: To get off the farm—where a native of Queens doesn't really belong in the first place. If I want to improve my communications companywide, the goal should be part of every contract with every employee from the CEO to the janitorial workers. A manager's contract might include, for example, a provision stipulating that he or she would "meet with each team member individually once a week for at least twenty minutes to discuss performance, outlook, and problem areas." As the leader, I can easily check that by asking individual team members to tell me when they last met with their manager. In turn, my contract with the manager should commit me to get together regularly with the executive to discuss and review his or her managerial performance, including the team's efforts to increase communications effectiveness, and offer any assistance. A contract must be specific, flow two ways, and entail actions that are verifiable.

This isn't a gun to the head kind of thing. Contract formulation should be a collaborative enterprise involving the individual and his or her direct supervisor. It's an excellent opportunity for the two of them to forge a close partnership: "Here's what we need from you, Mary, and here's how I will help you." There's no better way to avoid misunderstandings. In provides both sides with an objective standard for performance. A contract needs:

- Specific expectations, responsibilities, and terms of empowerment.
- Specific long-term and short-term goals with specific actions to meet them.
- Specific personal and professional objectives with specific actions to meet them.
- Specific career development plans with specific plans to meet them.
- Specific requirements to deliver 100 percent of the business plan and specific actions that will be taken.
- Specific actions to exceed 100 percent of the business plan.

A contract is useless if it is not be reviewed. Once a month, those who report to us should be walked through their contracts and asked about what's been happening with each item. If they are expected to sell five new Lexus cars a month, it should be in the contract and the manager needs to ask, "How come you sold only three?" And the next question has got to be, "How can I help you get up to the quota?" If this happens monthly, or biweekly, you won't end up at the end of the year twenty-four Lexuses in the hole. Spot the problem and move to fix it. A yearly review comes too late. During monthly reviews, an overly ambitious contract can be adjusted, but don't be too quick to back off requirements. Challenge your people to stretch and grow.

Some contract provisions must be nonnegotiable, such as ethics, elements of the mission statement, and essential provisions of the business plan. If people know what they're getting into up front, there won't be any nasty surprises. It's not a bad idea to use contract formulation as part of the recruiting process. By asking prospective employees to develop a contract based on their understanding of the job description and the contributions they can bring to it, you'll see where they're coming from. If you are committed to close teamwork, and if a hot prospect skates by it in his or her contract, there may be a blind spot in that area. Perhaps you need to keep searching.

In turn, as I lay out my contractual expectations for the new hire, he or she can see how I look at the job. If I'm being unrealistic, it would be great for both of us to find that out sooner rather than later. It's called communication—and it's not stupid.

The lack of a solid communication process both internally and with your customers leads to distrust and hinders your struggle against the competition. Not letting people know here they stand causes confusion and lost productivity.

The interpersonal, one-on-one, face-to-face laying out of expectations, soliciting feedback, listening to what our people and our customers are saying, and in turn letting them know where the company stands is imperative.

Communication is not e-mail, voice-mail, phones, etc. We depend too much on technology! It's an excuse not to face issues, employees, or customers head-on. The companies that use technology but keep it *personal* will win in the future.

CHAPTER EIGHT

Halftime—

Crossing the Bridge from Whining to Winning

*T*his chapter is going to function as a short review of what we've been doing. The problem with a book is that it's too linear. I can't hop around as much as I'd like. The last chapter is a good example. All that communications stuff could be scattered throughout the book to mix and match other subjects, like retention, training, and motivation. But if I did that, many readers would think that communications is only marginally important—and that *would* be stupid.

Or by tackling vision before communication, am I signaling that one is primary and the other secondary? Likewise, the way things are organized may suggest that people-ology is nothing more than a gimmick.

No way!

Think of each chapter in this book as functioning as a column—Doric, Ionic, or whatever—supporting the dome that is people-ology. The columns form a huge circle. There's no order of precedence. You can lose a few in a windstorm, or perhaps a couple are a little shorter than the others. The dome still has support, though. But if there's no people-ology, the dome falls away and what's left of the structure is wide open to the freezing rain and the burning sun.

People-ology: What It Is and Isn't

People-ology is a discipline based on the principle that people need and want caring, committed leadership to help them develop their full potential.

People-ology isn't a form of manipulation.

People-ology is value-centered and is dedicated to producing value in terms of direct financial and personal rewards, like strength, courage, balance, and fulfillment.

People-ology is not coercion.

People-ology is multidimensional and multicultural.

People-ology is not a luxury to be turned on when times are good and switched off when there's trouble.

People-ology is a necessity at all times.

People-ology is not PR.

People-ology is a set of working principles that recognizes that people are a company's number one asset and that every other product and service depends on the success of its people.

People-ology is not talk.

People-ology is action.

People-ology is not command and control.

People-ology is respect, responsibility, and accountability.

People-ology isn't for an elite few.

People-ology is for all.

People-ology isn't dull drudgery.

People-ology is electric and fun.
People-ology isn't about making do.
People-ology is about making history.
People-ology isn't only about making profit.
People-ology is about taking pride.

I know I promised to give you a review of the work in progress, and I will but I'm not ready yet. First I want to show you a people-ology organization chart and touch on the subject of creating a chief executive officer of people-ology, also known as the people czar.

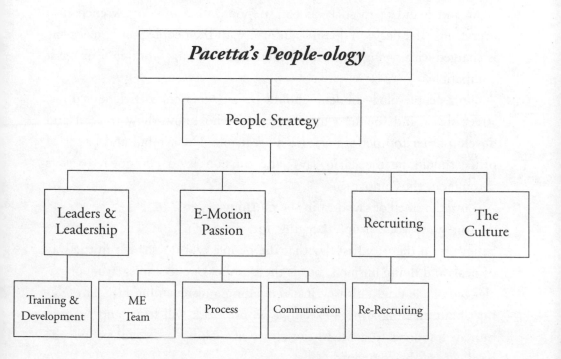

Pacetta's People-ology

People Strategy

Leaders & Leadership | E-Motion Passion | Recruiting | The Culture

Training & Development | ME Team | Process | Communication | Re-Recruiting

Message—"What a great company to work for."

The People Czar

I know, I know. People czar sounds too authoritarian, but anything else tends to sound like the product of a human resources group therapy session. Ideally, the CEO should function as his or her own people czar, but it will work to have another senior executive charged with the responsibility of driving people-ology through the corporate obstacle course.

This has to be one powerful, experienced dude, because he or she is going to be involved in every department and every nook and cranny of the operation. If a policy impacts people—and they all do—the people czar gets involved. Actually, "involved" is too mild a word. The people supremo signs off on it. No one gets to bypass the people czar, who has the right and mandate to stick an oar, a spoon, or a monkey wrench into everything. If a decision doesn't conform with the people policy, he or she is charged with saying so, saying it loud and clear, and working to make it compatible.

This people-ology honcho should be an experienced field executive, street smart and tough; a top performer who knows how to lead and develop other top performers. It's a great job. The symbol and badge of office should be the chain saw. The mission is to cut down barriers throughout the company.

Love the smell of saw dust in the morning!

You want your people begging for the chain saw. They'll see and believe from the very first day that the people czar doesn't get in the way of deals and doing business, but is the number one tool for getting obstacles *out* of the way. This isn't just retreading and renaming HR, I'm talking about creating a mega-executive whose work will focus and sharpen human resources to assist in the effort of making successful people the hard core of the company.

I'd have a contract with my people czar that's as brief as a haiku and as long as the Manhattan telephone directory. He or she would be held accountable for measurable improvements in every aspect of the operation, and would be rewarded commensurably. Since I personally believe that I can return a minimum of an extra 10 percent by practicing total people-ology, as a people czar I would be willing to commit to a 10 percent productivity and profit gain. In return, I get roaming rights over every square inch of territory. I won't have dictatorial power, just my leadership skills, access to the CEO, and the right and duty to tell it like it is:

- This policy, decision, or process helps—and here's why.
- This policy decision or process hurts—and here's a better plan.

Would CEOs see this as a threat? They shouldn't. The final decision rests at the top. As people czar, if I don't agree, it's my job to make it clear why I oppose a decision, lay out what I see as the negative consequences, and propose alternatives. If I'm overruled, the next move is to make people-ology as effective as possible within the new context. If that can't be done, I have to make that clear and, perhaps, get another job. Even so, I don't think that falling on your sword will become a way of life for the people czar. He or she will quickly establish how profitable people-ology can be.

Early in my career as a leader, I almost had a mutiny on my hands. All of my teams had effective managers except one. I knew it, but I didn't face up to my responsibility and make a change. I figured that I could finesse it by managing the manager. I was also ducking the blame. I had promoted her, even though I had doubts about whether she was ready for the job. Her team actually did well. They got their required numbers. But they came to me and demanded action. Why? Because the other teams were having all the fun and excitement beating the numbers. They wanted that too. They felt cheated. I didn't have a choice; I made the change. The story had a happy ending because the manager did extremely well in a new job within the operation and was far more satisfied with her situation.

That's the kind of effect the people czar will have on an organization. He or she would have been on my case earlier—"Frank, she's not ready," or "Let's move on this, Frank, your people feel cheated." All concerned would have been a lot happier and more productive months earlier. How can you resent, oppose, or attempt to politically stymie an executive who is going to make your life profitable, fun, and fulfilling? I'd want the people czar permanently camped in my operation.

Trouble? Send the cavalry. No, send the people czar. But you won't have to. She or he will be there already.

Serving Spaghetti and Meatballs for the Soul

My mother and father are the prototypes for the people czar. They practiced—and still do—pure people-ology. In the next four or five pages, I'd like to take you back home with me to experience leadership in its most robust, direct, and humane form. My objective is to dispel the notion that leadership is mysterious, manipulative, and the province of uniquely endowed practitioners, who are "born and not made." What I learned from my parents—from clarity of communication to strict accountability—is at the core of everything I do as a business leader.

Mom and Dad spent every waking hour working to create a family atmosphere where the very best things flourished and grew, where there was fun, warmth, love, security, and wisdom.

The Pacetta family never went on vacation or bought much; there wasn't enough money. But our little bungalow in Far Rockaway was stuffed full of priceless treasures.

My parents required my sister and I to do our best and keep our promises. They expected, inspected, and corrected. There were rewards for success and consequences for failure. It wasn't easy; my father started his business career as a bank teller with only a high school education and went to night school to get a college degree. As he worked his way to vice president at Chase Manhattan bank, he was always there for us. I was on the school baseball team, which played all over the city on weekday afternoons—Staten Island, Brooklyn, Queens, the Bronx—and by the third or fourth inning, I'd check the stands and Dad would be there cheering. I can remember how it made me feel proud, warm, and protected.

> ### For the Red Notebook
>
> A leader models the desired behavior.
>   Example: "Hey, Frank, it's only four o'clock, where are you going?"
> "To my daughter's game."

My father is a staunch conservative. He made it a point to drop by the school frequently to make sure the younger Jesuit priests weren't being too permissive with the students and letting us drift dangerously to the left. The school had a prefect of discipline, though. Father Hamel lined us up and checked our appearance every Monday morning. Long hair and other radical tendencies weren't going to slip by on his watch. Dad was his strongest backer. But he was more than willing to buck authority when his family was involved.

Before I got to Brooklyn Prep and was still in elementary school, Dad had a classic run-in with the teaching nuns. He always gave me a quarter to pay for milk. I'd put the coin carefully in my pocket. One day, a little girl complained that she dropped her quarter and lost it in the cloakroom. The sister asked the rest of the class if anyone had found it. I reached into my pocket and pulled out my quarter to show her. We were discussing money after all. I was immediately suspect number one. I wasn't about to give up the coin and I wouldn't confess, so the sister took me back into the cloakroom and made me kneel and swear on the cross that I hadn't taken the girl's money.

At supper that night I told the story. My father was furious; he gulped his meal down and headed for the convent to let the nun know that she was never to question his son's honesty ever again. Gene Pacetta's boy doesn't lie. "Don't mess with my family" was the loud and clear message.

Classic Italian-American, and about as far removed from the Mafiosi stereotype as you can get. My world was filled with relatives coming and going from the house, music playing in the background off the radio and, on special occasions, provided by Uncle Mike on the harmonica and Dad on the accordion. After the first bottle of red wine, as far as they were concerned, the Guy Lombardo orchestra had nothing on them.

One stereotype is true—food. It always took center stage. Every Sunday, pasta accompanied by gravy with meats—meatballs, sausage, or lamb. Stuffed? Wait. That would be followed by a whole chicken or roast beef, potatoes, and other vegetables. Dessert? Of course. "The Meal" was an event. It took hours to consume, what with the laughing and the talking and the crying. Usually, there'd be a break. We take a walk around the neighborhood, come back, and start again. I loved every minute of it. As a child, I was encouraged to listen, learn, and to make a contribution. And eat. *Mangia!*

Weddings, anniversaries, communions, name days were all celebrated with gusto. In between, if one of the family so much as cut a finger, the house was jammed with visitors to inspect the wound, provide sympathy, and offer medical advice. My aunts and uncles were second parents. They dispensed abundant love and discipline with equal authority. And there was Joey. Everybody *owned* Joey. He was tickled and teased and played with. Mom was so protective of him. In that deeply Italian combination of faith and superstition, she would tell Carm and me that because of what he had to endure, wonderful things would happen to us. And wonderful things have happened. To this day, when there's good news to share, she gets the first call, and I know Mom still says to herself, "It's because of Joey."

Joey's personal hero was Uncle Dom, a guy who never went to high school but didn't let that stop him from building a hugely successful home heating oil company. Joey loved to see Uncle Dom's trucks rumbling down the street. Dom died a few years ago but Joey still asks about him and those trucks.

My brother is in a resident nursing facility now, still unable to speak more than a few words or care for himself. At their ages, there was no way Mom and Dad could continue to take care of him. It was probably the toughest decision they ever made. On Dad's seventieth birthday, my brother-in-law Steve wrote and read this verse tribute at the party.

IF I COULD TALK FOR JOE TODAY

If I could talk for Joe today
I could never convey with mere words
What I'd like to say.
I tried to write this many times before
But tears would fill my eyes and I could write no more.
But now I think I know what to say
Even if it's only words I have to work with today.
If I could talk for Joe today
If I could talk for Joe today
There are three little words that are all I need to say.
Dad, I know it wasn't easy taking care of me
But you had a larger heart that only God could see
And that's why he put you here just for me.
If I could talk for Joe today
If I could talk for Joe today
The words could never make known
The patience, the kindness, the love that I owned.
You did for me more than I could expect
But it was never enough from your aspect.
I know it broke your heart to let me go
But it was best for me, but that you and I already know.
And although I live now with another family and friends
You are in my heart from morn till day's end.
Although these three words will be enough today
I will tell you more with my own voice someday
When you and I are in a far better place
If could talk for Joe today
So what are these words I keep rambling about
They are but the most powerful there is no doubt
Dad, I love you
There is nothing more I could say
If I could talk for Joe today.

Now I didn't reprint this poem just to make my brother-in-law Steve feel like Robert Frost. With a hundred words or so he captured the essence of leadership that has eluded the three thousand books on business leadership that are in print: "The patience, the kindness, the love that I owned." Pretty touchy-feely and fuzzy, eh? No, basic and human and grounded in the belief in the power of doing what's right. Mom and Dad knew there was no point in whining about Joey's condition, and so they went about the business of winning the best life possible for their three children and each other.

Got it tough at the office? Boss is a bastard? I'm sorry to hear that. But maybe we've forgotten what it really means to have it tough. While I risk sounding arrogant and unfeeling when I say, "Stop whining—and start winning," I'll take my chances because I know it works in far tougher situations than selling copiers, or whatever business we happen to be in.

But is all this ancient history really relevant to the every day cut and thrust of business? You bet it is. My parents were fiercely protective of their children. One of my fondest memories of my mother stems from an incident that occurred when I was ten or eleven. Joey was in his favorite spot, which was the front porch overlooking the street. He was probably out there waiting for one of Uncle Dom's trucks to pass by. A couple of teenage boys saw him and began to taunt him. In a flash, my five-foot-tall mother was out the front door and flying down the walk, brandishing her big metal pasta spoon like a sword. Don't mess with my family. They ran for their lives.

I can't think of a better motto for people-ology—*Don't mess with my family*. There was an incident in Xerox's Cleveland with one of our customers that came to be known as the "The Rescue." It was a classic "don't mess with my business family" situation. One of our sales reps called in from the field to say that a customer had just verbally abused her during a presentation. He had shouted and cursed her out about the price or some other aspect of the package she was offering. She was in the lobby of the building on a pay phone in tears. My administrative assistant took the call and immediately interrupted a meeting I was having with two other managers (Pacetta's first rule of setting priorities—if it's about a customer, the meeting's over). "Tell her to stay right where she is," I said. "We'll be right there." The three of us piled into a car and took off. On the way to the customer's office, one of my colleagues asked what we were going to do when we got there. "We'll tell him that his business is important to us, but not that important," I said. "He's not going to do that to one of our people."

We got there, went in to see the customer, delivered the message politely but directly, lost the deal—it was a nice one too—and left. Nobody messes with my family. And you know what? Word of what we had done spread like wildfire around the office. Our people loved it, hit the street even harder, and more than made up for the lost business.

That one was for my mother. By inviting you to come home with me via these pages to have spaghetti and meatballs for the soul, I'm struggling to put you in touch with your own deep attachments to others. Get hold of it! Please! There's incredible energy, strength, and value to be found in this soft spot. And it is so easy to forget or to be persuaded that it doesn't matter—that it's only business.

Only business? I'll take *don't mess with my family* any day. My business family will outsell, outwork, outperform, outrun, and outshine the cynics and gunslingers every time.

I love being Italian. We're taught to be emotional and proud of it.

We're taught to show and give affection.

We taught to honor traditions.

We're taught to offer respect to others.

We're taught to know and to show that our families can be seen through us and through the way we live.

Go ahead, look at me. Look at me and see my family.

But the marvelous thing is, you don't have to be Italian to practice people-ology. You just have to have a heart.

Rewind and Replay

Whoa! I should give you an 800-number to call for a CD of my father playing the accordion as a soundtrack for this chapter.

But let's switch to Steely Dan and do the review I promised a while back.

First, there's emotion. That probably comes as a big surprise. Seriously, emotion is the price we pay for going from good to great. That journey, that transformation isn't easy. There's so much work, endurance, and stubbornness involved in pulling it off, that without emotion—"passion" is the best word—the odds against success are enormous. Intellect simply isn't enough, and it never has been. Without emotion, there can be no bond or connection forged with others. We know that. There is strength in numbers. Its wisdom that is as old as the first family—and I'm not talking about the residents of 1600 Pennsylvania Avenue.

Make it personal. Forge a bond with your people by letting them know who you are and discovering who they are. Caring is the secret to building a care-full organization. Eliminate the question marks.

Practice people-ology. It offers the only genuine competitive advantage. Even if you got a lock on the secret of cold fusion, somebody else will soon come along and one-up the invention. Technological innovation is happening so fast, no one can count on staying in the lead for very long. That's why Bill Gates of Microsoft and Andy Grove of Intel are so crazed. They know some guy or gal in a garage is cooking up the next killer app. The only defense is having people who are just as smart, dedicated, and ready to make a difference. The social compact between the corporation and the worker is dead? It better not be. You take care of them, they'll take care of you. Believe me, if Bill Gates ever walks into the company's auditorium in Redmond, Washington, and says "Boys and girls, I need you to save Microsoft and we've got six months to do it," it will be fixed bayonets and helmets all around.

Work on your TAN. Take Action Now. All of the techniques and tips that I'm offering in the book work. I've road tested every one of them successfully. But they won't do you any good if you don't use them. It's not necessary to formulate a complete system or a methodology, so get started. And don't give me any of this, "Good idea, but it won't work here," stuff. In the remote chance that it doesn't work here, you lose nothing by trying and everything by breaking through the barrier of inertia.

Make promises and keep them. How else do you build trust? If you know a better way, let me know. Without trust, there's a dead spot at the core of your organization. People don't surrender trust lightly because it is such a precious commodity. They do it only when they see evidence that the investment will pay off. Making promises and keeping them is a demonstration of your sincerity. Breaking promises is a trust-buster.

Sincerity is the cornerstone of credibility. Liars are always losers. There are so many supposedly foolproof techniques for shaving the truth, spin doctoring, and manipulating reality. But the real proof is that those who use them are the fools because they lose the trust they're hoping to dishonestly gain.

Success is really very simple: people, passion, preparation, process, performance. Don't complicate your life. Identify your fundamental business purpose—what do you do that pays the rent? Then do it faster, better, and more productively. Get back to basics. Relearn the art of blocking and tackling. Rebuild a platform of success by reintroducing yourself to the customer. It is an uncomplicated truth, but customer contact is the soul of all business relationships. The less contact with the customer, the more soulless the business. Repair the bottom line by mending your soul.

Use a red notebook to record your leadership experiences. It's a good place to list dos and don'ts and maybes. Make an ongoing, thorough study of leadership. If you believe leaders are born, not made, you probably believe that taxes will be abolished someday. Leaders are made. We have to work at it and learn how it's done consistently and effectively.

Decontaminate your activities. Cut down on nonessential duties and activities. Ask, "What does this accomplish? Is it necessary to our success?"

Keep score. How do you know if you are winning or losing if you don't keep score? You don't. Track everything that's trackable. When you accomplish a goal make sure everyone knows it. And when you lose one, don't keep it a secret. People can become comfortable with failure if they are shielded from the consequences. Make sure they know what it means to win and to lose.

Never stop practicing the fundamentals. Basic training is just exactly that—basic. It's too easy to end up spending time and resources training for nonessential activities. Training is one area that is prone to contamination because nobody asks the trainees, "What do you need to be trained for?" Start asking.

Zero tolerance for defects and errors. Zero. You may never get there but you end up a lot closer if you try. Pursuing perfection generates passion. A 1 percent failure rate means that for every 100,000 products, 1,000 of them are disappointing somebody. It's a big country, but I'd rather not alienate a thousand people. Striving for perfection is the right thing to do.

Do your best, be the best. Don't settle for less. Who's passionate about being second or third?

Check your PQ—the Pride Quotient. There's no passion or high performance without pride. The best way to do this is to simply ask your people: "Are you proud of our company, our product, and our service?" Yes or no. Or give them a one to ten scale to use. Anything less than a ten is cause for alarm. Remember we're after perfection.

Make talent scouting and talent gathering your number-one priority. If you're pursuing perfection and out to be the best, you need the best people. I deliberately contradicted an early rule that you must identify the basic action that pays the rent and make that your first priority. Now you have two top priorities to juggle. You have to pay today's rent with the resources on hand, and you have build resources to cover tomorrow's rent—today.

What a great place to work! Find out if your people are saying it; if not, make hearing it your mission.

What a great company to do business with! Do your customers say it? If not, you have another mission to perform.

Compete, damn it. Complacency and failure grow out of a sense of entitlement. Go out and earn success every day. Beat the other guy to the business and revel in the victory. Impolite to gloat? No, it's imprudent to lose, and if we don't enjoy winning we'll learn to tolerate losing.

Say thank you. Succeeding is hard work. It's nice to be recognized when you pull it off. Take the time and effort to reward people for doing their job well. While you're at it, find out if your people feel appreciated and sufficiently rewarded. How? Ask them. You'll probably be shocked to learn that they feel underappreciated and overworked.

Have fun. There comes a point when the hardest working people need to kick back, laugh, and have a good time. As hard as my mom and dad made me work, I always knew Sunday was coming or a wedding, anniversary, or confirmation to celebrate.

Celebrate your successes. And remember to celebrate those who succeed.

Make 'em dance. Use music to create excitement.

Keep your people aware of the consequences. It's not about fear, it's about respect for the consequences of one's actions or failure to take action. In *King Lear*, Shakespeare wrote, "Nothing comes of nothing." And Lear's nothing was really something: civil war, murder, fratricide, and utter destruction. All because Cordelia wasn't willing to tell her father how much she loved him. Consequences.

Move fast. Don't wait to make a difference. Start solving problems right away. Trust needs to be established or it will sour and turn to skepticism.

Cut down barriers. They get in the way of your organization's speed, productivity, and performance. Make it your mission in life. Go for three a day, or at least three a week.

Make sure the first impression conveys who you are and what you stand for. Trust is so fragile, a leader may not get a chance for a meaningful second or third impression. The jury hands in the verdict and you're guilty of business as usual.

Ask for help. Tell them what's going on, why it's happening, and how they can contribute.

Know who your top performers are. Ask them for extra effort.

Create a vision and mission statement and live them every day. A vision without action is pure bologna. It's proof that you are insincere.

Demand to be held accountable for the vision. Cross check it against every policy, product, and decision.

Set a blistering pace by bumping up a key activity rate. Double, triple, even quadruple it. You'll quickly see where the problems are and what you have to do about them.

Over communicate. Tell your people everything—good and bad. Insist on full disclosure and a constant dialogue. Ask questions and demand answers.

Put it in writing. Every employee has a personal performance contract that spells out what's expected and how he or she promises to meet those expectations. And don't forget the second contract—yours and the company's—to help people succeed.

Become a feedback freak. Gorge on it for breakfast, lunch, and dinner. It's the report card of people-ology.

Admit your mistakes. Then fix the damage and move on.

Communicate with your customers. Ask them how you can improve the operation and serve them better! And actually follow their recommendations for change.

Using the Weed Whacker

I have to ask this question before we go any further: Have you done *any* of this stuff yet?

We've been at it now through nearly eight chapters. I hate the thought that even one reader is giving me a New York nod. Yeah, I know. You've been too busy. Things have been really wild around the office. Maybe next week.

Is it procrastination?

Is it laziness?

It is complacency?

Is it fear?

If you're still with me, I must be making a little bit sense. Either that or you like Italian food and you're hoping I'll print some of my mother's favorite recipes. Don't hold your breath. Those are going in the sequel, to be titled *Bella Deals, Bella Meals.*

I'll make it easy. Just close your eyes, run a finger back across the last couple of pages, and stop anywhere. Whatever item in the review your finger is on, do it. Or I'll choose one for you: Cut down barriers.

My favorite. I could spend every day just cutting down barriers. Have chain saw, will travel. Barriers are to a business what weeds are to a garden. There's always a fresh crop even in the most successful, well-run businesses. Because they proliferate so fast, barriers will get so thick that they will choke an organization. You spend all your time climbing over them, working around them, digging under them that there's no time for productive work. Barriers crowd out your cash crop.

I know a businessman who spent seventeen years growing barriers. At first, he was full of energy and talent. He'd leap those barriers with a single bound. But the business grew, and so did the barriers; getting over them started becoming harder and harder. Occasionally, he'd crash. No problem, the guy was good. He'd get back under control, but the barriers kept growing. Today, he is in his early forties, totally burned out, and looking to sell his company.

Have I got you interested in barrier busting? Kind of? Okay, go to the Joe DiMaggio of your organization. Everybody's hero, the home-run hitter. Ask her what slows her down (and I'm not kowtowing to the PC-gender police—in many of my organizations it's been Ms. DiMaggio who hits the ball out of the park day after day). She'll have a long list. Take notes, flag three of them—the easy ones—and get rid of them.

But don't run off just yet. Before you leave, ask her, "If I cut down these three barriers, will you give get me an extra 20 percent?" You may have to negotiate down to 10 percent, but your star is going to do a deal. She knows what it's worth to get rid of the barriers, even if you don't. Hold out for the biggest number.

"I need twenty, Sharon. You're going to be jet propelled with this stuff cleared out of the way. Plus, I'm going to work on the rest of the list too."

Does this sound too crass and undignified? Please. Leadership is a dirty business. There's nothing wrong with a quid pro quo. It's the essence of leadership. Moses promised his people a land of milk and honey (quid) if they gave up the golden calf and followed him into the wilderness (quo).

Repeat these words aloud: "If you deliver for me, I will deliver for you . . . I promise." Don't just say it—mean it.

Are you afraid that the barriers will turn out to be essential command and control mechanisms? Fat chance. But let's say they are, and not quibble about whether command and control is an oxymoron these days. Suspend the barrier for thirty or sixty days. Perhaps it's a burdensome paperwork requirement or a strict pricing formula that limits the field's ability to meet customer needs. Put them on ice temporarily to see what happens. Thirty days isn't going to cripple the company.

Besides, you have Ms. DiMaggio out there hitting for the fence. She's going to prove that the paperwork or the pricing formula were bad ideas. The effect will ripple through the rest of the organization; the other players will start getting base hits and scoring.

Still nervous? Try another selection from the review list: Have fun. You could use a break yourself. Announce that you're taking the whole operation for a weekend at a nearby resort for R&R. Throw your people together, let them golf, play tennis, swim, and party. Don't try any exotic team-building stunts, but at the end of the weekend call everybody together and ask if they enjoyed themselves. Tell them that you're going to do that sort of thing a couple of times a year from now on—if—if they pay for it by exceeding the business plan by 20 percent in the next quarter.

Bribery? No, fun. A lot of fun. But somebody's got to foot the bill. They're all adults and know that paying the piper is a fact of life. Plaster the office with the snapshots taken over the weekend, track your numbers, and tie them to whether they are getting closer to their goals or slipping away from them. Talk it up. If the extra numbers aren't coming in, tell them what's at stake and ask them to work on a plan to goose performance. Count it right down day to day to the end. If you don't make it, find out why, thank those who turned in the best effort, *and do not go to the resort.* Nope. But make sure you tell them why they're not going.

When I returned to Xerox's Columbus office for another turnaround assignment in 1994, my predecessor had promised that he would pay for a trip to the Virgin Islands. It was open ended, no quid pro quo. Their numbers were so cruddy, I said, "We're not going."

"But he promised."

"Yeah, he promised. And I promise you, we're not going with this kind of a performance." The message has to be clear: Have fun *and* perform. It was clear all right, and it was heeded.

Less than a year later most of those same people were on board the Radisson *Diamond,* cruising the Caribbean because almost the entire district had qualified for Xerox's President's Club, a reward for sales reps who exceed their plan by roughly 150 percent. We had gone from the bottom to the top to become the number one district in the United States—as I had predicted would happen my first day on the job as district manager. That's right. Prosaic, mild-mannered Columbus, Ohio, number one. Not New York City. Not Chicago. Not Atlanta. Not Los Angeles.

As we posed for a group picture on the main forward deck of the ship, there was so much exuberance and energy I think the captain was worried that the *Diamond* would go down bow first. What a moment! Those people were so proud and joyous about what they had accomplished. The entire boat was under charter to Xerox, and our fellow passengers were—I think—totally envious. You could tell the way they glanced sideways at our "Caribbean by sales. Columbus—number one" T-shirts and glared at us.

Recently, I recalled that moment in a video store where I happened to see a copy of *Glengarry Glen Ross,* the David Mamet play about sleazy salespeople that was made into a movie. By coincidence, at about the same time, the Tony Award–winning revival of Arthur Miller's *Death of a Salesman* opened on Broadway. Miller's play is a classic, but I despise it. And I'm no fan of Mamet's work, either. What is so vividly displayed on stage in both plays is, to my mind, not the death of a salesman. No way. It's the death of leadership and management—that's what destroys an individual and his family.

Nobody cared enough to rescue Willy Loman or the characters in Mamet's play. Nobody cared enough to set high standards, develop talent, and create the right atmosphere. Willy and the other salesmen were road-kill—casualties of good old-fashioned business as usual. If you want to see sleaze, turn the spotlight on those who hired them, paid their commissions, and established poisonous business cultures. When someone does care, there are moments like the one on the Radisson *Diamond,* and there are lives that are fun and full and rewarding in every sense.

As we move into the second part of this book, people-ology and caring are still the main themes. Now that I've laid out the tools that are needed to stop whining, we can set about accomplishing the rest of the mission—to start winning (if you aren't already, and I'm sure many of you are). Ahead there will be insights on recruiting the best talent and retaining it, team building, customer satisfaction, and—about time!—business process. Along the way, I'll continue to do my damnedest to help you attain effective, caring leadership.

Part II

CHAPTER NINE

Ross, Me, and
the Giant Sucking Sound

I was fortunate when I worked in the Cleveland district for Xerox. We had a lot of fun and great success turning a bad operation into a pretty good one. One spring, Lina, a district sales rep who was about to get married and transfer to Pittsburgh, got together for dinner with her best friend and their two fiancés. The conversation, as is so often the case, was about work. Lina told them about her whacko general manager and some of the things he did, like dress up in drag as Vanna White to play *Wheel of Fortune* or swapping the skirt for a god-awful plaid suit to look like Monty Hall of *Let's Make a Deal*, all in the interest of getting his troops cranked up enough to overcome their god-awful sales record.

It turned out that Lina's buddy was engaged to a reporter for the *Wall Street Journal*, who thought a story about this strange person would be a good idea. And so that's how I ended up on the front page of America's largest circulation daily newspaper.

And how I met Ross Perot. I probably seem like I'm ego-tripping and name dropping, but I am backing into an important chapter on recruiting. The "giant sucking sound" is a reference, of course, to Perot's comment during the 1992 campaign about the possibility that NAFTA, the North American Free Trade Alliance Treaty with Mexico and Canada, would cause massive losses of U.S. jobs. A colorful choice or words from a colorful and, I believe, immensely talented business leader and good citizen.

I'll leave debating the effects of NAFTA to others, but the sucking sound that I hear today is the talent that's being lost because most companies do such a poor job of recruiting, retention, and training. Ross Perot taught me a valuable lesson about recruitment that I want to share with you in his chapter. First, let me provide more context.

The story in the *Journal* came about because Jim Hirsch, the *WSJ* reporter, was persistent enough to overcome my skepticism about how much interest there'd be in the saga of people selling copiers for a living. Boring. He wouldn't take no for an answer, so I referred him to headquarters for permission, figuring that would end it.

A month or so later, I heard that corporate was thrilled by the idea. Free publicity. Let him in, I was told, but don't screw up.

I dutifully set up a two-day round of customer visits, employee roundtables, and a seminar on our mission statement and quality process. After spending time with my two management partners for administration and service, Jim Hirsch interviewed me for two hours and then went away for a couple of weeks. The subject still seemed boring to me and I thought Hirsch would find something better to do with his time and talent. Late one afternoon in September, the reporter called back and said there was good news. The *Journal* would publish the story the next day.

"What page?" I asked. Certain it would be buried behind the ads for fast food franchises and turnkey motel opportunities along U.S. Route 1.

"The front page." Hirsch's tone suggested that I had offended him.

Great! But Jim had some bad news. He said, "I'm going to make you famous outside Xerox and infamous inside it."

Oh? Why?

"You know that stuff about management partners, customers, and quality? My editors thought it was boring. They prefer a kind of rebel, bureaucracy-buster approach."

The next morning I saw exactly what he meant. Here's the headline:

Sales Force: To One Xerox Man, Selling Photocopiers Is a Gambler's Game

FRANK PACETTA, EMULATING HIS HERO VINCE LOMBARDI, INSPIRES LOVE AND FEAR

Cold Calls, Surprise Attacks[1]

[1] James S. Hirsch, "Sales Force: To One Xerox Man Selling Copiers is a Gambler's Game," *Wall Street Journal*, September 24, 1991, p. 1.

Jim Hirsch was right. I was famous and infamous. More than four hundred phone calls were logged in that day. The first one, at 7:30 in the morning, was from my father, who had just come back from hitting every newsstand for blocks around and buying up all their *Journals*. He was so delighted and proud, he had trouble speaking. My 2.4 *Lordy How Come!* at Dayton had been permanently expunged.

He couldn't get the words out and neither could I. We both choked up. Dad had spent the morning delivering newspapers to all the relatives and old neighbors.

The phone was madness. I was hearing from old friends and news friends, most of whom wanted to sell me something. I was suddenly the stockbroker's pal. It was impossible to get any work done. Paul MacKinnon joined me in my office and I took the calls on the speaker phone.

"Frank Pacetta?"

"Yes, it is."

"This is Ross Perot," a man with a high-pitched Texas twang proclaimed.

"Sure you are." I said, chuckling and thinking that whoever it was, he better not give up his day job expecting to replace Dana Carvey, the *Saturday Night Live* comedian. Ross must be used to that reaction. He gave me his private number. "Call me right back, I'd really like to talk with you."

He hung up, leaving Paul and me to sit there in shocked silence. Finally Padre snapped out of it and blurted: "ThatwasRossPerotandyou'regoingto-meethimandgetajobandtakemewithyouandwe'regoingtoberich—and no more copiers!" We calmed each other down and I dialed the number. Perot's assistant was waiting for the call and put me right through.

Remember, it's a little after 7:30 in the morning in Cleveland, which means 6:30 Dallas time, where, I guess billionaires get an early start to muck out the stalls and read the *Wall Street Journal*. Ross congratulated me for the article and said he was impressed by my leaderships skills, willingness to take risks, and the emphasis on creating a family atmosphere in the workplace. "I want to meet with you as soon as possible."

Paul, meanwhile, is beaming like a man whose ship has just come in and it's the size of the aircraft carrier *Enterprise*.

I was dumbfounded. Meet with me? My assistant wasn't in yet and I went out to rummage around on her desk for my planner. "Gee, my schedule's kind of full," I said turning the pages. What an idiot!

"Why don't I fly in tonight," Perot suggested. I thought, *Tonight? Not tonight, I've got to get my car washed.* Yes, that's what occurred to me. And yes, that was not a rational reaction. We ended up setting a date for the following week.

The day came, I was much calmer, but my wife, Julie, wasn't. Perot was not interested in an evening of business transacted exclusively at a fancy restaurant. He wanted to go straight from the private jet terminal at Hopkins Airport to the Pacetta home in suburban Hudson. To get ready,

Julie had our cleaning lady go over every inch of the house, then she cleaned it herself, and followed up with a backup cleaning lady to do everything all over again. When he arrived, Perot greeted me with a warm hug and said he needed a phone to make a call. I stood nearby and listened, impressed. "How are you," Ross asked the person on the other end, and then said, "Did we get any business today?" Sixty years old, a billionaire, and the guy was still hitting the street.

On the ride home to Hudson, I finally worked up the courage to ask, "Ross, why are you here?" The answer to the question was day number one in my postgraduate leadership education. He said, "When I meet, hear, or read about someone with your qualities, I want to personally get to know them to see if they can impact my business organization and our customers." Then, Ross Perot added, "Frank, it's all about leadership and people."

I knew that and so do you. Or we think we know that. The lesson Ross Perot delivered is one we really have trouble grasping on a level beyond its obvious common-sense appeal. On the page, the words seem obvious, even trite: "I want to personally get to know them to see if they can impact my business organization and our customers." His presence in Cleveland, in the front seat of my car, took those flat words and pumped them full of life. Ross Perot was engaged in important business. He talked the talk, but he was there on the ground in Cleveland taking direct action to implement his vision.

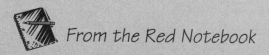

From the Red Notebook

"It's all about leadership and people."

—Ross Perot

"Frank, tell me this," Perot continued on as I negotiated rush-hour traffic with my Honda Accord, "Do you recruit?" What a perfect question. Home-run time. I explained our process from A to Z, how we assemble a pool or thirty to forty candidates, test them, pare them down by about a third, run them through a battery of interviews with all eight managers who must agree on the hiring decision unanimously, and then I come in for a final face-to-face session with the top candidate. Perot listened politely until I finished. "No, I mean do *you* recruit, Frank? Personally? Do you know the competition's best manager or sales rep?"

I . . . the best . . . roughly speaking . . . I could . . . There was no way around it. I had a process that my operation worked conscientiously to execute, but there was one thing lacking—real leadership involvement. Perot drove the point in deeper: "Frank, you're in this position for a reason. It's up to the leaders to be right up front and lead the charge to find the best people. You can't win without them."

 From the Red Notebook

"It's up to the leaders . . . to find the best people. You can't win without them."

—ROSS PEROT

But I had a damned good process. Yeah, and process isn't enough.

Perot, the teacher, wasn't finished. "Tell me this, if I called Xerox's CEO with a complaint would he call me back?"

"Of course. Paul Allaire would be delighted to talk to you."

"No, if John Doe, not Ross Perot, called, would the CEO return the call?"

"Somebody from his office would, and do it promptly. There's a process." That didn't satisfy my visitor. He wanted to know what the difference was between Perot and Doe. I tried to explain that Xerox had thousands of customers and that Paul Allaire couldn't call them all.

"Frank, that's what happens. We get too big, add so many layers, and we think we're too important. To this day, if a customer calls me I get right back to him. Or if a sales rep wants me to come along on a customer visit, I'll do it. What else would I do?"

What else would I do?

I've borrowed that question from Ross Perot and I use it all the time. It's really useful in this scenario: I'm doing my managing by walking around and hear someone talking about a problem with a customer. "When are you going to see them next?" I'll ask.

"This afternoon."

"Would you like me to come along?" The real answer may be no, but usually I'm invited. At the end of the day my colleagues thank me profusely for tearing myself away from important business—all those long-term strategy sessions and what-not. That's when I say, "What else would I do? What else is more important? What do you suppose my job is all about if I can't help you fix the customer's problem?"

 ### The Difference Between Willpower and Won't-Power

"I can't get away" means "I won't get away."
"I can't spare the time" means "I won't spare the time."
Say "can't," and you won't.
Say "can," and you will.

Do me a favor, write that Ross Perot question in your red notebook.

When we drove up to the house, Julie came out and Ross lost all interest in me. My wife is petite and about four-foot-eleven. She's always got a strong wind blowing at her back, and Ross's personality isn't bland, either. The two of them really hit it off immediately, and were perfectly matched in height, walking arm-in-arm up the driveway, like a couple of tiny figures off the top of a wedding cake.

My children were perfectly behaved, of course, though Frankie, then seven years old, was still a little sullen about being forced to bathe. Ross scooped up Alle, who was only one, and held her on his lap through the entire visit. I had stocked my liquor cabinet with standard brands for a

Southern gentleman—Jack Daniels, Jim Beam, and so on—Ross had bottled water. I put away about four scotches before we headed out to dinner.

As we walked through the restaurant to the table, I could hear whispers, "That's Ross Perot. What's he doing with Pacetta?" It was probably four hours before we got out of there. Ross seemed to ask hundreds of questions, mostly about our family, and told us all about his family and the early history of his company. At times, it was very emotional. His eyes would fill with tears as he recounted special moments of sharing and sacrifice.

For me the whole evening was special, as you can probably tell. There was no way to know at the time, but Ross Perot was on the verge of redefining himself, for better or worse, by plunging into politics. In the eyes of some critics who judge him solely on the basis of his eccentric performance in the 1992 and 1996 presidential campaigns, he's a flake. But what we saw was an authentic visionary and leader. Tough, uncompromising, principled, and devoted to his family—Ross Perot is the man he says he is.

In the winter of 1999, while writing this book, I was pleased to see that he hadn't changed. The IPO for Perot Systems was a huge success, billions of dollars were added to his net worth, and there was Ross telling the press that he'd return any customer or shareholder telephone call.

"What else would I do?"

Snare Jordans

Did he offer me a job? Not directly. But in due course, I was contacted and asked to consider joining Perot Systems, but I decided against moving my young family to Texas. Also, the company's culture required new managers to start over in some respects. I wanted more leadership and management responsibility, not less. It's one of those judgment calls that a person has to make and then wonder about. But second-guessing is a waste of time.

Thanks to Ross Perot, though, I am a reformed underachiever when it comes to recruiting and talent hunting. I never stop looking for talent, and it's one job I never delegate. I want you to test yourself, using Perot as a benchmark.

 Now-To

Get out the red notebook and answer these questions:

- Who's the Michael Jordan of your industry?
- Who's the best all-around leader-manager you've ever met, heard of, or read about?
- What are the names of your competition's five best people?
- If you could hire anyone—total wish list—who would it be?
- Name someone outside your own industry who you'd hire.
- Who's your most valued employee, and who would you hire to replace him or her?
- Who's your successor?
- If you are the CEO, who is your next CFO?
- Who did you personally recruit to join your organization?

Consider that last question. Until Ross Perot called it to my attention, I would have answered, "Everybody we hired in the last two years." And that wouldn't have been accurate. I met with the finalist who had been screened by my managers, but I didn't initiate the process or drive it through to completion.

Why not? I was too busy.

There we go again! Too busy.

And besides, I had a process to take care of that. Those are two lame excuses. It's like saying, "I was too busy to make sure my team showed up for work in the morning." Or "I was too busy to bother lining up new customers." Indifference to recruiting is the same as being indifferent about the future. If you don't adequately fill up the gas tank today, you're guaranteed to run dry tomorrow.

 *Now-To*

Find out who is in charge of the future and appoint yourself. Get *actively* involved in recruiting.

That is a big responsibility. If no one is in charge, that's frightening. I've run across operations that handle it with a filing cabinet and an administrative assistant. Need somebody? Check the latest resumes, make a few calls, do an interview or two. A slight improvement is to look in the yellow pages under "executive placement services." Maybe they'll have some candidates. The next notch up is to let human resources do the job, which will at least have a process. But without line or field responsibilities, HR ends up hiring by the book and the "book" can tend to be overengineered.

These aren't smart ways to go. The best way to start hiring franchise players like Michael Jordan is to hire one to run recruiting. And to work closely with that person. My personal choice would be Gary Hudepohl of Gary Hudepohl & Associates, a specialty executive search firm. I'd back up the Wells Fargo truck and let Gary help himself. He's definitely on my recruiting wish list. The problem is that Gary's happy right where he is, and his clients are even happier. GHA specializes in finding chief financial officers and chief information officers for a select group of major corporations.

What's the secret? Gary Hudepohl has a one-word answer—"retention." And you thought this chapter is about recruiting. It is, but we'll focus on the other R-word first.[1]

High retention is evidence of high people-ology. Companies that create an environment around strong leaders, who encourage high performance and work to develop their employees' full potential, are going to attract the best people.

This seems to fly in the face of the prevailing wisdom that the hottest talent is prepared to add lines to a resume the way gunfighters notched the handles of their revolvers. I believe young up-and-coming stars move frequently because they aren't getting the opportunities, the action, the excitement, the responsibilities, and the development that they need. Most surveys support me on that. To retain them, it's not enough to scout and sign the very best. You have to be a first-class talent-building organization.

 From the Red Notebook

Do you even know your attrition rate and how it compares to that of your major competitors? If you do—good. If you don't—find out!

Talent attracts talent, and talent retains talent.

A high attrition rate is a bad sign, particularly if it persists over a long period of time, or shows regular spiking. Making personnel changes or downsizing can happen, but it shouldn't be happening continually or in an off-and-on fashion. It can help to find out what is really causing attrition. How? Ask.

A system of exit interviews or follow-up contacts six to months to a year after an employee voluntarily leaves can yield valuable information. Do a Pacetta Poll. Ask them:

- Why did you leave?

And since you may be told, "I got a better offer," ask for more specifics:

- Were you dissatisfied by our management process?
- Were you dissatisfied by our product or service?

- Were you dissatisfied with our company culture?
- Would you have remained with us for more money?
- Would you have remained with us for more responsibility?
- Did you feel welcome, valued, and appreciated?
- Was your personal life and situation given due consideration?
- Were you mentored, coached, and trained adequately?
- Did you have a sense the company cared about your success and was willing to invest in it?
- Did anyone ask you to stay?
- Was a substantial effort made to meet and exceed the offer from you new employer?

These questions can provide a distinct profile of your retention strengths and weaknesses. The first—"Why did you leave?"—is an all-purpose clarification tool. Why isn't it asked? Few companies have a clear understanding of why people leave. They guess about it: Money, personality issues, family, and better opportunities elsewhere are the standard assumptions. Most of the time those assumptions are either flat-out wrong or only partially correct. To this day, Xerox has no idea why I decided to leave. They assume it was because I didn't want to make a lateral move to Minneapolis for yet another turnaround assignment. And since that was a precipitating factor, it was a good enough assumption, as far as my bosses were concerned. It allowed them say, "He's got his priorities, and we've got ours."

Fine. My point is that if you genuinely believe that the only way to produce and sell quality products is through quality people, you need to know what motivates a person to leave after spending twenty-four years with the operation leading teams that brought in hundreds of millions dollars in revenue. This curiosity doesn't mean that Xerox needs to beg Frank Pacetta to stay or to change any policy or procedure. The simple information value to be gained justifies the simple question—"Would you mind sitting down with us and explaining why you're leaving?" If the answer is no, okay. At least the attempt was made.

Now-To

Call or meet with three valued former employees and ask them why they left.

Listen closely to the reasons, and follow up to see whether their accounts jibe with the "official" explanation for their departure. Look for indications that structure, process, personalities, or other correctable issues were involved. If they were, they probably still are and need to be fixed—now.

By not asking, the message is sent loud and clear that we really don't care why an employee left and that individual effort and contribution is of little importance. *We'll just hire somebody else. More where that came from.* This attitude devalues and demotivates the people who remain. I don't care what the experts say about the new job-hopping career and economic paradigms. When most people decide to leave a job that they've held for more than a year or two, it is a major decision. Not caring about what went into that decision says to everyone in the organization, "We don't care about you." And the response that will come back from your people is, "And we don't care about you either."

That's poison, and your best people are the most susceptible to it. Don't believe the myth that the stars know they're so good they can and will go anywhere. Free agency in sports seems to confirm that. But in business we are all free agents, yet company loyalty is still the norm as long as it is deserved and reciprocated. Abby Joseph Cohen, to pull one name out of the hat, could work anywhere on Wall Street and name her price, yet the star financial analyst chooses to stay at Goldman Sachs.

I suspect the real reason that the question isn't asked more often is that we don't want to know. "You can't handle the truth"—a line from the movie *A Few Good Men* is right on the mark. It's tough to hear the truth because we then have to live with it or do something about it. And now we are squarely in the heart of the heart of people-ology. If my organization doesn't care about people, I want to know about it and fix it. So should you.

The other questions on the list are more specific and process oriented. Again, they provide useful snapshots of reality as seen by the ex-employee. Wouldn't you like to know if there are holes in the management process or deficiencies in the product? Consultants earn millions of dollars providing that sort of information. You can get it for free.

Were you dissatisfied with the culture? Picking up a bunch of yeses on that one should set off alarm bells—if you really care about the kind of culture that you've created. The money question is also revealing. Managers understand when the competition comes along and entices an employee away by offering more money. Over the years, I've surveyed friends and colleagues on the issue and found that the majority did see money as a major reason for making the change, but the amount of money tends to be ridiculously small. People change jobs, careers, cities, and disrupt their families for as little as $7,000 or $8,000 extra a year. Two things occur to me on this situation. One, there are other reasons for the decision beyond money. Two, if such pathetically small amounts of money are crucial, why didn't somebody say, "If we match the other guy's offer, will you stay?"

But we didn't want to get into a bidding war.

Come on!

Many companies do a cost-benefit analysis on whether to switch to a new brand of paper clips. Do one on your employees. Add up what you invested in training and development, add up salaries, fringe benefits, and bonuses, factor in a value to cover knowledge and experience, and compare the total to what the person brings in. I think you'll discover that the bidding war won't bankrupt you.

The Pacetta People-ology Ratio

(The PA/PE Ratio)

This is a variation on two standard Wall Street stock analysis tools: Book Value (P/B) and Price-to-Sales (P/S).

A company's book value is the share price divided by the total of all assets, less liabilities, per share. Price-to-Sales Ratio is the total sales divided by the share price.

To determine PA/PE, add up total assets and sales, and divide by the number of employees. The figure gives you a per-employee valuation and a rough measure of per-employee productivity as it rises or falls.

I'm not a statistician. The PA/PE ratio took all of ten minutes to dream up. You're welcome to it, or develop your own way to measure a person's real worth. Just measure it!

You'll discover that we are letting people walk out the door with your money. I hate that. I have an image of a guy with a wheelbarrow full of cash going down the elevator, moving through the lobby, out the front door to the parking lot, where he shovels my money into his trunk and drives off. All because I didn't say, "Can I match the offer?"

If he or she says, "Sure," and names their price, then I'll know whether to help with the wheelbarrow and wave good-bye or get out my checkbook.

A Communications and Retention Tool

Many times it's not even money. More responsibility and opportunities may cost nothing. Kick me if I have let someone leave who wanted more responsibility. Kick me again if I'm not offering enough opportunities. Both of these are issues that should be addressed in the individual performance contracts that were discussed in chapter 7. There is a communications breakdown involved if the first we know about this is after an employee leaves.

If a manager is conducting monthly one-on-one reviews of the contracts that he or she has with the team, the communications flow should have revealed the problem. If I want more responsibility, I can tell my boss and between the two of us we'll write contract provisions that realize the goal to meet the needs of both sides. The genius of the contract process is that it combines two sets of expectations into one action plan. The reviews allow the leader and the team member to collaborate on how best to achieve the desired results and to monitor the progress on a regular basis.

The contract is probably the best retention tool of them all. The questions that need to be asked after an employee leaves can be raised during the monthly reviews. If I have six or eight team leaders reporting to me, the contracts that we have—leader to leader—will stipulate that basic employee satisfaction issues are to be raised with the team members during monthly reviews. I go ballistic when a team leader says to me, "Frank, I think Jill is getting ready to quit."

"You think?"

"Yeah, she's been pretty standoffish and uncooperative lately."

"Maybe she's having family problems."

"I hear she's talking to Jeff Collier's operation."

"Why don't you ask her if she's going to quit?"

"Ask?"

That's right.

It's called c-o-m-m-u-n-i-c-a-t-i-o-n. Surveys show again and again that one of the principal reasons for attrition is that people don't feel they are appreciated. It could be that Jill has been working very hard lately, but her manager hasn't noticed. It may just be a one-time-only oversight, or it may indicate a pattern of poor management and leadership. By asking the question in a review, "Do you feel your work is appreciated?" the problem—if it exists—can be tackled.

Finally, "Did anybody ask you to stay?" What a question! What a question not to ask of a valued employee. I've had top performers tell me that they had no intention of leaving until they were approached by another company or head hunter. The money was a little better or other aspects of the deal slightly sweeter, but what tipped them to accept the offer was that their current employer didn't try hard enough to keep them. Simply asking them to stay is the minimum. At least it opens a dialogue with the signal that the employee is valued. And that may be enough.

Proactive Rerecruiting

The purpose of the postmortem questions is to bring your recruiting and rerecruiting process to life. By collecting answers from ex-employees about the reason they left, you can immediately set about establishing a rerecruiting process that will buttress your retention program. The goals should be to:

- Eliminate all barriers to retention that were highlighted by the surveys of ex-employees.
- Develop a list of high-risk likely defectors.
- Identify essential "can't operate without" employees.
- Thank each one.
- Upgrade their personal performance contracts, paying special attention to problem areas identified by the surveys of ex-employees.
- Provide extra compensation and other rewards from a specially established recruiting and retaining fund.
- Send letters home to their spouses describing the employee's contribution to the success of the company and expressing appreciation for the spouse's support.
- Tell each essential employee to come to you immediately if they are ever approached by another firm.

- If and when an essential employee attempts to leave, make a personal commitment to keep that employee—announce it publicly—and go all out.

Ho-hum rerecruitment leads to ho-hum retention. The vicious circle keeps spinning until it's wiped out recruitment, employee satisfaction, and high performance. A few comments about the last three bullets above before I double back to Gary Hudepohl. Sending a letter home to a spouse to praise their partner seems a little odd, doesn't it? Think about it, though. He or she carries a great deal of influence. I discuss everything with Julie, and she has final veto power. It's like that in many households. If you can encourage that spouse to say, "What a great place to work," the decision to leave may not be so cut and dried.

Dear Susan,

   I wanted to send you a note to tell you how much impact Ted has had on our team and to let you know that he made the difference in achieving record-breaking performance in the last quarter. I want to thank you for your support and let you know that I will do whatever I can to make this a fun and rewarding place to work for both Ted and you. Thanks again.

                                                         Sincerely,
                                                         Frank

---

Warning! Don't try this if you don't mean it. Don't overdo it. Don't make it formulaic. Don't assign it to your administrative assistant. Insincerity will cost you major grief.

The next bullet, "Tell each essential employee to come to you if they are ever approached by another firm," leaves you open to blackmail, doesn't it? Pay it, and the top performer will earn it back.

Finally, "Make a personal commitment to keep an essential employee who is about to leave" raises the stakes for both of you and puts the recruiting company at a disadvantage. The employee now must make a personal decision, not a strictly business one, to look you in the eye and say, "I'm moving on even though you have demonstrated this commitment to me." Furthermore, you are counterpunching the recruiting firm in a way that it can't match because the prospect does not have the preexisting relationships and this extraordinary personal commitment.

One final point about rerecruiting. If you lose a great one, don't rest until you get him or her back in the fold. Tell them that when they leave, tell the rest of the organization, and follow through.

Hurry Up and Wait

The leader must first *own* the retention and rerecruiting processes before there is a meaningful recruiting program. This involvement at the top is the first thing that Gary Hudepohl looks for when he establishes a relationship with clients. He wants to know who owns recruiting because it tells him about the firm he will be selling to his other client—the candidate. He needs to find the right fit for both. The wrong candidate for the right job is as bad as the right candidate for the wrong job. He's got to get it all right or else it's all wrong.

As far as I'm concerned, using an executive recruitment firm is the way to go if the client company and the consultant are committed to relentlessly pursuing a perfect fit, and if both sides expect nothing less. Gary's experience with working for a major midwestern bank is a good example. The bank hired him to fill a senior level vacancy that had been open for more than a year. Gary's associates had developed a list of twenty-five to thirty names, but he wasn't satisfied. The list had to be whittled down to the top five.

The bank—and this is an instructive detail—was willing to wait. A year had gone by and that was okay if they got the right person. Too often, there is such time pressure on the recruiting process that the whole thing falls apart. Gary's people took their time and eventually identified the five best people for the position. At that point, Gary personally took over, using his network of contacts, and worked the phones until he knew who was head and shoulders above the others. Not the one who was most interested or in the market for a new job. The best.

From the Red Notebook

In December my phone starts to ring every day with calls from headhunters who want me to recommend possible candidates to fill senior positions. "Let me guess," I ask, "you need them to start January 1?" It's a dead giveaway that recruitment is not a priority when such an important matter is allowed to slide to the last minute.

And that was the problem. When he called the guy, there was no interest. Zip. He was happy where he was. In fact, it took two months of telephone calls to get to that point. He wouldn't talk at all until Gary's sheer persistence wore him down.

Once there was telephone contact, Gary worked on establishing a face-to-face relationship. He made two trips to the candidate's home city and convinced to him to at least think about it. Gary finally decided to take a chance of irritating the candidate by bringing along the bank's recruiting manager. As far as the candidate knew, he would be meeting Gary solo.

It was love at first sight. The hiring manager said, "We have to find a way to get this guy." They totally revamped the bank's offer, broke through the dollar ceiling that had been opposed, and redid the rest of the package of benefits. When they went back to the candidate, they were afraid his company would make a counteroffer and that would be that. But the candidate liked the hiring manager as much as the hiring manager liked him. It was locked.

Now-To: Hire a Leader

He or she may draw some of their former top performing teammates to your organization. Why settle for one great recruit when two or more are available?

Know Thyself

Gary Hudepohl uses an eight-point checklist to guide the recruiting process. It belongs in your red notebook. Notice that the focus is on the company and the culture rather than on the individual's resume.

- What does the client need?
- What are the key behaviors?
- What's the management style?
- How do they treat their employees?
- What's the balance between home and work?
- What's the succession plan?
- What are the promotion and mobility possibilities?
- Compensation—can it be creative and flexible?

By answering these questions first, a recruiting manager or consultant has a basis for carefully screening candidates instead of madly scrambling for warm bodies with impressive resumes. If your company is not family-friendly, it's a good idea to recognize it, acknowledge it to all concerned, and avoid dangling jobs in front of candidates who take their parental responsibilities seriously. Why be turned down, or worse, end up undermining the recruit's family if they don't realize what they're getting into and try to tough it out after they're hired? Go for single men and women or those with children gone from the nest, who can handle the culture and its demands (better yet, become family-friendly). And if you are the one who is being recruited, don't you want to know the answers to these questions before you get way the down the road and discover that there's a slow promotion track or that you're not about to be included in the succession plan? Or that there's a glass ceiling for moms?

I'll add a ninth point to Gary's guidelines—a variation on the golden rule:

> ### *Recruit others the way you would want to be recruited.*

Simple, isn't it?

CHAPTER TEN

Recruiting Savvy—

Building a Network to the Talent

A pop quiz. What did a McKinsey and Company survey of six thousand senior executives identify as the number one corporate resource necessary for success in the next twenty years?

Tick, tick, tick . . . time's up.

Talent. I cited the survey in chapter 3 as evidence that businesses large and small are in jeopardy of losing the star wars of the twenty-first century. If you recall, McKinsey found that only 10 to 20 percent of the executives questioned felt that the improvement of the talent pool was one of their company's three top priorities. And 75 percent of them said their companies didn't have sufficient talent or that talent was in chronically short supply.

That's shocking evidence of ho-hum recruiting, and it's the reason why I've decided to do two full chapters on the subject. Anyone claiming to practice people-ology who let's recruiting slide is a fraud. I hear this complaint—"I just don't have the right people"—so often that I'm convinced that is it the number one business problem of our era, and next to nothing is being done about it. We're giving it the New York nod and the L.A. shrug.

Given the general complacency, something tells me that Ross Perot's stellar example as a hands-on recruiter isn't going to be enough to blast many readers out of this lackadaisical and self-destructive attitude. What will? Maybe a close look at a modern version of David and Goliath. This one is about how "Team David" survives, prospers, and wins.

Let me offer some additional background. When I was first planning to write this book, I decided to get expert advice from the masters of recruiting, those whose careers depend on, not the kindness of strangers, but the talent of strangers—college athletic directors and coaches. Why not Duke or Ohio State? The big time. But then it occurred to me that the approach would be similar to going to GE to interview Jack Welch or to Microsoft to hear from Bill Gates. Welch and Gates are such superstars that it would be like asking Jack Nicklaus for golf lessons. Everything he'd teach would be brilliant, but in the end the student would probably say to himself, "He's a genius, I'm not," and go back to playing the same old hackers game.

To avoid the trap, I spent time with Ted Kissell, the athletic director of my alma mater, the University of Dayton. With a student body of about six thousand, the school is small and not a sports power—not now, perhaps not ever (I should know, I go to all their home basketball games). But it's a study of how a small organization can dream big dreams and work conscientiously every day to make them come true.

Ted Kissell is relatively new to the job, and it's his first crack at heading up an entire sports program. Brother Fitz, UD's president and a member of the Catholic Marian Order, took a chance on him and he is obviously determined to succeed. Determined but not desperate.

What do I mean? Here's the background. Soon after arriving at Dayton, Ted met with a fervent UD booster and contributor. The guy told him that he hoped to see the school's basketball team, the Dayton Flyers, finish in the top twenty-five, but given the poor showing in recent years that would probably mean stretching the rules somewhat. Ted's reply was classic: "I guess we'll end up twenty-six then."

It was a comeback that went straight into my red notebook for use some day as a reminder that the greatest failures are the people who are prepared to pay any price for success. It wasn't a ranking that Kissell was after, it was pride. At our first meeting, he told me, "We had to create a platform where success is possible." To do that he set out to surround himself with the best staff.

Stop the story here for a moment, and think about that.

The best people, not the best arena.

The best people, not the best ticket sales.

The best people, not the best endowment.

The best people, not the best PR campaign.

How in the world does a small, relatively unknown school attract the best people? Ted Kissell had an answer: "I believe there are no limits. I believe in Dayton being the best in everything we do."

If you keep in mind some of the techniques we've been discussing, you'll see that Ted Kissell practices what I preach, and I didn't know that in advance of my request to meet him and spend a day taking a close look at his operation. For starters, Kissell, like any good businessman, had to figure out what his organization did to pay the rent and put concentrated effort into improving that requirement. In the case of UD athletics, basketball is the number one cash cow. There had been three disastrous seasons in a row. Ted Kissell needed to start winning basketball games, so he went looking for a leader, a new coach. It was time, he and brother Fitz also decided, for UD's men's basketball program to be led by an African-American, a decision in keeping with the school's commitment to diversity.

Kissell started by using what he calls "the network to the talent" by calling around to friends and colleagues active in college athletic programs around the country to find out who they regarded as qualified. The idea was to compile a list of the top African-American coaches and assistant coaches who were qualified and available. One name quickly bubbled to the top: Perry Clark of Tulane.

Ted Kissell didn't know Perry Clark, and no one in the network could offer him personal entrée. Kissell made two phone calls, but both times Coach Clark declined to meet with him. Instead of accepting that he was at a dead-end, the Dayton athletic director got out from behind his desk and traveled to Evansville, Indiana, when he knew Tulane would be playing the University of Evansville Aces. He waited courtside until Clark's team came off the floor victorious, and then pounced. It was probably the strangest and most straightforward job offer Perry Clark ever received. He listened politely to Ted Kissell, but declined the offer. It wasn't a wasted effort, though. Realizing that Dayton wasn't just going through the motions of putting a minority on the short list, Perry Clark offered to plug him into his own black "network to the talent."

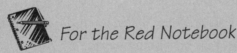 For the Red Notebook

Ted Kissell and Ross Perot had the same approach to recruiting. It is too important to leave to others.

See how this works? Want the best talent? Get personal, get on the phone, get on a plane—get directly involved.

As he worked this black talent network, Ted Kissell kept hearing about Oliver Purnell, a successful coach at Old Dominion University, who had turned their program around after getting impressive results in his first coaching job at Radford College. Old Dominion was Purnell's alma mater; he had been an All-American and an NBA draft pick. Coach Purnell had an excellent contract that paid for a good life, including a posh house on the beach in Virginia. He was a happy man.

Ted convinced Oliver Purnell to at least listen to the UD story. Not a small accomplishment, given the fact that the saga featured a team that had won just four games the year before, a university few people would call a hot, glamour school, and a city that was not on the "Ten Best Places to Live" list.

The mainstay of Kissell's approach proves my contention that 99 percent of success in business—any business—comes from building solid relationships. He worked hard on that. They played tennis, had long talks, and enjoyed many dinners together.

But when he finally asked for the sale, asked for a decision, Oliver Purnell begged off. He said his contract was substantial and UD, by no means a wealthy school, wouldn't be able to afford the buy-out. Ted Kissell said, "So long," and started thinking about the other names on his list. Purnell was right, he told himself, the money was going to be a problem for Dayton. Even so, he decided not to give up on his number one choice without a fight. Fifteen minutes after the disappointing phone conversation, Ted told his wife, Deanna, "I'm calling him back. He's the right choice, and we'll find a way of making it work."

Kissell had full empowerment from Brother Fitz. He knew it and it paid off.

Oliver Purnell finally agreed to visit the campus, meet with the president and the board or trustees, and make a go or no-go decision on the job. He'd bring his wife and family along too. Ted Kissell's wife, whom he calls "my executive assistant for recruiting," made all the arrangements. Everything was set, but at the last minute the recruit got cold feet and canceled. "Things were just going too fast," Purnell told me.

This aborted excursion to Dayton, by the way, was totally aboveboard. Oliver Purnell told Old Dominion what was going on. And that may have been the ultimate key to the deal. Purnell liked his job and had no intention of leaving, but Old Dominion apparently didn't make much of an effort to rerecruit their coach, whom they otherwise obviously valued. He was disappointed. It's a lesson to all companies: *Rerecruit your best people and keep rerecruiting them.*

It's also a lesson for those who are engaged in recruiting. Don't assume you will necessarily lose a bidding war—the other side may not bid. You never know what's going on behind the scenes.

With Purnell still on the fence it was time for a judicious shove. Ted Kissell had agreed as a condition set by Purnell himself that the Old Dominion coach would only be coming to Dayton to take the job as the university's first choice. No beauty pageants. Purnell wasn't messing around, and neither was Kissell, as it turned out. He sent word back to his prospect that it was time to decide yes or no. Kissell gave him overnight to think about it.

The second time around, Ted Kissell succeeded. His candidate said he'd take the job and agreed to come to Dayton with his family, make the usual rounds, and—unless something went horribly wrong—sign a contract. Almost there. Ted Kissell left nothing to chance. The Purnells had to make a change of planes in Cincinnati to connect to Dayton from Virginia Beach. To avoid another bout of second thoughts—a deal killer at that stage of the game—he arranged for his wife and two daughters to meet the Purnell family with a limo at the Cincinnati airport and drive to Dayton.

Kissell won't admit to premeditation, but that gesture was a masterstroke. The visit went well. All the preliminaries and legal niceties were wrapped up, and Oliver Purnell said yes. It was time for the always-dreaded first encounter between the newly signed coach and the local news media. This time, the meeting included a roomful of UD boosters and alums, as well; all of them were salivating for a basketball turnaround at any price. They desperately wanted a new coach, but at the same time wanted to show him who was boss—the boosters—and if that meant drawing blood, the knives were out and sharp.

Lights, cameras, action. A nervous Ted Kissell and Oliver Purnell crouched in the hot seat waiting for the first missile to zap them, right? Wrong. Try this: Up to the podium walked Ted Kissell's two daughters, Katie and Sarah. Katie, the youngest, who was only eight at the time, started the session by saying how wonderful it was that she and her sister could welcome the Purnell girls to live in Dayton and be their friends.

Hugging and holding hands, Oliver Purnell's kids, Olivia and Lindsay, joined them at the podium to say how happy they were to be in Dayton. The media tigers started to purr and the new coach was off to a great start. Ted keeps the picture of these little TV stars in his office. I think he missed his calling in public relations.

See what I mean about the limo from Cincy?

With the girls in the spotlight, Oliver Purnell's wife turned to him and said, "You can go back to Virginia, but we're staying here."

Ted got his man. Oliver Purnell pulled off a remarkable turnaround by winning twenty-one games in 1997–98, but there was turmoil and tragedy during the leadership transition. The team was forced to abruptly switch conferences, which is always disorienting, but far worse—the star player died in his sleep.

When I talked with the coach, I asked what he was thinking at the time.

"The death was such a blow! What a tragedy for that young man, his family, and for the whole university community. Personally, I wondered if maybe we had made a mistake," he said. "But my wife said we'd be all right, and that we'd be made stronger. We'll just pray on it, was what she told me."

Recruiting As Relationship Building

What I see in this Ted Kissell and Oliver Purnell story is a case study in people-ology. Kissell would never have gotten his man without personal involvement, a passionate commitment to finding the best person for the job, and the determination to overcome all the barriers that popped up. Clearly, from early on, the message Ted Kissell conveyed to his prospect was a passionate desire to get him on his team.

People want to be wanted. If passion is missing from the recruiting process it becomes ho-hum and the results deteriorate accordingly. The good ones, the best ones, get away.

When I went to the University of Dayton to gather material on recruiting, I expected to hear about how they prospect for athletes—and I did. As a leadership team, Ted Kissell and Oliver Purnell are just as passionate about bringing the best players to UD. Recruiting is a full-time proposition. Lots of money and time are spent just identifying prospects in their base, mostly Ohio and the Atlantic 10 conference area. They use recruiting services, the athletic equivalent of headhunters, but also know the territory personally. There are high school visits, talks with coaches, and scouting trips to summer camps and games. This process—just tracking who's out there—makes many business talent scouting and recruiting programs look weak by comparison.

What struck me most, though, was the effort involved in getting to know the kids *and* their families. The coaches go into the homes of the athletes to sell the program and build relationships, not with the recruits, but initially with the parents. They work with the kids and their moms and dads for three or four years establishing a foundation of sincerity and trust. It also serves as a way to view the prospect from another perspective—perhaps one that's the most revealing in terms of character and potential.

Businesses blow it in this way. We should also attract the best and brightest young talent by establishing relationships with them and their families in high school and college. Certainly for more than the typical two-week or month-long courtship. There's a host of extracurricular activities—and curricular ones too—that could be sponsored by business, not just for PR or commercial purposes, but with an eye to cultivating and attracting tomorrow's superstars. To briefly touch on an idea that I'll develop later, if we have basketballs camps, where are the leadership camps? For that matter, why aren't we, as business people, at the basketball camps, working with the young athletes who won't be going pro after college and who would be ideal candidates for recruiting into our own organizations?

We are so part-time and so sloppy on this, it's outrageous.

The family recruiting connection begs to be explored. I first became aware of it when I was interviewing a young Asian-American woman for a position at Xerox's Columbus operation. She was very impressive, and there was no doubt that we'd make her an offer. I asked if she had any questions for me. Her answer floored me. She said, "Yes, would you talk to my father about what it would be like for me to work here and get his permission?"

Huh?

Well, of course I talked to her father. I loved it! Why wasn't I talking to all of the prospects' fathers and mothers? Sure, there was a cultural tradition involved in that particular case, but if Oliver Purnell can sit in a living room and explain to a mother how he intends to help her son realize his full potential, what's stopping those of us in business from doing the same thing?

Nothing. Coach Purnell, by the way, tells parents, "I will treat your son like my son. Both good and bad. If I have to, I will take away what he wants—basketball—to give him what he needs (academics and discipline)."

Believe me, if I had a corporate recruiter look me in the eye and say that about Alle or Frankie, I'd be their strongest advocate.

It's high time business got smart about recruiting.

 Now-To

Invite a local college athletic director or head coach out to lunch (possibly pay a consulting fee or, better yet, make a donation to his or her school) and get advice on recruiting from someone who's been there and does that full-time.

Keeping Recruiting Honest and Engaged

One reason that leaders like Ted Kissell and Oliver Purnell have such an effective recruiting process is that their careers are riding on it. There's nothing quite so sobering as watching an eighteen or nineteen year old "running down a basketball court with your paycheck in his mouth," is the way Oliver Purnell described the feeling. Haunted by that image, few coaches let recruiting become ho-hum.

By tying recruiting to performance, and tying performance to compensation, the whole process of talent hunting and recruiting becomes very personal. That's why it's a mistake to allow recruiting to be conducted without the direct involvement of those who will be working closely with the candidate. At Xerox, each of my team leaders was required to interview a prospect and to sign off on the decision to hire. What kept the process honest and the executive personally involved was that the candidate could easily end up on his or her team. A major component of the manager's take-home pay hinged directly on how well the team performed overall and in competition with the other teams. This is a potent form of accountability. They knew that I kept the bar so high that a recruiting mistake would have immediate impact on performance and hit them right where it hurts.

However, if hiring is dictated by human resources or a recruiting manager, there's no direct financial incentive to get it right. In Cleveland, Paul MacKinnon, our marketing director, was the point man and initial screener. It seemed like every time I poked my head in Paul's office, he was meeting with another prospect. He kept feeding possibilities into the funnel at a steady rate so that we could count on doing interviews in batches of ten or twelve at a time or on a biweekly or monthly basis. There was no way our interviewing skills were going to get rusty with a flow like that. MacKinnon's pay was also tied to how well the district did, which meant that he wasn't about to slough off. To make sure that we were on our toes, he'd include an unsuitable candidate in each batch, but wouldn't reveal the ringer's identity. The preliminary filtering was such that the candidate pool was of extremely high quality, and we'd end up saying to each other, "Is this the one we're supposed to catch, or this one?" It's a good idea, actually. When the ringer keeps getting close to being hired, you probably need to overhaul the process. I'd be cautious with this technique, though. Paul MacKinnon is one of the few people I'd trust not to sit back and let me hire Jack or Jacquelyn the Ripper to see if I could teach them to do cold calls.

I probably could teach them to cold call, but I would have caught onto the Rippers with my favorite interview question: Who are your heroes? "Bluebeard" or "Lizzie Borden" would have tipped me off. Seriously, I've received more revealing answers to the hero question than to any other. My goal is to get the candidate off his or her script so that I can see the real person. Most of the time, I hear about their mother or father, a close relative, or a teacher. If they don't have heroes, I don't want them working for me. There won't be cultural compatibility with the organization. It's as simple as that.

I also like to encourage the candidate to interview me.

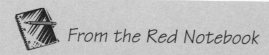 *From the Red Notebook*

When interviewing prospective employees, among other attributes look for self-confidence and communication skills. It's also important to assess energy levels and enthusiasm.

A prospective employee should know how I lead and manage a team. And I'm not offended when they ask about money. Please don't buy into this nonsense about how it's taboo to ask about compensation and other benefits. Most headhunters who pursue top executives will tell you that the five most frequently asked questions are: What's the company? Where's it located? What's the job? How much does it pay? and, Are you kidding?

Pay shouldn't be the first question, nor the last. I think we torture candidates by not including compensation information in the interviewer's opening presentation. Making the candidate raise the issue is sadistic game playing. *You're supposed to be more interested in the challenge than the money.* Excuse me? We are talking about the most materialistic society that the world has ever seen, with the possible exception of Babylon, aren't we? In an era when some top executives consider themselves poorly paid if the comp package doesn't exceed the GDP of Portugal, we should grow up and let prospective employees ask how much they'll earn.

But if you're going out for your first job, think ahead about what questions you would like to ask in the interview and the questions that you are liable to be asked in return. Once, I asked a young man why he wanted to work at Xerox. What a surprise! Should have been a slam-dunk.

"I'd like to work at Xerox because it's the leading computer company in the United States," he replied.

Xerox doesn't sell computers. I decided he was one of Paul's Rippers or ringers and passed.

 Now-To

Find out when job interviews are scheduled and sit in of them as observer.

Don't evaluate the interviewee, evaluate the interviewer. Get the leader. He brings people with him.

Commit to Becoming a Recruiting Company

I understand Southwest Airlines processes thousands of job applications a month. Good for them! Is that expensive? Oh, yeah. But they are bearing the cost to keep the door open to the best talent. At the same time, Southwest is compelled to stay in the recruiting business. There's no other way to handle such a flood of prospects. Full-time recruiters are exposed to the outside world, and they are constantly comparing internal expectations and perceptions to what the outside world expects and perceives.

Constant recruiting keeps you on the street and keeps you sharp. This is what levels the playing field and allows schools like tiny (a student body of five thousand), tenth-seeded Gonzaga University of Spokane, Washington, to almost break through into the Final Four and come within hailing distance of powerhouse Duke, as they did in the 1999 "March Madness" NCAA playoffs. Once you make the commitment to be a "recruiting company," lack of resources can be countered by energy, commitment, and passion. I could see that the University of Dayton was on to this secret. They worked their territory relentlessly, meanwhile, as Coach Purnell explained to me that the strategy was to pay the rent by building to a .500 record, then winning twenty-one games, knocking off a conference championship, and clawing upward rung by rung. Each win along the way provides entrée to higher caliber talent.

Some coaches make flashy recruitment presentations. Initially, Oliver Purnell favors the good cop/bad cop strategy, with a twist. It's more like good cop/quiet cop. He interviews the prospects and their families, accompanied by an assistant coach who handles the overview material about the school and the team. Purnell mostly listens and watches the reactions. He's interested in seeing whom the athlete turns to for advice. He refers to that person as the "primary influencer"—Mom, Dad, a coach, the minister, or some other adult. He then tries to get to know this influencer, not only as a channel through which he can sell Dayton, but as a way to evaluate the athlete's character and potential. It's closely akin to my question about heroes. Purnell is sizing up flesh and blood heroes and mentors in order to evaluate the heart and values of the young talent he's considering for the team.

One thing he listens for is whether the athlete talks only about himself. Is there any consideration given to the team or interest in what the overall college experience will entail beyond athletics? As a rule of thumb, he has found that if the athlete opens up and talks a lot, he's interested in Dayton. "The best recruits recruit themselves," he told me.

"The best recruits recruit themselves" went right into the red notebook.

Oliver Purnell clearly knows the difference between selling and recruiting. Even if an athlete can help his team improve, if he spots a problem with academics or attitude, he lays it out. The coach knows that he's the coach. He's going to have to work with the athlete for four years—problems and all. He knows how agonizing problems could be for him, the player, and the team.

For the Red Notebook

Use a recruiting manager, human resources, or a good headhunter, but the "coach"—i.e., the boss—must be directly involved in hiring key members of the team. After all, once they're on board, he or she will be spending a lot of time with them.

If the fit is right, Oliver Purnell "sells the dream" to get the recruit to come to Dayton. He lets recruits see that they can take part in building an organization and a set of traditions from the ground up. They won't just be one of a cast of thousands who've built a program at a power-house like Duke. These kids will be pioneers, the ones who set the standards that others will read about and attempt to live up to in the years to come.

The comment sparked a flashback for me: I'm walking down the hall-way in the Xerox district office in Cleveland. I've just taken over. Fred Thomas is with me, a sales manager I've inherited from the previous regime. The place is a horror show, and Fred is worried. He asks if I think he'll be able to make the cut. I tell him he's going to be one of the operation's super-stars and I repeat what I had just said to the whole office— "Our success will be so spectacular they will write books about us someday." Today Fred is a franchise player, handling an account—one account—that earns Xerox about $180 million a year. And two books have been written about Xerox's Cleveland comeback.

Sell the dream—and live it.

Better Than Gold

The dream was sold to Megan McCallister. She lives it every day at Dayton, as the assistant athletic director. "A career experience" is what this young woman bought. She was a member of the U.S. national volleyball team and Ted Kissell couldn't match the kind of money other schools were willing to pay. He persuaded her that she would be exposed to all the facets of the life of an assistant athletic director and be way ahead of her competition as a result.

"What's your goal?" I asked her.

"I want to be master of this job."

Megan explained that she came to Dayton because "there were no limits." Ted Kissell encouraged her to dream, but at the same time made sure that everything that the dream entailed was based on performance. She got autonomy and empowerment, but it came with the need to deliver. Megan had been recruited just the way Oliver Purnell, and the rest of the UD team, had been. There was a message, a vision and it had been communicated relentlessly. And Ted Kissell kept his promises.

He's great mentor, Megan explained, and he "gets you to the table." By this, she means that when there is a project to be shaped and presented, she's allowed to handle it from first to last, including taking it into the university board of trustees or Brother Fitz and making the presentation. Kissell's mentorship and empowerment allow her to build credibility and to see how decisions are made at the highest level. It's obvious that she loves her job, but probably what keeps her there is that she is given the opportunity to grow every day.

 For the Red Notebook

I'm going to steal a line from nationally syndicated radio talk show host Jim Rome: "This guy comes to work every day with a plan for getting better." "Romie," as he's called by his fans, was talking about a star NHL player. I see the same thing in Megan: This woman comes to work every day with a plan for getting better.

Kissell has delivered on his recruiting promises. He is helping Megan build herself into a future athletic director. That's the deal—and they both know it.

And does Ted Kissell have an eye for talent! I put Megan's comment directly into the red notebook: "To succeed at anything you have to be positive—believe in something that's beyond yourself."

There it is—the platinum rule of recruiting, leadership, and life.

CHAPTER ELEVEN

On the Fast Track—

Because the Train(ing) Doesn't Stop Here Anymore

*A*sk them.

If I could get away with it, I'd end the chapter right here.

Ask them.

It's my all-purpose answer to questions about how to develop an effective training program. Billions of dollars are wasted on training, and it's not because bad people are kissing off good and useful material. Nor is it due to bad material being thrown at good people. The fault lies with the unasked and therefore unanswered question:

What do you need?

Once they've seen a basic job description, even a rank beginner can meaningfully address the question. They know what they need. Well, most of them do. As a new employee, I sat through weeks of training at Xerox's magnificent training complex in Northern Virginia concentrating hardest on who among my female colleagues I would invite to join me for dinner that night (I was single at the time). I got back home to Ohio, a fully trained sales rep, but on my first call I was so scared, I drove around the I–270 beltway that encircles Columbus two full times—at an hour a lap—before I had the nerve to get off at the exit nearest the customer's office. Inside I was a babbling idiot. "I'm Frank Pacetta, what your name is?" is the way I introduced myself. Peter Rogers, another Xerox rep who was with me, still teases me about it.

Months later, I continued to be a high-energy disaster, more interested in finding out where that night's party was being held than getting serious about selling. My boss sent Peter Rogers out again to help, coach, and warn me—one young sales rep to another—that I was going to blow a great opportunity if I didn't pull my act together. It took marriage, Julie's pregnancy, and a $600 bank balance to end my days as an unreformed underachiever.

I was lucky that I didn't get fired long before Frankie was born. I really regret the wasted years. I burned off the middle portion of my twenties, which I could and should have put to far better use. I cheated myself and cheated my family. As a *reformed* underachiever I closely watch the younger members of my organizations to make sure they don't make the same mistake—not if I can help it, anyway. I've always relied on training to keep my teams focused, pumped up, and productive.

My point about asking people to tell us what kind of training they need stems from what didn't happen to me. Just that question alone, asked by my boss at the time, would have revealed that I was totally "CC"—Clearly Clueless. Or, which is even more central to the point, if my boss's boss had asked, "What does Frank need to get him on track?" it would have helped. Instead, what happened—and still does—is that a one-size-fits-all training program is brought into play that is only marginally useful. That is, if you're lucky. Many companies don't even offer any kind of training what-soever.

People want to learn what they can use—now. The issue is relevance. How can I, as a teacher—and that's what a good leader is—help you do your job better, have more fun, and become more successful?

If that answer is, "Learn to conjugate Latin verbs," you've lost them. The major complaints about training come down to this:

- It's dull.
- It doesn't relate to me.
- I know this already.
- I don't see a real-world application.
- There's no chance to practice.
- The trainer hasn't been there and done that.
- There's too much material.
- It's too complicated.
- It takes me away from family.
- It takes me away from my customers.
- What I was taught doesn't work.
- My boss told me to forget what I learned and do it his way.
- I didn't get a chance to use what I learned and forgot it.
- There isn't enough training.
- There isn't any training.

The last complaint wasn't an issue at Danka when the company acquired Kodak's high-volume color copier division. Kodak had an excellent training facility in Rochester, New York, that each new employee was required to attend for about three months. I made it a point speak to each class of trainees. I'd start by asking if they enjoyed the experience. "Oh, absolutely." "Okay, What did you learn? Do you remember all three months' worth?"

Meanwhile, the instructors were standing there and they wanted to kill me. It seems like a dumb question, doesn't it? Here's the vice president of sales asking trainees to tell him what they learned over the course of three months. Well, damn it, what did they learn? They better be able to tell me—and better than that—show me, or we've just wasted a lot of time and money.

Of course nobody is going to be able to spew back the entire curriculum. But what I heard in response to my question was so sketchy and spotty—and worse, so ho-hum—that I was alarmed. For some reason, few managers ask that question of trainees who have just returned from training sessions. Maybe it seems better not to know. But it isn't. Start asking. Find out if the training is dull, too theoretical, or doesn't pertain to the employee's job. Buck that information right up the chain of command.

The training bureaucracy will scream. Scream right back. If you don't insist on real-world evaluation of training programs, you're cheating yourself and your people. At Kodak, I suspected that the lackluster sales performance we were experiencing had nothing to do with training problems and everything to do with lack of customer contact. The idea of sales talent sitting in a classroom for three months bugged me, so I kept probing during bull sessions with trainees until we got beneath the "Oh, the training experience was absolutely great" to "Three months is kind of long to be away from my family" and "They threw an awful lot at us" to "I'd like to have a chance to try some of this before I forget it."

 *Now-To*

Sit in on a training session today. Ask yourself, how does it impact our customers?

No training being conducted today? How about tomorrow or sometime this week? If none is scheduled, you probably have discovered a barrier. Time to cut it down!

Newly returned trainees are a gold mine of information. Ask those who have gone through in-house or local training programs a series of Pacetta Poll questions:

- What was of most value?
- What was of least value?
- What subject would you like to have more work on?
- Did you feel there were gaps in the program, and if so, what were they?
- How would you rate the value received from your training experience on a scale of one to ten?
- Did you have fun?
- Out of all you learned, what have you utilized since you've been back?
- Has your manager or team leader reinforced what you learned, encouraged you to use it, and inspected its effectiveness?
- How does the training compare to what you received previously from us or from another employer?
- What would you suggest to improve the training program?
- Were your instructors passionate about their material? Rate them on a scale of one to ten.
- How will our customers benefit from your training experience?
- Did the training relate to our vision, culture, product, and customers all of the time, most of the time, occasionally, or not at all?
- How often would you like to undergo formal training of this sort: monthly, quarterly, annually, or I don't know?

There I go again with a lot of questions. And here I go again with my insistence that you do something with the information you gather. I don't want to hear, "But, Frank, training is not my area."

Make it your area. To practice people-ology, training cannot be delegated or relegated. Over the years I've heard tons of excuses, most of them are built out of prefab elements like, "My manager never did . . . ," or "Corporate refused to. . . ." My answer is, "So corporate tied you up in the basement without food and water, and there was no way you could go out and do what had to be done?"

Give me a break!

If training stinks, fix it. Look at the answers to the questions I've laid out above and develop a plan to correct the shortcomings. We've been talking about barrier busting, right? If your trainees tell you they haven't used their learning since they've returned, that's a barrier. You've lost their services for several days or weeks; somebody had to pick up the slack, which means you and their colleagues have paid a price for training that's not yet returning the investment. You can't let that go on for long without demotivating those who made the extra effort.

 For the Red Notebook

From about $5.6 billion to $16.8 billion is wasted annually on ineffective training, according to a Rutgers University study cited by *USA Today*—and I'll bet the actual figure is even higher.[2]

[2] Stephanie Armour, "Big Lesson: Billions Wasted on Job-Skills Training," *USA Today*, October 7, 1998.

Ask all newly returned trainees to develop a specific action plan detailing when and how they will utilize what they learned. Ask them to do it while they are in training. There's no sense racking up additional down time. Also, build in the requirement that the plan specify what learning will be applied the first day back into it.

Let's do it. Throw the ball! Training that isn't used won't be retained.

I'm not going to let poor training screw up my operation. Anytime a trainee answers the question, "What was of least value?" you've got important information to act on. If it's a vital area, bring in your superstars and top performers and use them as backup instructors. They can do this coaching one-on-one or in a group. The same goes for the question, "What subject would you like to have more work on?" It's an ideal mentoring situation. Mentor mania, here we go!

And what if—what if—the training gets the highest possible ratings and accolades? Count yourself lucky. Now, you can ask the trainees to pay for their superb training experience with *measurable* higher performance and productivity. That's the whole purpose, isn't it? Now you've got a chance to track ostensibly superior training to see how it translates in real-world terms. Do sales increase? Are customers happier? Is quality improved? Does the bottom line show a difference?

Don't tolerate what you can't evaluate.

By tracking the effectiveness of training, you can counteract a tendency that most of us fall prey to: We get to be old fogies. It's so easy to reject new ways of doing things because they're unfamiliar and seem to challenge our on self-worth as leaders and managers. If new techniques pass muster, shame on you for saying, "That's not the way I do business." Give new ideas a chance to succeed or fail. Just find out which is which.

 For the Red Notebook

Training "follow-up" is nothing more than another way to say "use it or lose it."

OFTS—Old Fogey Training Sabotage—can be a big program, but the manager's age is not the issue. It's all about attitude. A newly trained person who returns to the field and is told, directly or indirectly, that what he's learned has no validity is less likely to retain and make use of the material. According to Neil Sessoms, former director of curriculum development for the copier and duplicator division at Xerox's Leesburg training complex, this destroys the follow-up process that must occur for new knowledge to take root. The fault lies with the trainee's boss. "This manager not only does not reinforce, not only does not inspect, not only does not role model what the trainee has just learned," Sessoms contends, "but as a rule discourages or diminishes its importance. He insults its credibility in a thousand ways, whether it's an outright critical statement or by treating it casually—'Oh, that's interesting, but tell me where we stand on this month's outlook.'"[1]

Neil Sessoms is right. Veteran managers have been through so many iterations of the latest and greatest training they become callous and cynical. *Here we go again.* They roll their eyes and proceed to demean and discredit the training process both before it takes place and after.

Doc P's truth serum time again. You've done it, right? The thought of losing key people and scrambling to fill the vacancies while they go off into training never-never land is a major pain, not to mention a major expense. When they return, the last thing you want to do is listen to a bunch of new jargon and way-out theories. Totally New York nodsville. *Yeah, yeah, yeah. Just get back to work.*

Sessoms believes this leads to a self-fulfilling prophecy. The manager expects training to be a waste of time, and it is, because the trainee can't make full use of what he or she learned. The next step is for the demonstrably ineffective training curriculum to be revamped yet again, confirming that the manager was right all along. Vindication. Sessoms sees the manager's rationale unfolding this way: "That's why I didn't reinforce it, that's why I didn't learn it myself, that's why I didn't inspect you or pay any credence to it because I knew it was going away. And because I didn't do any of these things it was unsuccessful. Sure enough it went away. And here comes another." Effective training never gets off the ground. It's a vicious circle.

Time for Doc P to take some of his own truth serum. I used to do that all the time. I would look for excuses to keep my people from being dragged off to Leesburg. I wanted them on the job, but I was also reacting to negative feedback from trainees who came home and complained that they had wasted their time. What was needed was a mechanism for me to push back on Leesburg and get them to fix the problems on their end. But if I'm not conducting an evaluation—the one I laid out above—I don't have any ammunition. My bosses are going to give me the New York nod—and they did. What's more, if they are not doing an evaluation of me and my teams, top management will never know whether training is failing because the curriculum is lousy or because I'm sabotaging it.

All it should take is one "no" to the question, "Has your manager or team leader reinforced what you learned, encouraged you to use it, and inspected its effectiveness?" for my boss to be on the phone asking me what's going on. There's a fundamental disconnect here. Somebody needs to be held accountable for training. If I'm sabotaging training and my boss doesn't know it, he or she is as guilty as I am. The responsibility to expect and inspect runs right up to the top of the leadership hierarchy.

The Busyness of Failure

Training, like recruiting and retention, often is treated like a stepchild. When I conduct one of my informal and unscientific Pacetta Polls I keep hearing that "Training is weak, but we don't have time to do anything about it."

> *No time.*
> *No time for recruiting.*
> *No time for retention.*
> *No time for effective communications.*
> *No time to build trust.*
> *No time for leadership.*

We're too busy. What are we busy doing? I think I know: Managing the negative consequences of being too busy to do all the stuff that needs to be done. The winner is the person or company that doesn't bleed to death before crossing the finish line. This hemophiliac's marathon is as self-defeating as old fogey training sabotage. Those who can run fast and bleed at the same time are, by definition, superstars. The lesson learned—the wrong one—is to hire superstars, forget about the training, and get them out on the track clocking up the miles.

Unless there's unlimited talent and unlimited supplies of blood, it's the wrong lesson, for sure. But we're three-quarters right. Superstars are always worth hiring and retaining. Go ahead, but forget about training them in a generic one-size-fits-all mode. Get them out on the track racking up miles, and then study how they do it so the techniques can be taught to others.

 From the Red Notebook

When I first became a manager at Xerox, which uses a 1 to 5 performance-rating system, I told my dad that I was going to start spending time in the field with the 3s to help them develop. He said, "Frank, if there was trouble and you needed immediate results who would you go to?" I said, "The 5s." He replied, "Why don't you just get 5s then?"

He was right. Hire 5s and use them as templates to produce 5s throughout the organization.

Use training to clone your best people. They become the curriculum.

Let's work through that sequence. What's usually keeping most mediocre or failing organizations from total collapse is a cadre of hard working, high performing people. The same is also true of seemingly successful operations that could be and should be doing much better. In both cases, the top performers have figured out how to survive and prosper in spite of everything management does to bleed them to death. They may have cultivated superior product knowledge or a feel for the competition. In Cleveland, one of my managers had a brilliant tactical instinct for identifying the customer's decision-making priorities and process. I made two of his techniques standard practice for all the sales teams and trained them to make sure it happened.

Now-To

Identify the best practices of your superstars and make them SOP (standard operating procedure).

It's tremendously gratifying for top performers to have their techniques spotlighted and it benefits the entire organization.

Simply by asking your best people how they handle important business activities and observing them in action, you can get a training profile that's extremely useful, and is more relevant, specific, and field tested than anything an outside consultant could tell you. But go beneath the surface. If a top sales rep is making six or seven calls a day, that's useful information. Before you require all reps to make the same number of calls, find out what else the model is doing. Are her proposals especially comprehensive? Is his prospect base larger? How long does it take between initial contact and final agreement? How do you identify the decision maker? Those elements are all procedural and, as a result, teachable.

This isn't just sales stuff. It works for any business function:

- What do they do?
- Why do they do it?
- How do they do it?

Now there is one flaw to this, and it's a key reason why training is so screwed up. If you don't value what your top people are doing, it's pointless to use them as a training template. Until we come to terms with identifying what it is that we must do to pay the rent every month, we're probably training people to do things that aren't worth the time and trouble. It's not about identifying what we'd like to do or what seems like the trend of the future, but about knowing what do we have to do every day to keep the doors open.

Quick. What drives your business? I've been harping on this since chapter 3. Write it your red notebook. Until you can do that, forget about training. It's not going to do any good.

Learning for Performance's Sake

Training is not a panacea. Neil Sessoms reminded me of that. He said, "If you've got a bad compensation plan, you can't outtrain it. If your product line stinks, you can't make it smell better with training. If you've got a competitor with a distinct technological or price advantage, you can't out train that either."

He's right. But isn't it tempting to postpone the heavy lifting in the hopes that training will save the day? Many computer hardware and software companies follow this strategy: Train a huge support staff to deal with confused and irate customers who can't make the stuff work right instead of getting the bugs out before the product is released. No amount of training is going to counterbalance tens of thousands of people who feel that you've sold them an inferior product when, in fact, you've done just that. Roger Gittines, my coauthor, bought a computer directly from the manufacturer off the Internet. When he got it, the fax modem didn't work. After calling customer support, he learned that the fax modem shipped with the machine was incompatible with its operating system and that the company was aware of the problem at the time it filled the order. "You mean we paid nearly two thousand dollars and you knowingly shipped us a defective product?" his wife, Jane, asked the customer support representative. "I have entered the information about your problem and the company will be in touch with you," was the reply. I don't care whether that was or wasn't an example of a well-trained response, nothing short of "We're sending you a new computer and a dozen roses" was likely to work. No, training wouldn't help. The company had a product problem and the only way to solve that was to fix the product.

By treating training as an all-purpose panacea, we contribute to training bloat. There are training professionals who are more than happy to serve up a sprawling smorgasbord of learning experiences that are based on the academic model of learning for learning's sake. Neil Sessoms points out that business requires learning for performance's sake: "You don't care if they skip every class, as long as they can do it. And you don't give a damn if they have to take every class twice if that's what's needed for them to learn how to do it. There's no knowledge for the sake of knowledge. It's called criteria referenced instruction. Learning a whole lot of stuff and not being able to perform it is worthless."

What I like about Neil's approach to training is that he doesn't want to train you. He doesn't do smorgasbord. "Sell me on the idea of doing training for you," he says. "And then when you've convinced me that there's a positive goal for the organization, that the management hierarchy is supportive, that they're begging for it, and they need it, and they will play an active role in developing it and enforcing it and that they have a stake in it because it's in line with what they're being expected to do and deliver, then we've got something to start with."

Amen! Think how much better that is than having a training consultant or manager selling you a product that may be something you've heard or read about in a magazine. *Big name companies are signing up. All aboard.* Forget it. The key question is, does it fit in with what you need?

Begin the evaluation of your training programs by 1) asking recent trainees for their assessment of the experience, and, 2) determining how the training is actually impacting your business goals. If there's no impact—save your money!

The Express Train(ing) Track

Neil Sessoms is on my recruiting wish list. I want to hire him for my "situation room," a phrase the White House uses to describe the basement nerve center the president uses to stay in contact with the military chain of command during an international crisis. My situation room is more of a flight simulator, like the ones pilots use to train for emergencies. The simulator spits out a variety of "what-if" situations and the flight crew must respond without crashing.

For the Red Notebook

Here are some quotes from my interview with Neil Sessoms. It makes a great short course in the dos and don'ts of training.

"I think so many times people who are responsible for training start with the solution versus identifying the problem. Or it's a gap to be filled, a task to be accomplished, an objective to be served."

"There has to be an objective."

"What is our objective organizationwide? What role does training play in supporting the objective? How does that cascade through the organization? What are the inputs at all levels to the training? What are the responsibilities in implementing and following up? And if it is truly tied to the strategic objective, then it all hangs together."

"You have to be very specific with what you want to be accomplished with training. Then you have to be very diligent in its implementation and even more diligent in the follow-up."

"We do too much training sometimes, and it's absolutely counterproductive."

"Our little boy has been getting ear infections all the time lately. The doctors give him antibiotic after antibiotic, and he still gets ear infections. So what happens is that people have given antibiotics so much to kids like him that they've developed immunities and their diseases are invulnerable to antibiotics.

"That's the way training is. We've injected doses of training so often for wrong purposes and done it the wrong way with no follow-up so that people are immune to training now."

"If there are not a whole lot of people who support it and have a vested interest in it, it's probably not a good idea to use it in training."

"You can either buy talent, which is very expensive, or you can develop it. Take your pick. You're going to pay for it one way or the other."

"You can hire your competitor's best people, loading them up with nothing but money, but you're naked if another competitor comes along and offers them more money. Or you can develop an internal expertise to groom and grow the talent. And if you lose one, that's okay. Plug another one in and send them through the chute."

When I visited the University of Dayton to attend a closed basketball practice, Coach Oliver Purnell had the team concentrating on what do in close end-of-game situations. It was all "what if" and "what to do." He wanted those kids to know how it felt and what the options were so that when the real thing occurred they'd run through it smoothly.

Business people need the same sort of practice.

What if the deal falls through?
What if a woman calls and says we knowingly shipped her a defective computer? And she's right.
What if the client threatens to sue us?

Bring in the experts and savvy veterans and let them observe and coach as people role play through the scenarios. Do it on-site. Then send them out to work the street, work the Net, or work the line. Coach Purnell said he is always nervous about watching an eighteen or nineteen year old running down the court with his paycheck in his mouth. I think investors feel the same way about rookies running damage control or taking million-dollar gambles with stock dividend checks in their mouths.

What if the train(ing) doesn't stop here anymore? Just as I recommended that you become a "recruiting company," the next step to achieve and maintain competitive advantage is to become a training company or to go work for one that is.

CHAPTER TWELVE

Gaining Process*ability* to Close the Loop—

Connecting People to Profits

*T*he stalker has finally emerged from the bushes. Process. Everything that we covered so far rides on the back of process. Everything.

I hear you saying, "Now he tells me?"

Yeah, now. If I had overtly introduced process in chapter 1, there would be readers galore already billing themselves out at $2,500 a day as "Leadership Process" gurus. They'd gobble up the process and ignore the rest. Process is not leadership, but effective leadership depends on process.

Raw emotion isn't enough.

Is this Frank Pacetta speaking?

It's me. All the sincerity, trust, communications, family atmosphere, fun, high performance, people-ology, recruiting, and training aren't worth a damn without process. Process forms the wheels of people-ology and leadership. If you have a process phobia—and I believe more business people do than don't—hang in for this chapter! Process will not blunt your entrepreneurial edge.

The good news is it's simple to have an awesome process.

There's no bad news—except when there's a half-cocked process. Then the news is grim.

When I met Jaci Clark, the University of Dayton's women's basketball coach, I was startled by how many responsibilities she was juggling in a seemingly effortless way. "Doesn't it get to be overwhelming?" I asked. (I could tell it wasn't, but the dumbest questions get the best answers.) She said, "Not if you break it down."

Not if you break it down. Hello, red notebook.

That's what a process does. It breaks down a complex agglomeration of demands into manageable pieces. I have to have a process like that. I'm not smart enough to handle anything that has a high degree of intermittent synchronicity in a multimodular format. I can drive, talk, and tune the radio at the same time, and that's about it.

Therefore my process is simple and it works. There are four components:

- expectation
- execution
- inspection
- evaluation

You can clutter it up with subcategories, but why bother? Expectation, execution, inspection, and evaluation can also be expressed by basic questions:

- Where do we want to go?
- How do we get there?
- How do we know it's working?
- Are we where we want to be?

Great Expectations

This is the place where we get a chance to "dream big dreams." Or little ones. But there has to be a destination, both short-term—today, tonight, this week, next month, and so on—and long-term.

Don't turn into Carl Sagan on me and burn up billions and billions of brain cells planning a trip through the cosmos. There is entirely too much strategic thinking being done by people who should keep their feet on the ground worrying about the tactical considerations—like paying the rent and having enough left over to buy a nice U.S. Savings Bond or a promising Internet startup venture. Keep it simple until you get the hang of it. Where do we want to go? Try

What a great place to work!
What a great company to do business with!

Bill Locander of the University of South Florida's business school says that leaders take us on a journey. I like that metaphor. If we're going on a journey with a destination of "What a great place to work" in mind, how do we get there? The first decision involves the means of transportation. I vote we go in our own vehicle—let's travel in "The Business." Like most vehicles, it runs on fuel. Profits fuel The Business.

So now the question becomes, where and how do we get the profits we need to make the journey? This is a hard one, so think about it.

Right. The Business sells a *(product or service)* that generates a profit that fuels The Business.

I'm being excruciatingly simple-minded here because unless we embrace the radical notion that only by doing what we do as a primary business purpose, doing it well, doing it better, and doing it consistently over and over again in a manner that delivers high value to a customer is there any hope of getting to destination What a Great Place to Work.

Break it down. Everybody gets a piece of the profit generator. Do you design it? Do you manufacture it? Do you ship it? Do you market it? Do you sell it? Take your piece and break it down even further. What do you do to manufacture it? What do you do to ship it? What do you do to market it? What do you do to sell it?

Once you've broken it down to this point, the next thing is—stop. It takes too long to get to infinity and that's where we're headed unless we know enough to refrain from continually subdividing our basic profit generating unit.

In sales, that unit is customer contact. But, you might say, it's different for every business, isn't it? If you make Girl Scout cookies, it's . . . customer contact.

If you do E-commerce on the Internet, it's . . . customer contact.
If you practice medicine, it's . . . customer contact.
If you teach, it's . . . customer contact.
If you preach, it's . . . customer contact.
If you parent, it's . . . customer contact.

Well, what do you know? Customer contact is such a basic component of success because it provides an opportunity to accomplish four goals or steps:

1. To make a personal touch or connection.
2. Establish a relationship.
3. Make a good first impression.
4. And allow the relationship to grow.

My friend Doad parlays customer contact into a lucrative men's clothing business. I wouldn't let anyone else sell me a suit! He has the four steps down pat. When I first met him I explained that I hated going shopping and trying on clothes. No problem. He took all the measurements he needed, made several suits, and brought them to my home—on a Sunday. Into the closet they went, and I didn't try them on until I was ready to wear them. Every one was a perfect fit. Once I asked Doad for a specific style and fabric, wore the suit once, and decided I didn't like it, even though it was precisely what I'd requested. He took the suit back and never charged me. He is a charming, interesting guy, and a genius at making customer contact work. One of his secrets is he exudes pride and enthusiasm. The man loves being a tailor! Doad's passionate. He cares more about how I look than I do. When Doad makes contact with the customer, it's almost guaranteed that he'll sell a suit or sports jacket.

As for bullet point four—allow the relationship to grow—Doad is now not only making suits for me, he is giving me golf lessons for a hefty hourly fee. And my game is improving. Kind of.

Sure, there are other basic elements that link to and go beyond customer contact. Intel, for instance, has to make a superior computer chip if customer contact is going to yield a profit. But without sufficient customer contact the chip will not yield a profit on its own. Likewise, Doad has to be a skilled tailor (and golf instructor) to stay in business; that's a key link. You can decide which link comes first in the chain. Just decide. But in both cases superior people, with their commitment, enthusiasm, and expertise, provide the linkage that makes for the superior product and superior customer contact.

The next step it to find out how many chips or cookies or customer contacts are occurring currently. That's your preexpectation baseline. It's not going to enough to take you to the destination—What a Great Place to Work—because it barely meets the payroll, debt payments, and the cost of golden parachutes for your senior management.

The key tactical expectation becomes, what does it cost in basic profit generating units to get where we want to go? From that figure, subtract the current number of profit generating units. The difference is the "do-now" cost that will get you to the big dream.

Expectations must be specific, otherwise there is no basis for execution. I'm very reluctant to walk you through a detailed expectation-setting exercise because you will immediately revert to the old "Great idea, but we don't do it that way in our business." I hear it most from people who then add that their company or industry "is a lousy place to work."

So let's stay general. By estimating the cost of your primary expectation and translating it down to the required number of extra basic profit-generating units, you'll get a useful figure. When I first went to Danka, I determined that we needed a minimum of one more sales call a day from every rep. That's what I expected. It was the extra basic profit-generating unit that could get us to where we wanted to go as a company. Add that up. For two thousand sales reps that was ten thousand extra customer contacts a week, or over a half million a year.

How did I come up with that figure? I SWAGed it. SWAG is an informal military acronym for *Scientific Wild-Ass Guess*. I was out to jump-start lagging performance. That wasn't going to happen with, "When you get around to it, please do a couple of extra calls." I laid down a specific expectation and then insisted on execution.

The Executioner's Song

No, wise guy, "I did it my way" is not the executioner's song. It's more like "Row, row, row your boat." Execution is another word for action. Execution is the second most neglected part of the business process. *The* most neglected is inspection, and we'll get to that in a few more pages. When it comes to execution some of the most hard-headed people start conducting themselves like the absent-minded professor. They forget to write it down.

Here's where the personal performance contract comes into play. Expectation goes in one column (target), execution (actual) in another. The contract below can be adopted for use organizationwide, for operational units, and for each individual, and should be broken out on an annual, quarterly, and monthly basis.

Performance Contract

OBJECTIVE TARGET _____   ACTUAL RATING _____

COMMENTS:

Business Results

1. _____
2. _____
3. _____
4. _____

Activities

1. _____
2. _____
3. _____
4. _____

(Also include categories for personal development results and activities.)

The contract is basically a fill-in-the-blanks operation. Under Business Results denote what is expected, like revenue, total sales, sales broken down by product, and the like. Under Activities specify what actions are expected to occur: customer contact, face-to-face appointments, demonstrations, customer retention calls, cleaning the cookie cutter, and so on.

The format is usable at all levels. If there are ten regions, and everything else is equal (which it usually isn't), the regional manager's contract would be derived by dividing the national numbers by ten. Similarly, the districts would each get an appropriate slice, which would be parceled out to the individuals therein.

You probably know this already, but just in case I want to warn against breaking down a national performance contract into equal slices. There needs to be sophisticated statistical and tactical analysis conducted to set the numbers for each operational unit.

For the Red Notebook

Numbers are important, but also find out what's behind the numbers. Are the targets the right ones? Are you actually achieving bottom-line results?

If it is divided in equal pieces, a number may be unrealistically high for one unit and ridiculously low for another. You have to outlook the business, but that's the subject of a whole other book. Also, this is easier to apply if the individual team members have basically the same work situation and business opportunities. Even then, however, the manager and the individual have to work closely together to write a contract that is both realistic and challenging. One size does not fit all.

If I'm a district team leader, I have a contract with my boss that budgets the whole team at 810 customer contacts a month, for example (substitute your own business activity). I can divide that number by ten and assign it to each member of the team. And you thought I just got through warning against equal slices? I did, but I was talking nationally. It's a big, diverse country. Frontline teams need to be playing on the same field by the same rules. Unequal quotas within the same team lead to tension and resentment. Everyone should be pulling a fair share of the basic load. If they are properly motivated and rewarded, high performers will easily hit the plan's number and keep going. As for the team's overall targets, it's a judgment call, but in this case I would build in a 10 or 15 percent cushion to cover unforeseen problems. Better to shoot too high than too low.

The contract allows you to see expectation and execution at a glance.

The Expector General Meets the Inspector General

Expectation, execution, inspection, and evaluation happen when four questions—you've seen them already, but they bear repeating—are asked over and over again:

- Where do we want to go?
- How do we get there?
- How do we know it's working?
- Are we where we want to be?

Step back from a business orientation. When my daughter learned to ride a bike, we could have used the same formula.

1. Where do we want to go?
   Alle learns to ride a bike this summer.
2. How do we get there?
   Dad spends an hour each Saturday and Sunday coaching Alle and running alongside as she tries to develop balance.
3. How do we know it's working?
   Dad sees improvement each time out.
4. Are we where we want to be?
   The summer is half over and Dad is doing more watching than running.

Actually, Dad was on the golf course and Mom was watching and running. The truth squad would pull me over if I didn't make that clear right now. But this process makes dreams come true whatever they are. You have to have a means of systematic execution, inspection, and evaluation.

The performance contract that I showed you earlier combined both execution and inspection. By noting the actual number of business activities performed, the leader-manager is inspecting. By doing monthly reviews of the contract—yes, monthly—you engage in a regular inspection process. You just filled in the blanks, including a rating (which I'll explain in a moment) and comments. The individual should be prepared to verify the activity by bringing along notes or a planner in which he or she has recorded the details of the activity. Make this part of the drill for everyone, and that way it's not interpreted as distrust.

In the past, when I've bumped up an activity rate, I've asked all my people to turn in their planners each week to show me that the activity is booked. Ronald Reagan said it about dealing with the Russians—trust but verify. This is also the time to go beneath the numbers to ask specific questions about how things are going:

- When do you foresee closure?
- Can we speed thing up?
- What are the possibilities for additional business?
- Why haven't you demonstrated the new product?
- This number is at the low end of the range, can you bring it up?

Obviously, with my sales background, I believe in the importance of customer contact. The point is to take what drives your business and break it into a process that sets specific expectations, requires execution, and can be easily inspected and evaluated. If I'm wrong about customer contact, for instance, and business results start fading even though the customer contacts are high, I can then switch my emphasis or take the wheels off customer contact to see what's wrong. Perhaps it's a training problem or a product problem. If there's no process, however, I'll never know what works and what doesn't.

Many companies have huge process manuals that are never opened and never executed.

Take your truth serum. Am I talking about you?

This is precisely where we can put new technology to work. Information gathering is a piece of cake with PCs these days. If it wiggles, hit it. Get a number. In your red notebook, write down five important business results and five activities that are key to the results. Now you're ready to run the numbers. Don't run from them.

An Effective Process Is a Tool Box

It holds tools for

- communication
- setting expectations
- requiring execution
- shaping strategy
- satisfying the customer

The Value in Evaluation

Quantification is also necessary for effective evaluation. I use a three-level process: 1) green, 2) yellow, and 3) red. Here's the way it works.

Green is the highest level. It requires the expected business result or activity to exceed 100 percent of the expectation target. My goal as leader is to have everyone on my team with a green rating in every category. The yellow level is defined as performance that falls in the range of 70 percent below the target to just meeting 100 percent of the target. Yes, hitting the target merits only a yellow. Red kicks in at under 70 percent of expectations. I back this up with what I call "progressive discipline," which also uses a three-level escalator.

A level one, your yellow performers—hopefully, there will be some elements of green in the review—need counseling and coaching on their deficiencies. Document the unsatisfactory performance *in writing* and pair it with an action plan that describes specifically how the employee and the manager will address the problem. Lay out the responsibilities and expectations for both sides. This needn't be anything more than a memo.

But repeat after me: I will put it in writing.

The red performers will need more extensive coaching and a more detailed action plan, given their performance. If they are deficient in more than a couple of important categories, or the percentages are extremely low, take them immediately to the next step in the paragraph that follows.

If there's been little or no progress after a month, the individual should be given a formal letter of concern modeled on the one I'm about to introduce. Reds who received a letter of concern the previous month and failed to make progress should be warned they may face termination if specific goals are not met within thirty days. Do it in writing after alerting human resources and your boss. The reds who did not receive formal letters before, but who have failed to show improvement have to be given a letter at this point.

 Now-To

Find out how many people in your organization are falling below established minimum levels of performance.

What's being done to help them correct the problem? Do you even have established minimum levels of performance?

Large Mouth, Sharp Teeth

It's heavy, isn't it? But a leader has the responsibility to enforce discipline. It comes with the job. Take it from a reformed underachiever, you're not doing a favor to anyone whose performance is poor by avoiding the issue. There have been times when I've been thanked by employees for starting the corrective action process. Until that point they had been in a panic about what to do. Accountability closes the process loop. Everyone, top to bottom, must be held accountable. Not a few of the people all of the time, not many of the people some of the time—all of the people all of the time.

Progressive discipline backed up by the letter of concern comes as a shock only when it is infrequently used. If you bring it to bear early and often— but only when it's warranted—it becomes more of an administrative tool and helping hand rather than an invitation to a beheading. Most people will move quickly to get the troubles behind them. The whole idea is not to allow problems to fester until the individual's career is in jeopardy or the team's performance collapses.

A corrective action letter like the one I'm including should go out only after three conditions are met:

1. The manager has gathered all information about the individual's performance;
2. The manager has reviewed this information with his or her boss;
3. The manager has cleared the wording of the letter with the boss and alerted human resources.

Here's the context and situation for the sample letter: John is a sales rep with a good territory but he is below plan through the first two months of the year. His activities are low (measured by the contract) and this was discussed one-on-one with his manager at the end of January, the first time the problem had occurred. Don't let the example's sales orientation persuade you to say, "This won't work for my business." It will work. John can be an engineer or a truck driver. He has a contract with his boss, after the first month his performance falls short of the mark; the manager spots the problem and discusses it with John; they agree that February needs to be better; a month later the review shows that the improvement has not taken place. The corrective action letter follows.

Sample Letter of Concern

To: John Smith

Through February your performance vs. quota stands at 50 percent; the quota being $50,000 in sales revenue year to date. You've booked $25,000.

We agreed that your monthly activities would include:

5 customer demos per month;

10 proposals per month;

3 orders per month.

Year-to-date the results are:

6 demos;

15 proposals;

4 orders.

John, at this point I am concerned about performance, but more so by the fact that you've missed the activity numbers we agreed to on January 1. These activities are very much within your control.

I am pleased with your customer satisfaction surveys and was impressed with the customer demo I observed with XYZ Company.

In the month of March here are the requirements you need to achieve:

100 percent of the plan for the month;

15 proposals;

7 customers demonstrations.

You need to increase the activities we agreed on in order to move closer to plan. To support you in this effort, I would like to travel with you on three days this month. I would also like to meet with you *each week* to review how we might increase your activities and the quality of your presentations. We can also use that time to discuss any other help you may need from myself or the team.

John, failure to meet these requirements over the next thirty days could lead to further corrective action.

Sincerely,

Your Name Here

Don't leave out the next to last paragraph—the one that commits the manager to support the employee's efforts to improve. If a leader doesn't actively work to help a member of the team succeed, he or she is helping them to fail. If the day comes when an employee must be terminated you have to know in your own heart that you did everything within your power to assist them. Everything.

Putting it in writing means you are deadly serious.

Low Maintenance, High Yield

This process will not work if it is allowed to become an off-again, on-again thing. It seems complicated on paper, but once it's up and running, there's very little maintenance or hassle involved. Many managers fear that if they use corrective action, they'll cause conflict and hard feelings. Once it becomes part of the culture, however, it takes the onus off the leader. You're not being vindictive or mean—you are being responsible. This is a tool for achieving excellence. Don't be afraid to use it.

By putting your expectations in writing you avoid:

You never said that to me!
I don't remember that!
I didn't agree to that!
You never told me!
What a surprise!
This isn't fair!
Your putting words in my mouth!
It's news to me!

Businesses, families, schools, government agencies, and relationships are chock full of opportunities for miscommunications, misinterpretations, and memory lapses. The best process is one that takes this fact of life into account. The performance contract, combined with progressive discipline, accomplishes five key goals:

1. Establishes set activities and performance requirements for each individual on a yearly basis (but reviewed monthly);
2. Avoids side-stepping conflict because a manager may be reluctant to tackle these issues face-to-face;
3. Gives individuals clear direction and avoids surprises;
4. Brings in the next level of a management and HR into the loop;
5. Improves performance when done correctly.

The other requirement is that it must chain up as well as down. If I'm not being held accountable for holding (or not holding) my people accountable, the system is worthless. The people czar's job is to make sure the process has integrity and is being followed. For starters, he or she should have the assignment to inspect and evaluate the contract between each member of the board of directors and the corporation's share holders.

Yeah, I'm serious. The board then inspects and evaluates the CEO's contract, and down the process cascades until the place is awash in success.

X-ray the Business

Process is really very simple. A process is *the way* we live or *the way* we do business, whether we know it or not. As a business consultant, one of the things I offer my clients is an X ray of their business to get a detailed picture of *the way* they operate.

I'm not interested in what their process manual says they do, the only relevant information concerns what they actually do.

Answering the following questions will bring your business process into focus—for better or worse.

X-Ray Vision

- Year-over-year performance?
- What do customers say about you?

- Sales rep productivity, Y-O-Y and Y-T-D?
- What behavior does your compensation plan drive?
- Sales rep attrition?
- Management attrition?
- Major account program?
- Open territories?
- Market penetration?
- New products?

- Customer satisfaction results?
- Performance vs. the competition?
- What's the company structure?
- How do you measure?
- Performance broken into red, yellow, green?
- Top potential managers and leaders? Who are they?

- Channels of distribution?

- Recognition program?
- Field automation?
- Margins per product line?
- Inspection process?

- Goal for 2000?
- What do the company employees say?
- Product mix? What's selling, what's not?
- Customer retention strategy?

- Overall employee attrition?
- Top competitor?
- Market share?
- Open management slots?
- Training? How much? Who? What?
- Mix of new business vs. churn or retained customers?

- Are the right leaders in place?
- Describe the company culture?
- How do you drive results?
- How do you ensure accountability?
- Top performers?

- Review process? (Examples: Monthly outlook, monthly plan and review, product launches, employee contracts, daily activity reviews)

- What distinguishes you from the competition?
- Business plan?
- Communications process?
- Role of human resources?
- Barriers to employee productivity?

No matter the size of the organization, the product, or service, the answers to these questions define a process of doing business. It's all here. For each bullet, there are several more layers of questions to be asked. Go to it! By examining the operation in such detail you can spot strengths and weaknesses. Question marks and lack of specifics should be red flags. And please, "We don't do business that way," isn't acceptable. That's a cop out. The way you're doing business—what you, your customers, employees, and shareholders complain about—is the problem.

This is the kind of X ray Wall Street and individual investors should be doing as they conduct due diligence. I've attended my share of dog and pony shows for financial analysts; it's been disconcerting to see how easy it is for top management to brandish a few big numbers and projections to convince otherwise intelligent men and women to take huge leaps of faith. As far as I'm concerned a CEO who couldn't answer each one of the X-ray questions wouldn't get a dime of my money.

The direct link between data and revenue hit me during a meeting I attended in Boston at Fidelity, the number one mutual fund operation in the world. Before a packed audience of analysts and their support teams, the executive vice president evoked a *Star Wars* theme by putting up a slide that said simply: R^2/D^2. The message was, "square the revenue, square the data."

Brilliant. The two go in tandem. The revenue will never be squared without the additional data. And, besides, as Yogi Berra allegedly said, "If you don't know where you're going, you'll be lost when you get there."

Process delivers R^2 and D^2. A tight, consistent, in-depth process doesn't have to be a forms festival or an example of "analysis paralysis"—the disdainful words of one of my former bosses who ended up with paralysis that crippled his company because he scoffed at the need for analysis. Don't hide behind, "Too much paperwork. It takes too much time." It's not the case if you've got the right people and the right leaders. Process*ability* equals attain*ability* and sustain*ability*.

CHAPTER THIRTEEN

Sorry, Lou—

No More Team/Me

*L*ou Holtz, the legendary Notre Dame football coach started it:

TEAM

me

I remember first seeing this sexy hieroglyph and deciding that it was dead right. The perfect way to express every manager's deepest desire— cram all those unruly people into a Volkswagen-sized concept, chop off any arms, legs, and other inconvenient body parts that stick out, and step on the gas.

Go team!

I realize now I was half right—the *dead* part—Team/Me is dead wrong. And Coach, I hope this doesn't mean I'll never get your autograph.

Business has fallen in love with teams and teamwork. For good reason. Teams are an ideal way to flatten the hierarchy, shorten lines of command and control (but not eliminate them), increase flexibility and speed, enhance creativity, and allow for productive personal interaction.

Teams are good. But that doesn't mean individuals are bad. Unfortunately that's the way Coach Holtz's hieroglyph is interpreted. A team is a living aggregation of individual talent. Sure, its collective capabilities may add up to more than the sum of the parts. But if we forget to nurture and cultivate each part, the sum can never achieve greatness. I've found that many people—I'm willing to say the majority of American workers—are deeply suspicious of business's infatuation with teams.

Why? Start with the fact that the team will not pay your mortgage each month. The team will not raise your children, care for an elderly parent, or stand by your side in sickness or in health.

In those circumstance the rallying cry is Go Me!

Emotion starts with survival—fear and hope. The emotional bonds that sustain families grow out of the survival instinct. But in a healthy family, the individual never loses his or her identity; it is supported and sustained by the larger entity.

Team/Me diminishes the individual in the interest of a collective outcome. Family/Me, from birth to death grows, the Me bigger and stronger and smarter. As leaders, we sew distrust when we suggest that we are going to make the individual smaller in order to allow the group to get bigger and stronger and smarter. It is very threatening.

My starting point when I build teams is the individual. This is my answer to Lou Holtz:

T
ME
A
M

Me is the core of the team, not a danger pulled along in the wake of the more important entity. Me gives the team its center of gravity.

Making Teamwork a Priority

The best team leader who I ever worked with was former Xerox sales manager Neil Lamey. It was more than twenty years ago and I still consider him to be a mentor and a good friend. When Neil put me on his team, the first thing he did was to explain the benefits that would come my way. And I don't mean retirement *bennies*. Neil explained what was in it for me: money, experience, promotion possibilities, and long-term career development. Then he told me what my responsibilities were to the team.

By handling it this way—Me/Team—Neil allowed me to do a quick cost-benefit analysis and realize that it was in my interest do what had to be done to be a member in good standing of the team. From then on whenever there was something about the team that rankled me, I'd just reminded myself of the rewards that would come my way if I swallowed hard and continued to be a good team player.

Today, Neil Lamey still uses the same technique with his teams. He contends that pushing the *me button* first is the only way to attract high performers to your team: "I think *me* is always first in everybody's mind. It may be subconscious or instinctive, but it's always there. You have to appeal to that first."[1]

As a group, high performing individuals don't need teams. They'd succeed with them or without them. "They're not achieving because they want the company to be successful," Lamey says. "That's important but not the primary drive. They want to achieve because they want to achieve." Teams are incidental in his view: "If they have to be part of a team to achieve, they do what they've got to do."

Teams in and of themselves are no guarantee of excellence and high performance for many reasons. According to Neil Lamey, "If you've got somebody who's mediocre, they'll say, 'I want to be part of the team,' because that's what's expected . . . but they're not going to be the ones to pull the team off its ass and move it forward."

So where does that leave us? Right back in people-ology country. It's not the team, it's the people on the team—starting with the leader. Neil Lamey knows this, as do Coach Purnell and Coach Holtz. In Lamey's view, "It's the numbers. If my team doesn't perform, and I don't get the numbers—I'm gone."

In sports, the team doesn't get fired. The coach gets fired. And that's as it should be in both sports and business if the team is going to be more than a sham.

The Truth About Teamwork

I have no use for companies that talk a good team game, but don't play it. In my role as a speaker and business consultant I encounter organizations that are really much more comfortable with a command and control hierarchy than with teams, but they tell themselves and the world that they practice teamwork. It's a lie that hurts their customers and their employees.

The best reason to use teams is that they are an effective and efficient means of satisfying customer needs. Crypto-teams or dysfunctional teams can never achieve that. Whether it's backstabbing or poor coordination or a few hard workers carrying mediocre colleagues, everybody ends up frustrated, cynical, and angry. The customer isn't satisfied and the employees know it.

One frequent mistake is to assume that teams eliminate the need for supervision. The perfect excuse to eliminate layers of middle management. But in actual fact, teams require more leadership, not less. In a team setting, the primary responsibility of the leader is to create and maintain a culture of cooperation and collegiality, as well as to set expectations and hold the teams and their individuals members accountable for results. The suspicion that many people have toward teams, which I noted earlier, comes in large part from personal experience with teams that were poorly led.

Whenever I've undertaken a business turnaround assignment, one of my first statements to the entire group emphasizes that starting immediately, "Everyone pays the rent." The implication is that there will be minimal levels of expectation that *all* must meet. Without fail, I look around the room and a handful of people will be nodding their heads vigorously. They're usually the ones who feel they've been carrying a lousy team or that their well-led team is yoked to other poorly led teams that drag down the whole operation.

What could be more demotivating? I sweat so that you can loaf? My family gets cheated to benefit yours? My career is hurt because the company does not have the nerve to demand excellence from everyone?

Equally destructive is a culture that allows a portion of its teams to consistently turn in lackluster performance when, with a little effort and leadership, the individuals on those teams could be trained and developed to work up to their full potential. It's an outrageous waste of talent. Particularly since teams are a tremendously effective mechanism for individual development. A good team is a hothouse of synergy, mentoring, and cross-pollination. I've seen misfits and oddballs blossom in team settings, proving that they could bring unique skills to the table to directly benefit people who they might have little in common with. Competent teams dissolve the barriers that deny opportunities to women and minorities. Incompetent teams reinforce those barriers.

Nine times out of ten—no, ten out of ten—a lousy team has a lousy leader who doesn't know how to make each team member feel secure, respected, and nurtured within the team environment. That's where the trouble starts, and no amount of cheap, insincere blather about the joys of teamwork will fix it.

There are many classic signs of a half-hearted dedication to teams, among them:

- Major disparities between the performance of various teams within the organization that are allowed to persist;
- Insufficient rewards and recognition for overall team performance;

- Sporadic team activities and tasks;
- Off again–on again emphasis on teamwork;
- A recruitment process that does not evaluate a candidate's teamwork skills and history;
- Top management does not team.

 Now-To

Using the six points that I've just laid out, evaluate your organization for signs of "going through the motions" when it comes to teamwork.

Team Colors or Camouflage?

Teams can easily become hiding places if they are used as a way to blend high, low, and middling performance into some form of acceptable average. If that's happening it's really cheating your best people, and it will drive them away. They are thoroughbreds who should be allowed to run and win races, not function as wheel- and workhorses to make up for those who won't pull their share of the load. All the members within a team must be fairly tasked. The same goes for the all the teams within an organization. That doesn't mean, though, that the loads have to be equal down to the last ounce. But everybody pulls their appropriate share, given the assignment, and the business situation. Resentment and deep frustration are guaranteed if one team member clocks up a disproportionate share of the team's business, while other members are allowed to coast. Perhaps the high performer earns extra money for his or her effort—which is only just—but that makes a mockery of the teamwork concept and destroys morale.

When I was sent to the Xerox's Cleveland district there were excellent people still hanging on but it took a major feat of persuasion to keep them from bailing out. If I had been caught in a B.A.U. mode—business as usual—those people would have been gone in a flash.

High attrition rates always worry me because I suspect the ones who leave are just the people you need to keep. Neil Lamey says flatly, "The mediocre ones never leave. They never get fired. They never get promoted." My strategy is to always build teams around the highest performers and let them set such a blistering pace that the mediocre performers can't hide and chose to go someplace else where they're more comfortable.

One of the pleasures of a new leadership assignment for me is to rescue the top performers from teamwork hell and let them loose—but they're loose to move as a team, an effective team this time. And it is especially satisfying to liberate a young person who was stuck on a bad team. To me, knowingly assigning a newcomer, who is on his or her first job to be "broken in" by a weak team and team leader is a crime. The chances are you've ruined someone's career before it even got off the ground.

 Now-To

Take a personal interest in younger team members to make sure they are having the right kind of teamwork experience. You can't lose by sending the signal that you are ready to "invest in me."

Teams from the Top Down

Now that I have chewed up several pages badmouthing teams, it's time for a pop quiz. Answer yes or no: Frank Pacetta is a total Neanderthal when it comes to teams and favors going back to the good old days of command and control?

I hope your answer is no. I am crazy about teams; that's why I hate to see them abused and misused. When I was beginning to come out of my underachiever phase, I looked around at what I was really interested in and had the most passion for. It wasn't selling copiers or for sales in general. I had planned to be a lawyer, a dream killed by my own irresponsibility in the space of my first four months at the University of Dayton. I've never met anyone who set out to be in sales. Most salespeople had other plans that got sidetracked. *I majored in sales at Harvard* are words that are not likely ever heard outside of this book.

To find professional passion, therefore, I combined my two greatest personal passions—love for family and love for sports. I did what most everyone does—I looked inside myself and asked what I was going to do with my life that made sense and had meaning. It didn't take me long to realize that the places where I felt pride, exhilaration, and had fun and sense of purpose were at home, and when I played sports in high school and college. I wanted to feel that way every day. It seemed totally logical— and it still does—to take the best of the family traditions and the best from sports, put them together, and take the combination to work.

With a background like this, I consider myself a connoisseur of teams. The first thing I look for is the overall culture. Is it a genuine team culture, or isn't it? One way to tell is to determine whether the teams are cohesive both on and off "the field." If a team operates well in a structured setting, like meetings and presentations, that's one thing. The real test is whether the team continues to exchange ideas, support, and mentoring outside of this formal context. I'm not saying that becoming buddies is mandatory, but the best teams are those whose members seek out one another's company and expertise. Ideally, they become families within the family.

Teaming, for want of a better term, must start at the top of an organization and come straight down to the bottom. Anything less is fakery. Yet, as far as I can tell, few company recruiters bother to ask about a candidate's teamwork skills and experience. Why? It's really not a significant part of the culture. The talk isn't lived. Teamwork must be recruited, rerecruited, trained, and rewarded. As executives move up the ladder they should be held accountable for the performance of the teams that they led or were a part of. If "not a team player" is a damning indictment these days, "not a team leader," should be doubly damning.

In twenty-four years I was repeatedly trained at Xerox on teamwork. It was drummed in. The company has one of the best teamwork structures and process manuals that I have ever seen. It's fabulous. Even so, the corporate culture was not so entirely in tune with the demands of a team-based enterprise it could avoid falling into a "one-third, one-third, one-third" trap.

When I was with the company, roughly one-third of their districts fell below average yearly performance goals, one-third achieved the established goal, one-third exceeded the target. And it was usually the same districts in each category year after year. Like many companies that pride themselves on teamwork, Xerox's culture does not rigorously execute it. By definition, all teams and team members must pull their own weight. There has to be a disciplined process to ensure that that happens. Allowing one-third of your teams to consistently fail, one-third to do middling work, and only one-third to excel is pretty ho-hum.

Avoiding a Destructive Game of Hide and Seek

Earlier, I said that teams can become hiding places for people to burrow into, but they also serve as screens that top managers can use to protect themselves from accountability. If I empowered my teams and they fail—well, that's the price of empowerment is it? I'm an enlightened manager and can go on my merry way. Richard Sennett, the author of the *Corrosion of Character*, observes:

> Power is present in the superficial scenes of teamwork, but authority is absent. An authority figure is someone who takes responsibility for the power he or she wields. In an old style work hierarchy, the boss might do that overtly by declaring, "I know what's best, obey me." Modern management techniques escape from "authoritarian" aspects of such declarations, but in the process they manage to escape as well from being held responsible for their acts.[2]

Effective teams cannot exist without responsible and accountable leadership. That's where teamwork starts. You can have committees, bull sessions, and anarchy without leadership, but not teams. The term presupposes *coordinated* action. Likewise, accountability and the team process must stretch the full length of the organization. Only a culture-based teaming, driven from the top—practiced at the top—is strong enough to flow to the bottom and, on the return loop, back to the top, delivering all of its incredible benefits to the organization. When it does, teamwork can then measure up to the ultimate test: Does it positively impact the customer and make it easier for him or her to do business with us?

Hard Heads Versus High Walls

Teams can make a bad organization more tolerable. I know any number of team leaders who simply "paint the windows black" and keep their teams functioning superbly despite what goes on elsewhere in the organization. But it's a tough life and probably a relatively short one. Eventually, the culture clashes will intrude more and more on the team and interfere with its effectiveness. Eventually, a leader who has pounded his or her head against the wall will come to a point when it's not worth it any longer. As far as I'm concerned, I have only one head to beat against the wall. At least, I want a wall I can break.

Leaders can lead effectively only as long as their credibility is intact; if the culture won't let them keep their promises, it won't be long before the trust department is bankrupt. When the corporate culture is not aligned with team culture, fighting it out with the head office becomes a constant headache. When you're forced to use energy and time to manage up when you should be managing down, it is a sure sign that the team's days are numbered.

The best weapon, in that case, is performance. A well-run team may not be ultimately bulletproof, but it can take many hits and keep running. In the meantime, the team leader has to have three kinds of courage: 1), the courage to be honest with his team and explain why he or she is unable to clear barriers out of the way; 2), the courage to protect the team and its members from the fallout caused by unwise decisions from above; and 3), the courage to continue working relentlessly to get top management to change its ways.

It isn't easy. Some leaders—and Neil Lamey is one of them—simply make it clear before they are hired that part of the deal is that the boss is going to have to put up with getting an earful whenever he or she makes a decision that hurts the team. They may not like what they hear, but they're going to hear it. And isn't that what I've been saying from the start? Communication has to be based on full disclosure—up, down, and sideways. If full frontal feedback is expected on the loading dock and the warehouse, it has to be the policy right up to the boardroom.

I really believe that "the truth will set you free" and that if I keep telling the truth the message will get through and the right things will happen. It's cheating your team, and all the other teams in the organization if you stop "speaking the truth to power." Those two biblical injunctions give me courage to use my head as a battering ram.

If your head starts hurting too much, use vision to knock down the barriers. A company that thinks it believes in teamwork usually incorporates references to teams and teamwork into its vision and mission statement. Every time something happens that violates that vision make sure you point it out. It's hard to argue that you're not being a good team player by raising objections, when the objection is supported by the company's own cherished vision. "I'm just doing what's in the vision statement" is tough to gun down.

Talk Teams

The culture clashes that I warned about are often caused by a well-intentioned desire to become team-based that is undermined by an inability to execute the process of building and sustaining teams. One of the keys is to constantly talk about teams and teamwork.

Yes, talk. If you talk about it all the time, there's more of a chance you might do it. As a rule, hardly a piece of paper was issued in my name without the word "teams" and "teamwork" included in the text. I never ran a meeting without talking about teams and teamwork, and few conversations ever occurred without the subject being mentioned.

Here's a copy of an overhead transparency that I have used for years to remind my team leaders what their mission is all about:

Team Building

- Hire team players
- Communicate: Tell them why they need to work as a team
- Benefits of team play
- Customer

- Learning
- Bottom-line

- Fun
- Recognize and reward the team as well as the individual

- Feedback
- Share the best practices
- Each player has a responsibility to the team

- Provide the leadership
- Put them together

- Set common goals
- Measure and communicate results vs. goals

- Instill pride in the group
- Don't tolerate bickering or back stabbing

- Challenge them
- Promote them

- Empower them
- Direct and inspect them
- Create team environment

As you can see, team building is a full-time job and it is never done. Teams are works in progress. When you think you're finished team building—the team is finished. Kaput!

Neil Lamey reminded me of this when I asked him to contribute his thoughts on teamwork and leadership for this chapter. He said teams get stale. "Ours in Columbus never lasted for much longer than a year." New blood was always being added and people promoted up to other positions. That was one of the draws to be on one of Neil's team's—he puts you on a fast career track. We knew that and were dying to work for him. I don't think his teams ever really got stale, but some do; even successful ones get too comfortable and fall into ruts. Businesses change, customers and teams need to change as well.

And keep this in mind: Selfishly holding a good team together by holding good people back from promotions and career opportunities elsewhere is an act of betrayal that will end up hurting you in the end.

In or Out

Two additional points about teamwork need to be addressed before I wrap up. The statement on the overhead transparency, "Recognize and reward the team as well as the individual," deserves a place in your red notebook. Talking is essential, but so is rewarding team behavior and performance. It seems like such an elementary concept, but it is ignored time and again. If there is nothing in it for "us," what's it to me? It's true for laboratory rats and for human beings—we get the behavior we reward. By asking for teamwork and then neglecting to recognize and regard those who comply, we signal that teamwork really isn't all that important.

Finally, "each player has a responsibility to the team." There are no exceptions to this rule. Dennis Rodman can't play for my team. I don't care how many games he can help me win. Lone wolves and teams can't coexist. The wolf will devour team spirit and cohesion. It's up to the leader to domesticate the beast enough to allow him or her to make a contribution and still be an effective performer. One of the best ways to do this is to appeal to their highly developed aggressiveness by devising incentives that can only be captured through team play. Thank them publicly for their contribution, and make sure they know how important they were to the team's success. It may take time. I have worked months turning solo acts into team players, but it's worth it.

My, What a Big Nose You Have

High people-ology requires teams. It's not optional. But I think many of our brightest, best, and most aggressive business executives see teams as a threat to their success: It seems to smack of power sharing and loss of control. Also, teamwork requires leadership skills that have taken a back seat to management techniques fostered by the command and control era. And, of course, *there really isn't time for teamwork*.

Make time. We can't afford to reserve top management positions for the wolves and teams for Little Red Riding Hood. Unless we start practicing people-ology built around real teams, Red's going to stop coming to visit Grandma, start her own cottage industry, and kick our butts.

CHAPTER FOURTEEN

The Art of How—

The Leadership Difference

Several years ago somebody told me that there was a study out that indicated that "leadership" is a word the most people can't relate to, and that if it's used in the title of a book, the author's own mother would find an excuse to read something else. As a salesperson, I can solve that problem by using one of the oldest, grungiest maxims of sales—"Don't sell the steak, sell the sizzle."

Here it is: Sweaty people in expensive clothes, dancing. That's my idea of leadership sizzle. The leader's job is to run the strobe light, crank up the volume of the music, and play a little air guitar. Interested? Send your resume, references, and salary requirements to P.O. Box 10–5–2.

While I wait for the mail, there's just enough pulp wood growing in northern Wisconsin for a few more chapters. I'm going to make a final run at leadership because I owe it to your kids and mine. I owe it to them to recruit you and rerecruit you on the rewards of leadership and its absolute necessity.

When I began writing this book, my son was moving full speed ahead toward his sophomore year in high school. He brought home an impressive catalog of courses. I went through page after page and discovered that there wasn't a single course or extracurricular activity on leadership. Nothing.

I guess they don't have time for leadership in the Upper Arlington, Ohio, schools. A lot of time for computers, though. They are winning the battle for computer literacy, which is fine. I'd just like to know that Frankie and Alle have some exposure to high-touch activities like leadership, along with high-tech. In a country where leaders are made and not born, we're awfully indifferent to the means and methods of learning how to lead our own lives, and lead our families, churches, communities, business organizations, and the nation itself.

Leadership is fun, fulfilling, rewarding—and necessary.

I'd prefer my children and yours got on the Internet to learn leadership skills rather than to learn how to make pipe bombs, or used the PC to play in a leadership "situation room" working out what-if scenarios that sharpen interpersonal skills and problem-solving abilities instead of having their heads filled with gory visions of Doom.

I've written about the need for dreaming big dreams and then systematically living the dream. How about these big dreams?

- What a great life to live!
- What a great place to live!

But we must learn *how* to live those dreams, not just luck into them. That's the art that leaders have mastered and that those who aspire to leadership must learn: the art of how. At the moment, a good place to start learning it is the University of South Florida. The school, located in the Tampa–St. Petersburg area, is creating a leadership center that could serve as a model for other academic institutions to follow. When I visited the campus not long ago I was impressed by the hip, media-savvy approach that Dr. Bill Locander and other faculty members of the business school use to help students create what Locander refers to as a "mental model of how they see leadership in different environments." In one class, students are assigned to watch five films: *Flight of the Phoenix, Norma Rae, Hoosiers, Bridge Over the River Kwai,* and *Lord of the Flies.* Each student must design and lead a presentation that showcases the key leadership styles and techniques in the selected film.

It's a great exercise. Rent those films from a video store and see for yourself.

There are also field trips to area companies in which students are cut loose to interview people about which leadership techniques work and which don't. But the most innovative approach is Leadership House, which amounts to total immersion in real-life leadership experiences. It's based on the philosophy of Robert K. Greenleaf's book *Teacher as Servant,* an account of life at the fictional Jefferson House, a college dormitory that is open only to students who agree to take an active part in building and running a leadership-centered community with a mission to serve and to share. The University of South Florida's Leadership House is the real thing and it was the first of its kind (Butler University in Indianapolis launched a similar program in 1997). Forty students, drawn from all over the campus, become residents of the house for the school year, and most stay two or three years. There is an ongoing program under one roof involving weekly meetings, service projects, speakers, and other leadership-oriented activities. The whole facility and its programs are run by the resident students, using leadership methodologies that are studied as they are practiced. In the first year, there was a small hitch. The students decided on a "no leader" approach and anarchy reigned.

Since then, the students have chucked the "no leader" model and learned to be adept at consensus building, conflict resolution, and communications.

Question: Are you inadvertently following a "no leader" model in your business, family, or community? Perhaps that explains the conflict and chaos.

With my love for sports, I was tickled to discover that Leadership House has also used its team-building skills to become an intramural sports power—including winning the university's intramural coed football championship a few years ago and becoming the first dorm to ever win the "intramural triple crown." Even better—although there's good news and bad—a community has evolved which acts as a magnet for young area business leaders who, I was told, regularly visit the house to take part in the programs to gain leadership skills that they are, unfortunately, not getting a chance to hone on the job.

If you run a business near Tampa–St. Pete, take some truth scrum. Are your young leaders headed for Leadership House after work? Good for them. Shame on you for not building a Leadership House under your own roof.

 Now-To

Establish a leadership center in your own company (or in your own home). Set aside space where people can go to read leadership books and articles, watch videos, and hold discussions. Make leadership one of your "products."

One of the things I really like about the U of SF program is that the close camaraderie is like a fraternity house, but instead of a bond created by beer bashes and *Caddie Shack*–style stunts, the glue is a common interest and commitment to leadership issues and the idea that leaders serve the community. And since the students are a mix of majors, there's a rich diversity and a valuable intermingling of disciplines.

One of the advantages of the University of South Florida's approach is that it isn't totally textbook dominated. Leadership is a hands-on skill that has to be learned on the job, mistakes and all (as the kids discovered with their "no leader" experiment). While Robert K. Greenleaf's strong spirituality isn't to everyone's taste, I'd like to see versions of Leadership House on college campuses and in high schools all over the country. Something similar could be offered to elementary and middle school students as well. If we can teach marketing, public relations, accounting, and law, we can teach leadership—and we should start early.

Leadership centers could serve as a the ultimate training grounds and clique-busters in our high schools. Being a leader is about

- communication, not alienation
- rapport, not rejection
- cooperation, not conflict
- achievement, not anger
- building up, not tearing down

Why not establish a team-based leadership culture within our schools? It works for athletes. Those jocks have a wonderful time; there's pride, self-confidence, and a sense of accomplishment. But you don't need to be running around on a ballfield to feel all of that. Why not let every student have the same thrill? Assign them to teams on the first day of school—athletes included—deliberately mixing personalities, academic skill levels, and social backgrounds. From then on, they work, play, and succeed together. Kids would be graded for their individual development, as well as the way they function as team members and team leaders. Their parents would be part of the team and expected to help coach.

Let's stopping knocking the jocks, and start clocking the jocks. Figure out how the coach makes Johnny run, try the same techniques and maybe Johnny will read and write and talk about his problems. Leadership builds self-esteem and self-awareness. By exposing children to "nerds" like Bill Gates and the other successful men and women who might have been considered "strange" by their peers at one time, an understanding and respect for diversity can be fostered that can only strengthen our communities. A leadership program is a way to let the popular football players find out real quick that someday soon they could easily be working for the geeky kid with the big vocabulary. By mixing and matching the teams properly, the athletes and nonathletes can form common bonds—*he's not so dumb, she's not so flaky.* The sooner a child realizes that value is measured by who you are and what you do, rather than what you wear or how you look, the better it will be for all of us.

They ought to hear my friend and mentor Neil Lamey's views on workplace diversity: "I'd don't care if they're purple with three heads, if they can sell copiers I want them on my team." Kids need to be introduced to the real world. Leadership programs in schools can do that.

But like business teams, it can't be half-baked. The culture of the school from the janitor to the principal has to support a team-based leadership culture. The message must be communicated over and over again: *This place works as a team, and we're building a great place to go to school!*

Say it over and over again. Do it over and over again.

No time for leadership in the schools?

We better start making time for the sake of the children. The baby boomers took over college administration buildings to demand an end to the Vietnam War. Their children should take over administration buildings and principals' offices demanding a start to the leadership war.

Systematic Leadership Training

In business organizations, the people czar would be involved in creating and running leadership centers dedicated to supporting and building leaders within the operation. This would provide an ideal mentoring environment and practice ground for young managers and those who need their skills polished. The "situation room" concept that I introduced in chapter 11 could be up and running to allow for quick "what-if" scenario training.

One of the problems with on-the-job leadership training is that the novice leader's mistakes impact real people. I would have loved having had a couple of rounds in the "situation room" before one of my Xerox employees walked into my office and began talking about committing suicide. Tell me about on-the-job training! I sat there listening so intently, I thought I could feel my brain cells coming to a boil. I did my best to be sympathetic and to calm him down. When he left, I was on the phone immediately to human resources for help. Together, we got him into a counseling program.

It worked out fine, but things like that are so fraught with the potential for tragedy that "situation room" training or something similar should be available to every leader and manager. As it is, Xerox holds panel interviews to evaluate those who are hoping to be promoted to the first rung on the management ladder. Oddly enough, candidates are asked a whole battery of "what-if" questions, but there's no standard operating procedure for them to prepare themselves before the interview takes place. It amounts to a psychological exam to see if you have the right instincts or have learned what you need by osmosis. I was rejected twice because my instincts and osmotic learning curve were at odds with Xerox policies.

My father finally had to explain to me that any company has the right to expect its managers to know and adhere to its standards. The end of instinct and osmosis. I had one of my peers "what-if" me until I could satisfy the promotion panel that I was ready to lead. My question then and now is, what's wrong with actually helping those who seek leadership roles to get ready for their new responsibilities? Why instinct? Why osmosis?

 For the Red Notebook

If we train for sales skills or customer service ability, why don't we train our leaders? And I mean extensively trained, not just a few once-over-lightly classes?

With my own experience in mind, I set up a training program in Cleveland for aspiring managers. We'd go over "what-if" scenarios and other material one night—*after* the close of business—a couple of times each month for eight or nine months. Initially, the participants pushed me to hold the classes during the day, but my comeback was that as managers they were going have to learn how to juggle many, many conflicting demands and *still* take care of business.

The training allowed me not only to keep the leadership pipeline full, but to see close up who was really able to master the work and who was struggling, and do it without making the discovery the hard way when it was too late and mistakes were being made that hurt the customer. Group leadership training has the additional advantage of allowing individuals to see their peers in action, and perhaps realize that Dan or Sally really did merit the promotion (when it eventually comes their way) based on talent and hard work. Training can be an effective reality check.

Flight Lessons

I'm willing to be the poster boy for reformed underachievers because I know how aspiring to a leadership role and being allowed to live that dream changed my life. I went to my first Xerox recognition meeting in October 1976. I can fix the date because we were kicking off the fourth quarter. I think my responsibilities for the event were such make-or-break assignments as carrying in the boxes of plaques and checking the microphone. As my colleagues were called to the front to receive their awards for helping make the third quarter a success, I recall thinking that while getting one of those plaques was nice, what I really wanted was to be my boss, who was up there handing them out.

Something clicked at that moment. Frank Pacetta, the lone wolf and party animal, started paying attention to what it meant to be a leader. Until then, my attitude had been, "Well, I'm a top performer and you're not." Pretty snotty! Neil Lamey, my mentor in Columbus, warned me that I was going to have to lead a team composed of many different personalities, and if I tried to turn them into Frank Pacetta clones, I was bound to fall flat on my face as a leader.

I was determined to succeed. And the desire to be a leader was strong enough to make me realize that I would have to learn tolerance, to value diversity, to listen to criticism, and to enjoy the interplay of personalities as its sparks creativity, excitement, and fun. What a personal transformation it was! The opportunity to lead changed me for the better. The magic of leadership works both ways because you get back more than you give. Learning to fly is profound. Teaching others to take wing is sublime.

Evaluating Aspiring Leaders and Students

Sometimes to motivate, one has to irritate. I know there are readers whom I've irritated so much that they've tossed the book away. Good for them! Now I'm going to irritate others by telling you to stop reading this section unless you're under the age of twenty-five. But there is an exception to this edict. If you're planning on helping young leaders learn their craft, you can stay. If not, I'll see you in a few pages.

Okay. If you want to lead, you've got to "mind the gap." If you've ever been on the London Underground, you've probably heard the recorded announcement warning passengers to "mind the gap" between the plat-form and the subway car door.

Minding the gap as a would-be leader is to realize that there is percep-tion and there is reality. When I first set out to be a leader at Xerox, I knew how good I was going to be at convincing my team to sell copiers by the freight-car load. But I was essentially told by my bosses, "Yeah, Frank, we know how you'll convince them—'do it or you're fired.'" For some reason, they didn't think that was a desirable leadership quality. And they were right.

There was a gap between my perception of Frank Pacetta's leadership skills and their perception. Since they controlled promotions, their percep-tion was reality. What I had to do was change their perception (and my atti-tude), and in the process, change reality. Ever since, I have been acutely aware of the gap.

I like you to take use the Gap Evaluator. How strongly do you exem-plify the following characteristics?

	Always		Sometimes		Never
Adaptable	1	2	3	4	5
Articulate	1	2	3	4	5
Careful Planner	1	2	3	4	5
Caring	1	2	3	4	5
Compassionate	1	2	3	4	5
Collaborative	1	2	3	4	5
Courageous	1	2	3	4	5
Creative	1	2	3	4	5
Decisive	1	2	3	4	5
Effective Coach	1	2	3	4	5
Effective Listener	1	2	3	4	5
Energetic	1	2	3	4	5
Fair	1	2	3	4	5
Highly Focused	1	2	3	4	5
Highly Motivated	1	2	3	4	5
Honest	1	2	3	4	5
Loyal	1	2	3	4	5
Patient	1	2	3	4	5
Perceptive	1	2	3	4	5
A Person of Vision	1	2	3	4	5
Positive Role Model	1	2	3	4	5
Recognizes Other's Contributions	1	2	3	4	5
Relentless Pursuer of Goals	1	2	3	4	5
Risk Taker	1	2	3	4	5
Sincere	1	2	3	4	5
Tough	1	2	3	4	5
Willing to Give and Take Explicit Feedback	1	2	3	4	5
Willing to Share Power and Responsibility	1	2	3	4	5

It's a truly staggering list. Honestly assessing yourself on each character-istic will give you a personal checklist of what your strengths and weak-nesses are as a leader. If I were twenty-five again, I would probably have given myself a long string of ones and a few twos for the sake of modesty. More than likely, I would also have awarded myself a one in "Willingness to give and take explicit feedback." I'll bet you did too.

Now I'm going to see if you are who you say you are. Go to a copier—make it a Xerox, please (even though I knock them, I am still extremely proud of being a Xerox guy)—make twenty copies of this same list, and give them out to your friends, relatives, colleagues, professors, and boss. Yes, the boss. Don't forget him or her. Ask the group to evaluate you.

You are not going to like this experience. But it will make you str . . . never mind. It will make you a better leader because you will be able to see the gap. If you can see it, you can mind it, and close it.

At Xerox, managers were rated by their employees (using a different set of questions). I would get high ratings even when I was pushing my teams hard. The reason for that was the negative comments from those who resented the pressure tended to be more than counterbalanced by the positive ratings from those who loved the challenge. The feedback coming up from below made me feel great, but then I asked my boss for her opinion of how I was regarded from above. It was crushing. The gap was enormous. She and I worked well together. There was no problem there. But she gave me an honest reading of how more senior manage-ment regarded me: too emotional, a troublemaker, not a team player, and those sorts of things.

At first, I was furious. Then I realized that it was valuable information. Why? Perception is reality, even if the perception is not accurate. I set out to change that perception. I probably wasn't completely successful, but I worked on it. And by the way, there were areas I didn't work on because I knew that if I did I would weaken characteristics that made me an effective leader. The ratings I was getting from teams demonstrated that I was skilled at leading and managing *down*. Managing *up* is fine, just don't let it interfere with the real job of leading and managing your teams.

The advantage you have with this Gap Evaluator is that those who are doing the evaluation actually know you. The feedback I got was mostly based on hearsay because many of the people my boss quoted had had very little personal contact with me. That's probably not enough consolation, though, when the evaluation is negative in areas that you consider to be your strength. But all I can say is, grow leather skin and work to improve.

From time to time, hand out the evaluation sheets again and see how much ground you've gained. But save the first one as a reminder of how far you've come.

Now the fun part. Use the same sheet to evaluate your boss or profes sors. You're the judge, but if you assign more than ten or so fives and I think it's time to transfer or look for a new job. Pay careful attention to this next suggestion: If you didn't ask for your boss's evaluation the first time around—or if you did and also gave yourself a one for courage—send the evaluation you did of the boss to him or her. If you'd like to preserve your anonymity, wipe the fingerprints off the envelope.

Congratulations. Both of you now possess valuable—actionable— information.

An Anthem for Leaders

All readers are welcome to come back. Actually, I hope those over twenty-five eavesdropped anyway. The Gap Evaluator is a great tool for self-assessment, no matter where you stand in your career. When I use it to test myself I never get a perfect score—not from myself or from the others I ask for an assessment.

When I've received a particularly troubling rating, I've taught myself to ask why they feel that way and what they believe I can do to improve. But don't try this if you are in a bad mood or looking for a fight. The point is not to persuade someone that their assessment is wrong or unfair. If you try, they'll probably never be straight with you again.

The Gap Evaluator is an effective tool for leaders to use to assess team managers who report to them. First, record your impressions of the manager, then ask his or her team to do the same thing anonymously. Don't expect people to put their names on the sheet. But you can ask for more information by following up on a personal basis. If Greg or Carol got a string of fours for honesty, energy, or some other important area, select a few team members and probe them for background and more information. The Gap Evaluator is exposing a problem you can't ignore.

I started the chapter with leadership in a disco mode—"Sweaty people in expensive clothes, dancing." So I'll close by giving a recent hit tune a small twist. When I fill out one of these evaluations with numbers that look good, and there's progress being made, I sign my name and then add a postscript in invisible ink: "P.S.—I believe you can fly."

This belief is what makes the true leader different from the manager and what gives the leadership difference such potency. It's not that the product or the process will fly. If we do our jobs as caring, committed leaders by practicing the *art of how*—how we set goals, how will achieve them, how we make this a great place to work and a great place to live—the people will soar and take the product, process, *and profits* with them.

CHAPTER FIFTEEN

Understanding the Implications of a Faulty Employee/Customer Paradigm—

Or, Pissing Off the Customer Is a Real Bad Idea

Not long ago, I was coming back to Columbus on America West Airlines after making a speech in Boston. It was late and everybody was grumpy and fed up. Another lousy day of trying to make a living. But I'm talking about the America West cabin crew, not the passengers. The passengers were positively cheery by comparison.

The flight was way behind schedule, of course, and the crew had missed a meal break. They were unhappy and openly venting about how insensitive the airline was to their needs. "Bad day?" I asked one flight attendants who was moving down the aisle, doing her best not to make eye contact that might lead to a request for service. "Awful," she said. And preceded to tell in detail just how awful it had been. "Funny," I said when she paused for breath, "I was just reading an America West newspaper ad trumpeting a J.D. Power and Associates survey that designated the airline number one in short-haul frequent travel satisfaction." The ad, I was informed, was a crock. And I don't think she meant a crock of dry roasted peanuts.

For once, I held my tongue, which I'm not in the habit of doing when I am dealing with an airline, and customer satisfaction feedback is in order. There's a United ticket clerk who may still be mulling over the lecture I gave her when she too informed me it was a bad day and, pointing to a nearby group of casually dressed passengers, said, "It really annoys me when tourists expect the same service as business travelers." I won't repeat the whole sermon, but I suggested that maybe they had every right to expect service and that perhaps they were hard-working business people who had earned frequent flyer points on her airline for their much-deserved vacations. "They may look like tourists, but they're still customers," I reminded her.

So the America West lady got off lightly, but I really should have told her that as a customer I didn't care to hear about her grievances with her employer even though she may have had legitimate reasons to gripe. I sat there wondering if the pilot was also having a bad day.

I probably would have forgotten the story if I hadn't experienced a sequel with a far different plotline involving Southwest Airlines. On a subsequent business trip, I was passing through the terminal in Columbus just after most of the outgoing flights had departed. I noticed that the Southwest counter was free of customers and that five clerks were standing there chatting. I couldn't resist.

I walked over and said, "I'm writing a business book. I've been to seminars, read the case studies, and heard all about what a great company Southwest is to work for. I won't use your names, but tell me—is it?"

In unison the five fairly shouted, "Yes!"

"Why?" I asked

"Because of Herb," one of the men said, referring to Southwest's CEO Herb Kelleher. They all nodded in agreement. In turn, the told me how "innovative" he was, "down to earth," "fun," and "terrific to work for." All of them had been employed by other airlines and they contended that none even came close to Southwest as a great place to work. "We love it here," one woman said, and told me that during the departure rush that had just concluded the airline employees at the adjoining counter had complained about the noise made by Southwest employees and their customers laughing and talking.

 For the Red Notebook

Herb Kelleher thinks he's CEO of Southwest Airlines, but he is actually its people czar. I'm naming my annual People Czar of the Year award "The Herb," and the first recipient to mark the new century is—Herb.

Poor things! They had to listen to somebody having a good time. And I'm being only half sarcastic. It is too bad, and they'd be smart to shoot off a resume and a job application to Southwest to get in on the fun.

I could hear it at that Southwest counter: "TGIM—Thank God, it's Monday. I can't wait to go to work." Every customer should cock an ear for the same solid-gold sound of satisfied employees. There isn't a better way to determine whether or not you're going to be satisfied with the product or the service. I hear it every time I walk into Starbuck's and Office Max, for instance. The atmosphere is bright and upbeat. There's almost a hum of electricity. It says to the customer that something special is happening: *I'm having a good experience working here, and you'll have a good experience shopping here.*

Value Delivers Value

When Roger Gittines and I were outlining this book, he asked me what I planned to write about customer satisfaction. "The whole book is about customer satisfaction," I said. And it is.

It is nearly impossible to consistently deliver value to the customer if the employee is not deriving meaningful value from the work experience. In their book, *First, Break All The Rules: What the World's Greatest Managers Do Differently*, Marcus Buckingham and Curt Coffman report on a 1997 survey of employee satisfaction at a national chain of three hundred retail stores. The results were tallied up and compared store to store, and then tracked against profits at each outlet. Those in the top 25 percent of the survey ended the year 14 percent higher than the targeted figure in the individual store's budget. Those who finished in the bottom 25 percent undershot their profit target by 30 percent. Even more startling, the employee retention ratio between the two groups was such that in total those in the bottom 25 percent lost a thousand more employees than did the top 25 percent. The wasted training costs came out to almost $30 million.

Buckingham and Coffman conclude that the disparity was caused by an inconsistent culture, but that the good news was the company was "blessed with truly exemplary managers" in the stores that turned in high employee satisfaction numbers:

> These managers had built productive businesses by engaging the talents and passions of their people. In their quest to attract productive employees, the company could . . . find out what their newly highlighted cadre of brilliant managers was doing and then build their company culture around this blueprint.[1]

Rewind: "engaging the talents and passions of their people." I couldn't have said it any better myself.

A Little Dissatisfaction Goes a Long Way

There is a formula that estimates that every disgruntled customer tells an average of twelve other people about the experience. That's a lot of damage for starters. But if I had an employee dissatisfaction problem among my two thousand person salesforce to the tune of just 10 percent, with each of them contacting five customers a day, the damage potential would be hair-raising. Do the numbers: Two thousand reps, with a 10 percent dissatisfaction rate, contacting five customers each day over a five-day work week could directly sour five thousand customers, who then spread the word to sixty thousand others. That's just one week! If the malcontents were as eloquent as the America West flight attendant, and if they gave each of five customers a day as negative an experience, we'd be looking at nearly a quarter million people who have gained a poor opinion of the operation a month. Next month it could another 240,000, and on, and on, and on until my administrative assistant buzzes me:

"Frank, your mother called."

"Put her through."

"No, she hung up after telling me how much she hates our company."

In reality, those numbers wouldn't accumulate as rapidly. Word of mouth spreads slowly and the negative impact dissipates as it moves away from the original dissatisfied customer. But it's interesting to note, in 1994, Southwest Airlines estimated that just five customers per flight—3 million out of a total of 40 million customers—meant the difference between profit and loss for the company. Consider how much daily customer contact a single flight attendant has. Somebody like Ms. Sunshine at America West would have single-handedly put Southwest into chapter eleven. Pissing off the customer is a real bad idea.[2]

Sarcom's Peter Rogers told me that his company's policy on customer satisfaction is that "everyone owns the account." That makes sense as insurance against handcuffing a valuable customer to someone who might be having too many bad days in a row. But the best insurance of all is to stay on top of employee satisfaction.

You don't really need to pay for formal surveys. Keep asking them how they feel about their job. Listen and take action to correct the problems. Buckingham and Coffman—they are part of the Gallup organization—asked twelve good questions in their survey. You might take a look at their book for the wording. But I'll give you a one question survey to be answered with one word followed by a brief essay.

Is this company a great place to work?
Yes or no. Please explain why.

Taking a Meter Reading

When I did my interviews of the coaching staff at the University of Dayton, I kept hearing the same two phrases over and over again—"there are no limits" and "there is no ceiling." Limitless opportunity is a powerful employee satisfier. Jane Fichem, vice president for human resource development at Bass Hotels and Resorts says that, in general, lack of opportunity is one of the most frequently cited reasons that employees give for leaving their jobs and going elsewhere.[3]

And here's a good survey question: "Are you satisfied with the opportunities for advancement and career development that we offer in this company?" In addition, another couple of questions occurred to me during my conversation with Jane Fichum, who reported that the principal complaint from those who quit is, "I didn't get any feedback on how I was doing. My boss never established what I was expected of me." You're probably already writing the questions in your red notebook:

- Are you satisfied that your manager has told you explicitly what he or she expects from you?
- Are you satisfied with the amount of feedback you are receiving on your job performance?

If you combine these questions with the Pride Quotient Test in chapter 3, it will make for an effective survey. Or use the ho-hum meter:

To: All Employees
Subject: Employee satisfaction, the Ho-Hum Meter

Please fill out the following chart, circling 1 to 5. No names.
No repercussions.

1—Extraordinary   2—Good stuff   3—Ho-hum   4—Broken   5—*Fahgetaboutit*

Company leadership	1	2	3	4	5
My boss	1	2	3	4	5
Company vision	1	2	3	4	5
My company cares	1	2	3	4	5
Company training	1	2	3	4	5
Company product	1	2	3	4	5
We have fun	1	2	3	4	5
I love what I do	1	2	3	4	5
My views are listened to	1	2	3	4	5
I'm outta here!	*never*	*don't know*	*maybe*	*soon*	*yesterday*

Anything that draws threes, fours, and fives from more than 10 percent of the workforce is a barrier that needs to be cut down immediately. Then, start delivering the message: "There are no limits."

Staying out of the Penalty Box

If you are a manager, try this. Choose the name of someone who works for you. Go the file and pull out his or her personal development plan. You've got two minutes. I'll wait.

Doc P's Truth Serum is served. Did you not bother to get up and look in the file because you knew that a personal career development plan wouldn't be there? Or did you look and come up blank?

 Now-To

Work with each team member to draft a personal career development plan.

Or, if there are plans on file, review them, evaluate progress to date, and update them.

If there are no plans on file or the ones that are there are outdated, the penalty is that you're going to have to go back and reread the book from the beginning. People-ology is not breaking out all over. Among other things, there is a fundamental communications problem. People are not being asked what they want and expect from the relationship. Or if they are being asked, nobody's listening and helping them to achieve their dreams. The highlights of a personal career development should be part of the employee performance contract that is reviewed monthly.

Say it—"Monthly."

I know: There's no time. But the time you save by escaping from the misunderstandings and lack of productivity that comes from not doing monthly reviews will more than cover the initial squeeze that you may feel.

Back up the contract up with a second, more detailed document that will take an employee five, ten, or even twenty years into his or her career.

I'm not so sure that the conventional wisdom is so wonderful that we've got to get used to being job-hoppers. If it's truly a great place to work, I want my gold watch, thank you.

 Now-To

Establish career development plans for *all* your people.

Encouraging Mentor Mania

Mentors are another antidote to employee dissatisfaction. It's better to have a unhappy team member crying on a mentor's shoulder than venting with a customer. Mentors offer solace, support, second opinions, and kicks in the butt when necessary. And that last function is an important one. Sometimes it's the only way to learn. Coaching is fine, and I'm all for consensus building and the Socratic method, but sometimes more forceful communications techniques are required.

Bill Duffy, remember him? He was my football coach at Brooklyn Prep. One day at J.V. practice I was particularly inept. Inept? I was horrible. We were running our pass offense against the second team's defense. I was throwing interception after interception. After each play, the quarterback was supposed to leave the huddle and consult with the coach about what would happen next. Coach Duffy would patiently explain what I was doing wrong. After several more interceptions, and as I turned to go back to talk to him, Coach Duffy yelled, "Don't turn around, Frank. Stay right there. Don't talk to me. You stink!" Reflexively, I kept turning toward him. "No, you stink. Stay there. I don't want to talk to you." The other kids in the huddle had all they could do to keep from laughing out loud.

My game instantly improved a thousand percent.

I call this the "Needle." Leaders have to be willing to use the needle when all else fails, but use it judiciously, deliberately, and without intended malice. Also, as much as a I loved Coach Duffy, use the needle one-on-one so as not to embarrass anyone publicly. Or, use it in a group setting without aiming it an individual.

Example: "Fred, five years ago you would have had this done by now. I think you're slowing down. But that's okay, it happens to the best of us."

Fred will be hugely miffed. And the deal will get wrapped up in a flash.

Example: "I brought this with me today (hold up a gas can)—this team is running on empty."

The team will be hugely miffed. And their energy levels will zoom.

Example: "Frank, are you going to give us the same old shtick today?"

When Ron Nelson, one of my managers, needled me that way prior to a team meeting he had asked me to address, I responded by delivering a exhortation that made Gen. George Patton and Shakespeare's Henry V seem like tongue-tied wimps—or so it seems to me upon modest reflection.

Most people know when they're being needled and don't let it bother them deeply. But there's enough of a jab to motivate.

Even the golf pro at my country club uses the needle. We were out one day working on my hopeless swing and testing the new set of clubs he had sold me. It was hot, we were sweating, and I was not making progress. If anything, I was getting worse, not better. "It's this new driver," I said lamely.

That did it. Vic crossed his arms and stood back. "No, Frank, your problem is loft," he snapped.

"Loft?"

"Yeah, L-O-F-T: Lack of F—ing Talent."

That hurt! But in this case, the needle hasn't worked yet. When it comes to golf, loft is still a problem. But every time I tee up, I hear Vic say, "Frank, your problem is loft," and I try my damnedest to hit the ball long and straight.

Finding the Missing Message

There is something missing in this chapter on employee satisfaction and how it impacts on the customer. I wonder what it is? Help me with this. We've been working on pride and passion and talent. No problem there. The ho-hum meter goes after vision, training, caring, and so on. Manager mistakes—that's taken care of. Career development is covered. Buckingham and Coffman's survey even asked if the employee has a best friend at work. Good idea. What's missing?

From somewhere just south of Yipsalanti, Michigan, I can detect the distant sound of a reader screaming. "Money, you idiot!"

Oh, yeah. Money. Like sex, we think about money all the time but don't like to admit it out loud.

Stop Whining—and Start Winning's dirty secret about money is that you get what you pay for. I'm sorry that it comes in the form of such a clanking cliché, but those are the breaks. Every dollar that is paid in the form of compensation bears a message in addition to "In God We Trust." Usually it's not just one but several messages, ranging from "We expect you to show up for work at nine o'clock in the morning," "Be part of the team," "Make Mr. and Mrs. Bliven very, very pleased to be doing business with us" to "By the way don't screw up."

There's nothing wrong with those four messages, but 44 messages, or 444, get to be a problem. Which one is the most important? Where do I start? In what order do I tackle them? There is message overload; we don't know what we're getting paid to do. And it makes for a lot of conscious or unconscious dissatisfaction.

The quickest and easiest way to sort this out is to hire a consulting group. Most of us have horror stories about consultants, and so do I. But with a well-defined mission and careful controls and inspection, consultants can bring value to the table. I found that to be the case with the Alexander Group, a business consulting firm that specializes in compensation plans. I know it sounds like a advertisement that's out of place in a book dedicated to a balanced, unbiased, and unopinionated presentation of scholarly research—and it would be in a book of that sort. My mission is to tell you about what works. These guys work. I've hired the Alexander Group in the past and the firm did a great job of helping design a world-class compensation package.

One reason for my high customer satisfaction was consultant Mark Donnolo. He's the one who explained to me how important it is to identify and deliver the message that is explicitly and implicitly part of compensation. Donnolo does a lot of work with sales organizations that tend to use some form of a variable-pay plan—that is, sales commissions. But I think variable-plans—bonuses and incentives—are the only way to go for business organizations. Hell, any organization, for that matter. Pay the priest or preacher based on how he's managed to increase the size of the congregation, and the school principal according to how test scores have improved.

And that's what I think Donnolo means by a message. What do I expect? How much is it worth? How much do I pay to get it? Who do I pay to deliver it? Answer those four questions and you are on the way to having a message. You're not quite there yet, though. Before you pay, you have to ensure that the organization can play.

"You can't do compensation," Donnolo says, "if you don't have the organization designed correctly. So if you have a flawed sales operation in terms of how it's designed and how it aligns to the markets, the compensation plan is not going to work correctly. You've got to understand the job, and you've got to understand their objectives first of all."

I get it. "You, you, and you go sell this stuff" is not much of a message and not much of organizational design. What I also got from Mark Donnolo is confirmation that structuring compensation requires rigorous analysis before the package is finalized and while it's in service. This is not a subject that can be handled casually or in a one-size-fits-all manner.

It comes down to the questions I've asked again and again throughout the book:

- What do we want?
- What do we do to get it?
- How do we know that we're getting it?

The compensation message and the message have to align. If 100 per-cent employee/customer satisfaction is the message that has to be translated into dollar terms in the compensation plan in order for the two messages to square up. You pay for what you get.

Mark Donnollo says it without resorting to a single cliché:

> You've got to keep the message very simple because the reason you design a compensation plan is that a variable-pay plan is not intended to pay people lots of money. It is because you want to communicate a message. And if you don't want to communicate a message, you'd probably just pay them base salary because it's a lot simpler to administer. But if you're going to have pay-for-performance, you want to keep the message very clear. So you want to say go out and sell, get revenue, or get profitability, or sell certain products, or sell to certain markets.[4]

My reading of this is that too many companies don't know what mes-sage they're sending with compensation, and if they did know it would turn out to be a garbled contradictory message that undercuts the results and hurts employee moral.

"Don't ask for one thing, and pay me for another" is the lament. Or, "If it is so damned important, why aren't they paying me for it?"

 *Now-To*

Find out what you're paying for.
What's the money message that's being sent?

Pay for what you want. Pay for what you get. But this doesn't mean to serve what Donnolo calls a "buffet" of compensation: *Do this for $1,000 extra, do that for $500, maybe this for $1,500 . . . that'll take too long. I'll go for $500, it's quicker and easier.* Incentives must be focused and significant in terms of what they contribute to the individual's overall income.

Another key point: The size of the incentive must relate to how much influence the person has on the objective. Don't load people up with incentives that they have no way of earning. Conversely, withholding incentives from someone who's in a position to directly achieve the desired outcome is also foolish. In sales, management is often fond of imposing "top stops," which curtail commissions once they hit a certain amount. To me, top stops are insane. What's the message? Stop selling. And the response from the sales team is, "Top stop? I will stop."

The playwright George Bernard Shaw said, "Lack of money is the root of all evil." I say, lack of a smart money message is a dumb way to do business.

Compensating a Soccer Dad

In the final analysis, employee satisfaction is all about compensation. Southwest Airlines issues two kinds of paychecks, one that can be taken to the bank and cashed, and another that comes in the form of pride and professional respect. Effective leaders recognize the need for both. Maybe I sound naive—but I'll risk it: Money, no matter how much of it there is, never compensates and never fills the void that's left when prides dies.

My daughter gets the last word on satisfaction and compensation in this chapter. The two of us were on our way to a soccer game one Saturday morning. Alle was in the middle of the backseat. Sports is not one of her big things, but she's fast on her feet and well coordinated. I was giving her coaching about how to handle the game, stuff like "stay on the ball" and "keep your head up." Advice Manchester United would pay me big bucks to deliver to their stars. I was rattling on the way I do with her brother before a big game until I heard a sigh. "Dad," I looked into the rearview mirror that framed her gorgeous eyes, "you know, it's really not that big a deal."

She was right. Racking up the points, going for the numbers isn't such a big deal. I took a deep breath, exhaled slowly, and took another look at the mirror to admire those bright eyes again, and felt very satisfied indeed.

CHAPTER SIXTEEN

The People-ology Payoff—

No Limits

*T*he last chapter. I feel like I'm in the final few minutes of a football game and quickly running out of time to score. Coach Duffy would probably tell me to stick to the plan, throw the ball to an open receiver, and pray.

Sounds good to me. Here goes.

Change—how's that for an open receiver. One of the most talked about and written about topics in business today.

Change must be really, really difficult, judging by the number of *change meisters* who are available for hire. But I don't get it. Change isn't hard if you do it every day. Small *constant* changes are the way to go.

It's probably my short attention span, but I don't want to keep doing the same things over and over again. It's boring. I don't care how successful we've been. Keep asking:

- How can we do this better?
- How can we do it faster?
- How can we be more productive?
- How can we provide more service?
- How can we have more fun?
- How can we create more customer value?

Nothing is perfect. Everything can be improved. The whole process of driving constant change creates energy and electricity. Change becomes part of the game. People look forward to it. However, change becomes overwhelming when we are allowed to settle into a rut, even a successful rut. But Coach Oliver Purnell of the University of Dayton puts it well: "What made you successful today won't make you successful tomorrow."

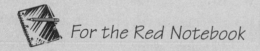 For the Red Notebook

To bring about successful change:
- Know your objectives.
- The change project team must have a mandate and be committed.
- Secure buy-in from first-line managers.
- No tolerance for different political agendas.
- Obtain buy-in from front-line employees.
- Be open to course corrections.
- Listen carefully to the reaction to distinguish between road noise and real problems.
- Know that a great change design that's poorly implemented has no chance.
- Get a "Hammer."

One good thing about constant change is that nothing you do is going to burn the place to the ground. But when change is postponed and allowed to accumulate, major upheavals occur and there's no chance to back off. If I tweak my process and it produces too much paperwork, I can re-tweak it in thirty days or less. Constant change is like a regular savings or reinvestment plan. The effects build over time. But spend some of the capital on worthy causes. Many managers try to hoard their success. Go ahead and rack up victories, but then take some risks. You've earned the right. If you lose, the previous successes will cover it. Don't squat on a pot of gold.

A Simple Tool Will Do

Small changes won't cut it? First, get a hammer. "Hammer" is a term I first heard from consultant Mark Donnolo. I love it because it perfectly captures the tool that you're going to need to force meaningful change through the organization. The hammer is a senior executive, preferably the CEO, who is committed to making the change happen successfully. *If there's no hammer, there's no chance.* Zip. At Xerox in the 1980s, David Kearns was the hammer. He made sure change happened, and without him Xerox probably wouldn't exist today.

If the CEO declines to be the hammer, it's a bad sign. But whoever he or she is, make sure your hammer has a nice long contract. There's nothing quite so maddening as going halfway through a change process and having the executive leave, taking the commitment to change with him or her. It leads to a *this too shall pass* attitude that sabotages change efforts from then on. But even if the hammer is locked in and totally committed, there has to be a concentrated effort at rounding up buy-ins from managers at all levels and unofficial influence leaders.

There are numerous individuals within an organization who exercise influence without portfolio; they're the old hands who have been around for years, maybe a few of the up and coming stars, or executive and administrative assistants plugged into a network of support people. Listen to what they are saying about the changes, sound out their advice, and then ask for help selling the program. This part of a major change effort, from my experience, is usually badly botched. The organization is told, not sold on, what's going to happen. Tell people what benefits they will derive from the change.

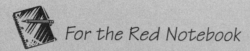 For the Red Notebook

Go ahead and change. But don't take your eye off the ball. Whatever it is that you do to pay the rent can't be neglected.

No matter how important the change may be in the long run, you'll never get there if the basic core business is allowed to slip. Double trouble comes when a company's change process and its fundamental business process are both mediocre.

Do you know why this sales job doesn't happen? Answer number one: Often management doesn't really know what the benefits will be. They have a rough idea, a good guess, but nobody wants to go out on a limb. That's the problem with drastic change—and why I recommend avoiding it if you can—consequences are unpredictable. I'm not risk averse. I am failure averse. I want to know what the pitfalls are in advance. Then I want to know how we'll get out of them in the event that we fall in. If I receive the L.A. shrug on that one, I'm nervous. Closing your eyes and jumping isn't prudent risk taking—it's a form of roulette the Russians wouldn't even subscribe to. Maybe they would, but you get the point.

Answer number two: They know, and the news is not going to go down well with the troops. The whole process is permeated by dishonesty. Remember, if you can't sell it, you have to force-feed it—and that's an ugly way to do business. Force-feeding can be self-defeating. While it wipes out resistance, trust is also damaged.

But sometimes there's no other way. Or so it seems.

The Worst Day of My Life

In 1994—get ready for ancient history—Xerox had its best year ever. The company launched a classy national advertising campaign and became a sponsor of the U.S. Olympic team. Profits soared, the stock prices rocketed upward, and it decided to lay off about ten thousand people.

As the district manager in Columbus, I was ordered to eliminate about 10 percent of the operation's workforce. There was no consultation, discussion of options, or warning. I was given a list of names and told to pull the trigger. The carnage was the worst among the support staff, people who had worked hard for the district's success without much recognition and with comparatively little financial reward.

The downsizing came as a special shock to all of us because Columbus, like Xerox itself, was having a spectacular year. Our performance, which had been near the bottom when I took over, was closing in on the number one position nationally. The reward for success came in the form of pink slips and a brutal downsizing. If I had it to do all over again—I wouldn't. No, I'd be the first one out the door. I don't like telling people who have done everything they were asked, and more, to clean out their desks and leave.

Corporate America, cheered on by Wall Street, has become entirely too casual about this kind of butchery. *Strong medicine is needed to strengthen the company* is the rationale that's heard over and over. Okay, I'll buy that. But before waking up one day and announcing an across-the-board cut of 10 percent, how about asking for 15 percent more productivity? Devise a turnaround plan, sell it corporationwide, and execute it instead of launching a sneak attack. A 10 percent cut in executive salaries—mine included—wouldn't hurt, either.

Meat-ax downsizing is all about failure. It's emblematic of poor leadership, bad management, contempt for people, and disdain for the customer.

Forced reductions happen to the best of operations. There are mistakes, miscalculations, and changing market conditions. But Xerox made a decision to take a shortcut back to the glory days of the 1960s and '70s.

It bought into the idea that the problem was people. Wrong P-word. The problem was—and still is—productivity. Roughly one-third of Xerox's sales districts had been allowed to fail year after year, while one-third turned in so-so performances, and only one-third exceeded their goals. If Xerox was going to practice teamwork, which is what it has preached since it committed itself to the concepts of the Total Quality Movement, the right thing to do was make sure that all of its teams pulled their weight.

But there wasn't time for that. There was only time for a bloodbath.

I've used variations on the phrase "no time for leadership" throughout this book, usually followed by the admonition—make time! If we don't, we invite the kind of casual slaughter that occurred so frequently in the 1990s, accompanied by the applause of those who believe it is a necessary and altogether wholesome feature of the new economic paradigm.

Get a load of this hit list, showing layoffs as of May 1994—not halfway through the year:

IBM	85,000
AT&T	83,000
General Motors	74,000
U.S. Postal Service	55,000
Sears	50,000
Boeing	30,000
NYNEX	22,000
Hughes Aircraft	21,000
GTE	17,000
Martin-Marietta	15,000
Dupont	14,800
Eastman Kodak	14,000
Philip Morris	14,000
Proctor & Gamble	13,000
Phar Mor	13,000
Bank of America	12,000
Aetna	11,800

GE Aircraft Engines	*10,250*
McDonnell Douglas	*10,200*
Bell South	*10,200*
Ford Motor	*10,000*
Xerox	*10,000*
Pacific Telesis	*10,000*
Honeywell	*9,000*
U.S. West	*9,000*

Don't expect me to total it up. It would make me vomit.[1]

But not to worry, that was 1994. Downsizing is really old hat, or so I've been assured—not something that hip readers really care about anymore. Better start caring. As I write this, layoffs for the first half of 1999 are running 40 percent higher than the year before, which set a record high. Currently, there are about sixty thousand announced layoffs each month. The figure, though, is probably low because it only counts large companies that are required by law to report plant closings and massive job cuts. Silicon Valley and other startups are excluded from the mix.

But of course everyone also knows that Silicon Valley follows a new paradigm. How about these figures in that case: Between 1993 and 1998, the computer industry announced 273,000 job cuts, about the same as the old paradigmers defense and aerospace, which have been struggling since the end of the Cold War.

Last time I checked, the years from 1994 to 1998, and on to 1999, were part of the longest peacetime expansion of the American economy in history. Hmm. Logic suggests that firing people is really, really good business. And it is—for somebody else's business.

The implication of these figures is that the initial bloodbaths of 1994 fertilized the new economy. Xerox and other large corporations dumped people who promptly got up, dusted themselves off, and went to work elsewhere or started their own companies. There was an infusion of motivated and recharged talent ("Okay, kick me out, but you can't hold me down").[2]

The big boys jumpstarted their own competition. They are still at it too. The Labor Department estimates that 50 million workers, or 40 percent of the labor force, changes jobs within a year. Check that. Fifty million people are so dissatisfied, restless, fed up, or bored that they leave the job after less than one year. That tells me that American business is doing an atrocious job at people-ology.

If I were reading this book, I'd throw it down and rush to rerecruit my best people right now! I'd also start worrying—as Silicon Valley should along with all the slick Internet startups—that my new paradigm is in danger of turning into the old paradigm. Thisisnotyourfathers.com? Guess again. People power and technology have been driving the new economy. But if people stop being an asset and start becoming disposable—á la Xerox and the other kings of downsizing—isn't the Cinderella economy likely to turn itself into a pumpkin?

Maybe, maybe not. As a businessperson and someone who has to work for a living, my tendency is to go with maybe. And as an author, I hope that you take these figures as a serious warning. Can you afford to discard talent and stay in business? If you're counting on Prince Charming to bail you out, you do believe in fairy tales.

As for me, I believe in leadership.

In 1994, the year of that horrifying lost of job cuts and the worst day of my life, and again in 1998 when there was another drastic downsizing—it's not only vampires who develop a taste for human blood—aggressive leadership could have energized Xerox's people to achieve the desired outcome. If I had been asked to deliver an extra 15 percent from the Columbus district, Xerox would have had its number without a single layoff. My teams would have delivered that on a platter, and had a ball doing it. But I wasn't asked, I was told. I was managed, not led.

The same would have been true for the other top performing districts, and the same could have been true for the other two-thirds of the poor to middling operations—had there had been time for leadership. In those cases, some people would have lost their jobs or been moved out to other positions. But only because there had been no time for training, recruiting, a high-quality disciplined process, and the other requirements of leadership that had been sliding for years.

You're probably sick of hearing my mantra—"What a great place to work!" Xerox was a great place to work and could be again one day if it is willing to take the time for leadership. And it would be so simple. What worries me, though, is that a more difficult feat is underway. First, let your technological edge slip away; a mission largely accomplished by 1985. Then, crush your greatest asset, the one that kept you from going belly up—people. That goal is now within reach. Finally, take a company founded on one of the most astounding inventions of the twentieth century and turn it into a me-too Internet clone in search of the next killer app.

Nice work.

Solve the People Problem

I know that most of my readers could care less about Xerox's fate, and that really isn't the point. I'm riffing on Xerox to explore a deeper theme: the need for people-ology. Xerox and many other great and small companies are faced with a real dilemma. They want to get rid of people, but they can't do it and survive. To use Lincoln's famous expression, it amounts to a half-slave, half-free mentality. The result is mood swings that range from mellow to maniacal and back again.

My suggestion to Xerox is to fire your best people. Get rid of them; they are more trouble than they are worth (to you). Go to Wall Street and the venture capitalists to raise money, which won't be a problem, since your stock will zoom past Pluto when you really get serious about downsizing. Take the cash and bankroll the people you've just fired. Let them do the stuff you're not interested in anymore. Go be an Internet company, lean, mean, and pony-tailed. Meanwhile, the business of selling copiers and printing technology, even manufacturing, can be profitably outsourced.

Xerox would still control the brand and dictate the terms of the culture. There'd be strictly delineated agreements between the corporation and its vendors, backed up by a disciplined process to see to it that Xerox always gets its share of the revenue. But there'd be no limits, no ceiling on the independent operations that are supplying the talent. Xerox would go from being an unhappy, reluctant employer to a demanding, happy (or else!) customer that is on the receiving end of the kind of high-quality, service-based culture it once tried so hard to provide until deciding that the only suitable delivery vehicle—people—was too much trouble.

Forget about Xerox. Any company that doesn't have time for leadership should do the same thing. Have a last fling. One humongous downsizing, get it out of your system. But don't throw those people away. Set them up so that you become their customer. Perf! I'm not advocating a new form of corporate colonialism. These would be fully independent entities that serve as investment opportunities and suppliers of goods and services under the originator's trademark and oversight. Somebody's got to do it. Might as well be people who are willing to work hard, make money, have fun, and say, "What a great place to work!"

Inside the Women's Locker Room

I've mentioned Megan McCallister a couple of times. She's the assistant athletic director of the University of Dayton. I was impressed by her intelligence and leadership ability, but there was one question that she asked during our first meeting that still haunts me, and I think it always will. She's a champion athlete, a former star on the U.S. national volleyball team. Her hero, by the way, is Diana Niade. When she chatted about that part of her life, the subject came around to the old complaint that women in business don't share the same sports culture that men do, which puts them at a disadvantage, and, as a result, that culture should be toned down and made less combative.

Megan didn't buy into that. "You should visit a women's locker room sometime," she said with a laugh. The only "break" Megan asked for was, "No limits . . . no ceiling."

As I was getting ready to go, Megan finished a review of her impressive management accomplishments at the university, looked me in the eye, and said, "Frank, will I ever feel the rush again that I got from sports? You know, that feeling . . ."

She really brought me up short. I told her she would, and that it would be even better. I've been thinking about what I should have said ever since. Here it is:

Megan, you'll feel the rush again, and it will be even better. I know because I have sought that same thing. I wanted to feel that powerful mixture of pride, exhilaration, gratitude, and fatigue. To be uplifted, to float in a bubble of triumph, to stand side by side with a band of brothers, happy together, satisfied that we'd done our very best. Megan, the rush in sports doesn't compare with the rush you get in real life when you're asked to do your very best—and you deliver. I used to say, it's all about winning. No, it's all about doing your best. That's the real rush, the very best rush of all.

Family Is Forever

Publication of the *The Force*, David Dorsey's nonfiction book based on the several months the author spent observing Xerox's Cleveland district, confirmed the prediction I made on the first day I arrived to lead the operation that our success would be so spectacular that books would be written about us.

Dorsey's portrait of us was what a book a reviewer might describe as "sharply etched." To the point that if my wife ever gets hold of him, the outline of her foot will be etched permanently on a tender portion of his anatomy. David was out to write a new *Death of a Salesman*. The last line of the book comes at the end of party at my house to celebrate one team member's promotion. It's two o'clock in the morning, we're in the kitchen standing shoulder to shoulder singing to a James Taylor record: "For a moment, no one is selling anything to anyone."[3]

He didn't get it. Not at all.

On the wall of my office at home, going on ten years later, is the only memento I have on display out of all the awards, certificates, and pictures that I've accumulated. It's a corny poem that I got at my farewell party when I left Cleveland. While I hate to telegraph my punches, I'm going to end the book with that poem. My purpose is to break away from many of the themes that we've been dealing with in the later chapters like recruiting, training, teamwork, and so on. Those are all key parts of the whole, but that whole rests on people, leadership, process, and emotion. In its own way, the poem confirms that fact. If you were a real glutton for punishment, you could go back and reread the book from the beginning and assign specific lines of the poem to chapters and sections. The title itself reflects my passionate conviction that good, strong business families make for good, strong businesses and careers. It's all there. The trust, the sincerity, the communications, the preparation, the expectations, the accountability. You probably know the list by now.

I was tough on those people. I made 'em dance. Most remain among my very best friends. Many hold down senior executive positions in Xerox and other corporations—No limits!—which just thrills me. They could have given me a fancy fountain pen or gift certificate. Instead, it was a poem that doesn't scan too well as verse, but, if you read it slowly, you might hear the heartbeats:

FAMILY IS FOREVER

Family is forever; others come and go.
We shared three years through joy and tears,
And wanted you to know you taught us how to reach the stars
that seemed beyond our grasp,
To "stretch up on our tiptoes,"
And be the very last to complain about
What would not work and which plan made no sense.
For after all, it all comes down to
"Perseverance, hard work, and confidence."
"You raised the bar," "We took the hill,"
And I guess we all could say
The teamwork and camaraderie made light
Our twelve-hour day.

We blitzed until the cows came home
And when the eve was night
The troops regrouped with karaoke, and lots
Of pizza pie.
Family is forever; others come and go.
We wrote the book—We made our mark
And one thing we all know:
Your leadership made the difference,
You made our dream come true.
Northeast Ohio is special,
And that special leader was you.
Family is forever, Frank.
In case you didn't know
You won our love and respect, wherever you may go.

They got it, and that's what matters. Is it emotional? You bet it is.

Notes

CHAPTER THREE

1. Charles Fishman, *The War for Talent* (**CITY:** Fast Company, August 1998), 104.

CHAPTER FOUR

1. Daniel Goleman, *Working with Emotional Intelligence* (New York: Bantam, 1998), 9. Also by Daniel Goleman, *Emotional Intelligence* (New York: Bantam, 1995), chapter 10.
2. Robert K. Greenleaf, *Teacher as Servant* (The Greenleaf Center for Servent-Leadership, Indianapolis, 1979).
3. Richard Carlson, *Don't Sweat the Small Stuff* (New York: Hyperion, 1997), 65.

CHAPTER FIVE

1. Frances Hesselbein and Paul M. Cohen, eds., *Leader to Leader: Enduring Lessons on Leadership By the Drucker Foundation* (San Francisco: Josse-Bass Publishers, 1999), 279.
* Financial data and *Fortune* magazine information from Whole Foods Market, Inc., 1998 report to stockholders.
2. Rhoda Thomas Tripp, ed., *The International Thesaurus of Quotations* (New York: Harper & Row, 1970), 206.

CHAPTER SIX

1. "Nortel Networks Marketing Campaign Signals Aggressive Approach to Building a Brand," *PR Newswire* (12 March 1999).

CHAPTER SEVEN

1. Stephanie Armour, "Failure to Communicate Costly to Companies," *USA Today* (30 September 1998).

CHAPTER NINE

1. Gary Hudepohl, of Gary Hudepohl Associates, interviewed by Frank Pacetta, January 10, 1999.

CHAPTER ELEVEN

1. Neil Sessoms, interviewed by Frank Pacetta and Roger Gittines, January 27, 1999.

CHAPTER THIRTEEN

1. Neil Lamey, interviewed by Frank Pacetta and Roger Gittines, January 15, 1999.
2. Richard Sennett, *The Corrosion of Character: Personal Consequences of Work in the New Capitalism* (New York: W.W. Norton & Co., 1998), 114.

CHAPTER FIFTEEN

1. Marcus Buckingham and Curt Coffman, *First, Break All the Rules: What the World's Greatest Managers Do Differently* (New York: Simon & Schuster, 1999), 37–39.
2. *LuvLines: A Corporate Newsletter for the Employees of Southwest Airlines,* November 1995.
3. Jane Fichem, vice president human resources development, Bass Hotels & Resorts, interviewed by Frank Pacetta and Roger Gittines, January 27, 1999.
4. Mark Donnolo, of the Alexander Group, interviewed by Frank Pacetta and Roger Gittines, February 12, 1999.

CHAPTER SIXTEEN

1. "The Pain of Downsizing," *Business Week,* May 9, 1994.
2. Michael M. Weinstein, "Economic Sucess: Cream in Labor Market's Churn; Why Job Losses Are Rising amid Job Hunters' Nirvana," *The New York Times,* July 22, 1999.
3. David Dorsey, *The Force* (New York: Ballantine Books, 1994).

Index